D1593662

Partners at the Creation

for Ruth and Jim

Partners at the Creation

—

THE MEN BEHIND POSTWAR GERMANY'S DEFENSE AND INTELLIGENCE ESTABLISHMENTS

—

In Memory of Jim

James H. Critchfield

Warm Regards,
Lois

NAVAL INSTITUTE PRESS
Annapolis, Maryland

Naval Institute Press
291 Wood Road
Annapolis, MD 21402

Library of Congress Cataloging-in-Publication Data
Critchfield, James H., b. 1917.
   Partners at the creation: the men behind postwar Germany's defense and intelligence establishments / James H. Critchfield.
   p. cm.
   Includes bibliographical references and index.
   ISBN 1-59114-136-2 (alk. paper)
   1. Germany. Bundesnachrichtendienst—History. 2. Intelligence service—Germany—History. 3. National security—Germany—History. I. Title.
   HV8208.7.B86C75 2003
   327.1243'009'045—dc21

                                              2003006058

Printed in the United States of America on acid-free paper ∞
10 09 08 07 06 05 04 03   9 8 7 6 5 4 3 2
First printing

TO LOIS

Contents

Acknowledgments

THE LATE Richard Helms, whom I met in Germany in 1946 and who was instrumental in my decision to leave an Army career and join the new CIA, was the guiding force behind practically every twist and turn I took—first in Germany in the development of the Gehlen Organization into a German national intelligence service, and later in the Middle East during the tumultuous years of the 1960s and 1970s. Richard rises above all others in his wise counsel and total support of risks he and I both felt worth taking. My appreciation to him has no end.

During the course of writing this book, a period spanning more than ten years and numerous drafts, I have had support from former American and German colleagues, and family and friends too numerous to mention. To all of you who helped me refresh my memory and fill in gaps, I sincerely thank you. Special thanks are due to Hans Buechler who, as the BND archivist, gave me enormous assistance and who, after his retirement, continued to be of invaluable help in document research and manuscript review. My thanks go also to Dr. Hans-Georg Wieck, who as the president of the BND supported my effort to get this story out. Close friends from Reinhard Gehlen's inner circle—Gerhard Wessel, Heinz Herre, Conrad Kuehlein, and Eberhard Blum—devoted many hours helping me, as did their wives Rosemarie, Christa, Astrid, and Putchen. I deeply appreciate the help and hospitality of Mrs. Val (Hannelore) Rychly, who graciously opened her beautiful home to Lois and me during our many trips to Bavaria. To the four children of Reinhard and Herta Gehlen—Katharina, Christoph, Marie-Therese, and Dorothee—and their families; I treasure the hours we spent together, reminiscing about their father. That goes as well for Annelore Krueger, Gehlen's lifelong assistant, who has been gracious in helping me remember. Thanks also go to Siegfried Graber, who bridged the historic connection between the Abwehr of Admiral Canaris and Gehlen's organization. Graber helped me understand the important relationships between the two.

My wife Lois has been by my side since the start of this project and has patiently seen it through to the end, providing much needed editorial help. Thanks also to daughter Ann, who remembers her time as a child in Pullach and who helped with many different research projects. My close friend and neighbor Dr. Gerold Broock not only helped edit the manuscript, but provided moral support until it was completed—and beyond. Countless friends and colleagues helped along the way, such as Ruth Ellen McCullough, Ed Petty, Sam Halpern, Mary Ellen Reese, Dave Murphy, Dr. Kevin Ruffner, Henry Pleasants and Virginia Pleasants, Bill Graver, Merrill Kelly, Gen. DeWitt Armstrong, Clarence Schmitz, John Bannigan, William Spaller, Sean Fitzpatrick, Ross Ford, Mike Geoghegan, and Stacy Edwards.

May this effort be a contribution to the history of the period.

Partners at the Creation

Prologue

IN LATE 1948 I arrived in the small village of Pullach, Germany, located a few kilometers south of Munich. I had just joined the newly formed Central Intelligence Agency (CIA), leaving behind a career as an officer of the U.S. Army. My assignment was to evaluate the postwar German intelligence operations based at Pullach, which since the end of World War II had been under the sponsorship of the U.S. Army. The army was pushing the CIA to assume responsibility for this group. I anticipated staying only a month, but my mission in Germany was ultimately extended to eight years—and provided the firsthand knowledge of events described here.

This story is about two men: German Army General Staff officers Reinhard Gehlen and Adolf Heusinger. The two men joined the General Staff of Ludwig Beck in 1934, and continued with his successor, Franz Halder, from 1938 to 1942. Both Beck and Halder had principal roles in the opposition mounted against Hitler within the German military. Ludwig Beck died in the chaos that followed the failed plot against Hitler of 20 July 1944, and Franz Halder narrowly escaped execution by the Schutzstaffel (SS) in the last days of the war. The SS, the enforcement arm of the Nazi movement, controlled all police, security, intelligence, and paramilitary forces that were called upon to perform systematic surveillance, terrorism, oppression, police measures, and a wide array of other actions, including planned genocide.

The Korean War provoked both U.S. president Harry Truman and German chancellor Konrad Adenauer to take remarkably farsighted actions that eventually gave the North Atlantic Treaty Organization (NATO) military alliance real credibility as a deterrent force to any possible Soviet move against Western Europe. A few weeks after the crisis in Korea, Adenauer established contact with both Gehlen and Heusinger without prior consultation with the Americans; in 1950 he appointed Heusinger as his principal military advisor.

On 5 May 1955, a year before the end of my Pullach assignment, the German Federal Republic became a sovereign state and a member of NATO. In 1956 Gehlen emerged as president of Germany's new Federal Intelligence Service, the BND. Heusinger became the top general in the new Bundeswehr. About 150 officers, all of whom had served with Gehlen and Heusinger in the German Army's General Staff, passed through the BND in their return to senior positions in the armed forces and the intelligence service. (I might add that not one of these 150 officers was among those assigned guilt and responsibility at the Nuremberg trial.)

In my eight years in Pullach I was both an observer and a participant in Germany's transition from an enemy to an ally. How did this remarkable transition occur? I believe it was through the enlightened policies of the United States and the political and economic framework that had evolved out of World War II and the Occupation. But much of it also came from German initiatives created by individuals sensitive to changes and trends in U.S. policies—the basis for this story.

1

The Last Days of World War II

IN EARLY March 1945 Allen Dulles, the wartime head of the Office of Strategic Services (OSS) station in Switzerland, traveled to the U.S. Seventh Army headquarters of the Saar district to meet with the Seventh's head of intelligence, Lt. Col. William Quinn. Dulles wanted to discuss with Quinn the deteriorating Nazi position in Italy and on the western front, particularly two reports received from a German agent who had periodically visited Switzerland. One of those reports stated that Adolf Hitler was building a fortified position from which to make a final stand in the Alpine region south of Munich. The Redoubt, erected and manned by the German SS (including troops of the heavily armed Waffen SS), was being supplied for a long siege. The second, possibly related, report concerned Reinhard Gehlen, a relatively unknown one-star German general described as the head of the German Army General Staff intelligence group stationed on the eastern front. It was reported that Gehlen was actively operating in the same area as Hitler's Redoubt.

Quinn was skeptical of both reports, but he did have information that Gen. Paul Hausser, the commander of the German Army Group G (which was facing the U.S. Seventh Army), had been reassigned to a military coordinating role as retreating German troops converged from all sides into the Alpine regions of Germany, Italy, and Austria. Supreme Headquarters–Allied Expeditionary Force (SHAEF) intelligence had reported the orderly transfer of part of the German

High Military Command (the OKW), which at one time had served Hitler, and other staff and command elements from Berlin south to Bad Reichenhall on the German-Austrian border near Salzburg. A second comparable OKW-led contingent under the command of Gen. Alfred Jodl was being relocated from Berlin to a location in the state of Schleswig-Holstein. Prudently, Quinn distributed the report of the alleged Alpine Redoubt.

The U.S. Seventh Army's offensive momentum had carried Allied troops through the Siegfried line in northern Alsace and, on 24 March, across the Rhine against the somewhat disorganized defense put up by German forces. It appeared to Quinn and Seventh Army commander Gen. Alexander Patch that Hitler's Army Group G, though it blocked the way across Germany to the east, was showing signs of disintegration. The character of the war was changing rapidly. The Wehrmacht forces located on the western front were no longer seriously attempting to block the advancing Allied troops. German officers were anxiously listening to news of Soviet advances into Germany, Czechoslovakia, and Austria. A conclusion of the war with victory firmly placed in Western rather than Soviet hands was on the minds of most German commanders.

I crossed the Rhine on 28 March as commander of a mobile task force built around the Second Battalion of the Texas 141st Regiment, which was part of the Thirty-sixth Division. The 141st traced its history back to the Mexican destruction of the Alamo and the annihilation of the fort's defenders in 1836. The motto "Remember the Alamo," the Texans' battle cry throughout the war with Mexico, was inscribed on the insignia of our regiment. From the first moments of our H-hour landing in southern France on 15 August 1944, our battalion had been in almost continuous combat and had sustained an enormous number of casualties. During the next month after the Rhine crossing we joined other major U.S. forces in advancing across most of southern Germany and met little resistance along the way. My task force led the rest of our regiment as it moved along not more than a few miles behind us and was prepared to reinforce our group in the unlikely event we encountered significant German resistance.

During the late afternoon on 29 April my map indicated we were passing a village called Hurlach, close to the larger town of Dachau and a few miles north of the autobahn leading east into Munich. For several days we had advanced unopposed by German troops; suddenly the lieutenant commanding our leading reconnaissance unit broke the silence in my radio operator's headset with the call "Rondo White Six." ("Rondo" was the code name for the 141st Regimental

Combat Team; "White" designated the Second Battalion; I was "Rondo White Six.") The lieutenant reported their encounter of a freight train slowly moving east along the edge of a forest less than a thousand yards ahead.

The train consisted of a large number of boxcars pulled by one steam locomotive. I ordered the lead tank to move up to the halted reconn cars and to fire a warning round across the front of the moving engine. The tank gun's fire brought the train to a halt. A few train guards in black uniforms jumped from the train and disappeared into the woods; no other German troops were accompanying the train. Infantrymen riding atop the lead tanks broke open the doors of the boxcars and a ghastly cargo of emaciated human beings wearing soiled black and white striped prison uniforms spilled out into the arms of the stunned American soldiers.

At first glance the prisoners seemed more dead than alive. Virtually all of them simply collapsed to the ground. It was our first encounter with inmates of a German concentration camp. Nothing had prepared us for the sight. Remarkably, we had received no briefings, no intelligence, and no instructions on how to deal with this terrible contingency. Few of the prisoners were coherent; most uttered only incomprehensible sounds and no understandable words. When we asked in German, English, and French who they were and where they had come from, a man still strong enough to remain on his feet mutely pointed back down the track.

In the company of two armored cars and two tanks that carried most of a squad of infantrymen and several members of my staff, we set off down the track to the rear of the train. In less than a mile we found the still smoldering remains of a prison camp surrounded by a tall barbed wire fence. On one side of the enclosure was a railroad siding and platform from which the train had obviously just departed. Several bodies of prisoners had been left on the platform; more bodies were found in some of the smoldering dugouts in the camp; outside the fence on the north side of the camp many more bodies were stacked, unburied, in the woods. It clearly had been a hurried departure. Years later I read a report that described the Hurlach camp as an annex to Dachau—where the sickest, weakest, and oldest prisoners were sent in the last weeks of the war. It was a holding area pending shipment out by rail, probably to an uncertain destination to the east. The entire system created for achieving "the Final Solution" was obviously collapsing in the face of the enemy troops advancing from all sides.

At first glance there was no sign of survivors in the just-evacuated camp; even those close to death had been put aboard the train. As we deployed our small force at a spot just short of what appeared to be the main gate into the camp, I heard shouting in the woods to the south of the gate, then observed two inmates wearing the black and white prison garb pursuing a single person wearing an unfamiliar black uniform. The two assailants finally brought the fugitive to the ground within a hundred yards of our halted vehicles. We watched the drama in shocked silence, trying to put it all into perspective. As U.S. soldiers approached, the two former inmates fell exhausted to the ground a few feet from the motionless body, and lay there sobbing with apparent physical and emotional exhaustion. The man in the black uniform had been choked to death. I wondered at the time where the two inmates had found the physical strength to destroy him with nothing more than their emaciated hands. The dead man was a member of the special SS force—the *Totenkopfverband* (Death's head units)—that operated the concentration camps. The camp's SS administrative building and guardhouse stood intact, just outside the main gate. There were no barracks or other permanent facilities near the Hurlach camp. We later learned the SS troops at Hurlach were part of the large SS force stationed at Dachau. In the company of several members of my staff I walked the length of the camp, seeing row upon row of partially burned-out dugouts—the undeniable evidence of terrible living conditions and a hurried departure.

Upon our return to the site of the halted trains I found that in response to my initial radio report, both the division and the regiment had sent medics and a variety of other support units to relieve me of responsibility. I was directed to regroup my force and move south across the autobahn and resume my advance toward the Redoubt, which was rapidly taking the form of a myth. My mission was to keep moving. We bypassed Dachau, unaware of what was taking place there. I radioed to my deputy, Maj. Parkhurst Hough, an abbreviated report of our findings at the Hurlach camp and the situation at the train. We passed the still steaming locomotive and set off through the fields to meet up with our unit.

The story of the Dachau concentration camp reflects the deterioration of the entire German command structure within both the Wehrmacht and the SS in the last days of the war. Himmler was far too late in ordering that Allied troops be denied evidence of the atrocities. Indicative of the confusion was that as I captured the train departing from Hurlach that was evacuating to the east the dead and dying Dachau inmates, American troops approaching the main camp at Dachau discovered a train that had arrived loaded down with hundreds of inmates that had been evacuated westward from concentration camps in Poland —people locked in the train for days without food or sanitary facilities of any kind. It was probably the train from Poland, still loaded with its ghastly cargo, that emotionally incited soldiers of the Forty-fifth Thunderbird Division to take extreme isolated actions against Wehrmacht soldiers and members of the SS within the Dachau camp. Considerable confusion among the U.S. commanders of the Forty-fifth and Forty-second divisions and unclear responsibilities of the Third Army and the Seventh Army existed in the seizure of the huge Dachau camp, and a loss of command control and discipline at the lowest levels resulted in numerous incidents in which Americans entering the camp shot members of both the Wehrmacht and the SS.

For many years I attempted to track down rumors that American troops had lined up against a wall and executed some captured Germans still present in Dachau. Until recently I had found no evidence to support this claim, and for fifty years was unsuccessful in acquiring a credible account of what actually went on at Dachau on the same day that I captured the train at Hurlach. The story finally appeared in the last chapter of Flint Whitlock's book, *The Rock of Anzio from Sicily to Dachau: A History of the U.S. Forty-fifth Infantry Division,* published in 1998. Whitlock states that in 1945, immediately following the military action at Dachau, the IG and JAG of the Seventh Army proposed a court-martial of offenders at Dachau. Gen. Wade Haislip of the Seventh Army and Gen. George Patton of the Third Army rejected the proposed court-martial for actions of any kind linked to Dachau.

I SET a new course for our unit that would take us south of the two lakes that lie between Munich and the Alps, the Starnberge See and the Ammersee; our next objective was Bad Toelz, where the regiment was to regroup after the long advance from the Rhine and before entering the actual Redoubt area. Again we encountered no signs of an organized enemy defense.

It was snowing on the morning of 2 May when we reached the west bank of Starnberge See and moved on through the village of Seeshaupt at its south end. This region of Bavaria was a picture-postcard land and most of the farm villages we passed showed virtually no trace of the war. Only when we reached the road running along the forested slope of the Alps did we begin to draw small arms fire from SS troops that had taken refuge in the protection of the trees. We arrived in Bad Toelz in late afternoon to discover that the First Battalion of our regiment had arrived from the open northern areas and had encountered no resistance getting through. Bad Toelz was obviously not the fortress gateway to the rumored Redoubt—the German troops on all sides were waiting only for the formality of an official cease-fire. Second Lt. Joseph Burke, a platoon leader from the First

Battalion, found Field Marsh. Gerd von Rundstedt there, who had been fired by Hitler in March 1945. He was having dinner with his family in a villa that was part of a hospital for senior officers. When Burke met him, von Rundstedt was dressed in the full regalia of his rank. A man of seventy years, von Rundstedt had worked from the rank of private up to his current rank during the fifty-three years he had served in the German Army. When told that he was at that moment a prisoner of war of the United States, von Rundstedt quietly acquiesced. In addition to the German troops, hundreds of Nazi collaborators were being picked up by our troops right and left.

It had become quite clear to us that the reality of a defended Redoubt was actually a myth, possibly a deception to cover other Nazi operations. Agents reporting to the OSS by clandestine radio locations in the Alps found no evidence of any fortified or organized sites from which the Nazis planned to make a last stand. The OSS and the Seventh Army had at that point lost interest in the story, though the intelligence had not yet filtered down to stop moving troops further into the Alps. By that time we were skeptical of any reports of a German final stand. However, the report on the presence and undefined activities of Gen. Reinhard Gehlen was accurate. We missed an early opportunity to contact his organization, but once the story of the existence of a Redoubt was discredited there appeared to be no real interest (by OSS or Army Intelligence) in pursuing the Gehlen story.

REINHARD GEHLEN, a single-star general, served as the wartime head of the German Army's General Staff intelligence branch on the eastern front. Although the German Army was not prepared to take a last-ditch stand in the Alps in May 1945, this general had assembled his experts and their extensive files on the Soviet armed forces with the intent of turning them over to American intelligence—wholly unknown to the Americans. In the weeks before the end of the war Gehlen had ordered that the files of Fremde Heere Ost (Foreign Armies East, FHO) be carefully packed in metal cases and stored in precisely the same Alpine area as the alleged Redoubt. Gehlen and about a half dozen of his associates were hiding in a ski hut there, waiting for the war to end. Two other FHO groups were hiding elsewhere, waiting to make contact. Gehlen planned to surrender to the Americans in the nearby village of Fischhausen, where he would ask to be put in touch with a senior American officer with whom he would arrange the assembling of his experts and their files. In fact, on 3 May my task force stopped to refuel at Fischhausen, not more than one and a half kilometers from the Elend

Alm where Gehlen was hiding. I had never heard the name Gehlen and had no orders to search for any group. We were ordered to continue pushing through the Alpine area even though resistance had all but ended in most of southern Germany. After refueling we moved out. Just east of Fischhausen the road divided; the right fork led up a wide hard surface road to a high mountain pass and then past a small lake, the Spitzingsee. I briefly considered sending a small armored reconnaissance patrol to investigate the area even though it was not relevant to my mission. In deciding not to send a patrol up that road I probably delayed meeting Reinhard Gehlen, whom I finally met face to face more than three years later and under totally different circumstances. Gehlen in fact had waited a full two weeks after the cease-fire before he descended from the Elend Alm to surrender to the small U.S. Counterintelligence Corps (CIC) team attached to troops in the area.

By dusk on 5 May we had advanced through the supposed Redoubt, traveling virtually unopposed since leaving Bad Toelz seventy-two hours earlier. Our regiment had been engaged only sporadically by small and isolated groups of SS troops. We had heard numerous reports taken from POWs that the SS had been harassing and sometimes terrorizing any members of the Wehrmacht who showed an inclination to surrender. But we had seen only a few members of the SS and surprisingly fewer civilians. The Wehrmacht had prudently withdrawn from our route through the Alps and had not fired a single shot in our direction. The Wehrmacht seemed to have stacked arms.

Then at 1900 hours on 5 May a new voice cut in on our tactical radio net: "We have a message for all troops. All troops are to cease-fire, halt in place, and not fire unless fired upon. We repeat, we have a message . . ." We did not need to hear the message again to understand it fully. We had just received the most welcome order of the entire war: the war was over. I ordered all our radio communications to remain open and alert until we knew more. Nothing else needed to be done. A light but steady rain had been falling from the cloudbank that hung low on the slopes of the Alps. Breaks in the clouds to the west and the sight of the setting sun cast a red glow on the snow-capped Alps. In later years I often heard the residents of the Alps refer to this phenomenon at sunset as the "Alpine glow—a sure sign of better weather tomorrow."

Several hundred yards back along the road we discovered that the vehicles of our command group, perhaps a half dozen jeeps, had pulled off the road into the courtyard of an abandoned roadside inn. I found my men assembled in the inn's main room. There was little conversation and the atmosphere was somber.

The apparent resignation of German troops had ended the war in unconditional surrender, and we were all experiencing a kind of shock—an inability to grasp the full significance of the moment. For these combat veterans, some of whom had landed with the division at Salerno in September 1943, it had been a long war. There was no sign of exuberance, but I did notice that many of us, as we moved about, paused to momentarily place a hand on the shoulder of another. Such was the extent of our celebration. Each appeared to be buried in his own thoughts of family, friends, and, especially at this moment, those men who had fought with us and had not lived to share it. For the first time in months I sat quietly and permitted myself to think about the future.

I had come all the way across Germany without having had a single conversation with a German, beyond terse exchanges with German officers who had insisted on surrendering their forces and had peacefully and tactfully pulled off to the side of the road as we passed. I never projected my thinking beyond the day-to-day conduct of military operations. I assumed that other Americans would be coming along behind us to deal with defeated and occupied Germany. Now that the war was over I would return to the United States to rejoin my family and resume my career as an officer at whatever army post, camp, or station was appropriate. The future of Germany and the German people did not, in those first hours after the cease-fire, have a place in the mind of a professional soldier who like myself had become conditioned to the day-to-day conduct of the war.

Just before midnight I received orders to visit the headquarters of the First German Army located at St. Johann to assist in arranging the details of the cease-fire. Now, I thought, I would have my first real conversation with Germans. We arrived just after daylight at a crossroads in the center of the village of St. Johann, a few kilometers north of Kitzbuehl. We were immediately escorted into a building and introduced to several German officers, the most senior of whom was Col. Albert Emmerich, chief of staff, First Army. Because Emmerich and one or two others spoke adequate English, we dispensed with the assigned interpreters. Emmerich said that the army commander, Gen. Hermann Foertsch, had been gone for several days, involved in some hastily made shifts in the German command structure. Later I learned that Foertsch had been called upon to perform the dubious honor of surrendering several major German commands to the entire galaxy of top commanders in the Allied Sixth Army Group. The German officers briefed us on the confused situation of the entire region. We in turn conveyed to Colonel Emmerich our instructions for maintaining command of and tight control over German troops, including the SS, by assembling units through a minimum of movement on the roads and establishing guarded weapons and ammunition assembly areas. In all matters they were cooperative. We occupied a small house opposite the German First Army headquarters and established communications with Allied division headquarters, which was handling the cease-fire from a location in Kitzbuehl. A few days later the 141st Regiment was withdrawn from Austria and assigned to temporary headquarters in Ulm, a destroyed city and rail center between Stuttgart and Munich in south central Germany, as part of a move to withdraw the entire U.S. Seventh Army to Wuerttemberg Baden. The Seventh's withdrawal left only the U.S. Third Army in Bavaria, but both were subordinate to the new headquarters of the U.S. Forces–European Theater (USFET) established in Frankfurt.

After 8 May, the official V-E Day, the totality of the German acceptance of defeat and unconditional surrender was quite remarkable. In the days immediately after the cease-fire and during the Occupation I never saw any meaningful sign of German armed resistance. The specter of a powerful communist military presence that had advanced all the way to the Elbe (the Soviet forces) was a strong moderating influence on the attitude of the SS. By early summer I had been left in temporary command of the 141st Regiment, with our headquarters located in a villa on the eastern edge of Ulm. Our battalions were occupying villages and towns near the city. Ulm was on the main rail line of Paris–Munich–Vienna and, when Europe was not a war zone, was part of the route used by the famous and luxurious Orient Express from Paris to Istanbul. There was no Orient Express in 1945; in fact, no trains were running, and throughout all of Germany only a few rail lines had not been destroyed.

Ulm had been heavily bombed by the U.S. Air Force during a ground-level raid on 17 December 1944. Due to the fog that day the bombers had been forced to split formation on the approach to the Ulm cathedral; buildings situated on both sides of the cathedral were demolished but the cathedral itself was untouched. Only after the late spring thaw was it possible to carry out cleanup operations, and the warm weather brought the overwhelming stench of bodies out from under the piles of rubble.

Early one morning as I walked through the vast rail yard in the city, I stopped by a huge bomb crater to observe two German electricians attempting to match several hundred wires of many sizes and colors with an equal number of wires coming out of conduits on the opposite side of the crater. After observing them for awhile I foolishly asked how they were doing. The perfunctory response was one used to describe almost everything going on in Germany that summer: *"Krieg kaput, alles kaput*" (War finished, all is finished). Indeed, the war had finished off a great deal of what had once been Germany. In the weeks after settling into Ulm the regiment had little to do but observe the efforts the Germans were making to survive. The movement of the German troops into U.S. POW camps was an almost self-executing operation, since captivity as a Soviet prisoner of war was a wholly unattractive alternative.

With no more battles to fight and no thought of serious training, our combat forces were willing to leave the Germans to the newly organized U.S. Military Government in Germany. But in the early summer of 1945 few Military Government officers were in place and all of our troops in the smaller towns around Ulm had pragmatically established ad hoc relationships and solutions to local problems. Eisenhower's "nonfraternization" order was well understood but at times circumvented by the ingenuity of the American soldier. Life in the countryside went on, often protected from the chaos and turmoil prevalent in all the severely damaged larger cities and communications centers. Somehow these stop-gap arrangements seemed to work. We were all marking time, waiting to see what the future held. When the war ended the typical American GI in Germany was a civilian in uniform who had served his country and was counting "points" that would determine the date of eligibility for return to the United States—he wanted nothing more than to resume a life that had been interrupted by war. He knew little about American policy in occupied Germany and had little interest in learning it.

That summer someone at home had given thought to the idea of entertaining the troops awaiting discharge. The celebrities of the motion picture world and the New York stage and several big bands were on the road generously doing what they could to entertain the millions of American military still abroad. One day late in June 1945 a large four-door German-made sedan pulled up to my villa, which previously had been the home of a German industrialist but that was serving the nobler purpose as a requisitioned residence and headquarters for the commanding officer and staff of the 141st Infantry. I happened to be standing just outside the front entrance when the car came to a halt and the driver stuck his head out of the window and greeted us with a cheerful, "I'm Benny." The statement didn't mean anything to me. I said "I'm Colonel Critchfield." Getting out of the car the driver made a second effort: "I'm Jack Benny and this young lady is Martha Tilton and the lady in the back seat is Ingrid Bergman." In the meantime a distinguished-looking man had gotten out of the car and extended his hand to me saying, "We have obviously surprised you, Colonel. I'm Raymond Massey." By then I had gotten things correctly into focus. I acknowledged that I had not been informed to expect them but immediately extended a warm welcome and invited them into the house. Reinforcements arrived in the form of several members of my staff and the mess sergeant, bearing hot coffee and miraculously produced small sandwiches. I had sent up smoke signals to summon the special services officer, a staff captain who dealt with entertainment for the troops. I offered to our visitors every convenience and comfort our villa had to offer. In doing so I made no intolerable sacrifice. I vacated my large and comfortable second floor bedroom for Miss Bergman. When I checked later to ensure that she had found everything in order, she was sitting on the balcony that overlooked the garden. She asked me to sit with her and talk about the war. She had a hairbrush in her hand and asked if I would mind if she brushed her hair while we talked. Drawing on my training as an officer and a gentleman, I joined her and we talked. For the moment the war seemed very far away; I was glad that I had not followed my first impulse to offer my room to Jack Benny. (For fifty years now I have been fondly viewing reruns of *Casablanca*.) Most of the group of entertainers performed for two nights and then moved on. Raymond Massey stayed with us for two weeks and organized a performance of *Our Town* using talent that had until recently done nothing but carry M-1 rifles. That two weeks was certainly one of the brighter times of that summer.

Throughout the summer there were mass movements of people of all Eurasian nationalities in every direction. No interference or help came from any German authority, police or military—the German military had ceased to exist and the German police had disappeared. Allied military police, other than the few who accompanied combat troops, had not yet appeared. Since the railroads had been completely disrupted, displaced persons either wanting to get home or searching for security elsewhere had commandeered anything and everything with wheels. Trucks loaded with flag-waving men and women clogged the damaged highways. With the gas-guzzling U.S. Army no longer on the move, we had plenty of gasoline to spare, and both it and innumerable captured trucks were generously made available. Of the six million displaced persons in the Western zones of Germany in May 1945, by autumn four million had mysteriously left— many of them, about two million, into hastily improvised displaced persons (DP) camps. Massive numbers of Russian DPs were on the run and hiding out to escape forced repatriation home. The congenial Soviet liaison officers who during the day were enjoying the free benefits of our American messes, clubs, and hotels, were by night hunting these fleeing Russians, who at some point in the war had found their way to the West.

Jewish refugees from all of west Eurasia—from the English Channel to the Ural Mountains—were uprooted and on the move out of Eastern Europe and into the occupied areas of western Austria and Germany. Among these were the few thousand survivors that at one time had been in the hands of the German extermination system that was forcing the remaining Jewish population toward Auschwitz and other end stations in the system. The United Nations Rescue and Relief Agency (UNRRA) and an array of Jewish aid agencies that were active all over Europe were gathering these large number of Jewish refugees, many in need of medical attention, into Jewish DP medical facilities in the occupied areas of Germany and Austria. In the summer of 1945 mere survival appeared to be the main motivation of Jews who had gotten a last minute reprieve from the concentration camps and gas chambers. They were by far the most highly organized and goal-oriented element in the millions of displaced persons on the move all over Europe. American occupation forces shared with President Harry Truman and most American citizens a sense of guilt that, until the last days of the war, the fate of the European Jews had remained largely unacknowledged and outside their consciences. As a result, few American military men were inclined to interfere or unduly complicate the efforts of the Jewish agencies that had mastered the art of cutting corners in meeting the needs of refugees. The U.S. occupation forces nonverbally agreed that help should be generously provided.

Most Jews who survived World War II in Europe lived in the areas of Eastern Europe and the Soviet Union that were under the control of Stalin and the Red Army when the war ended in May 1945. Of the 4.7 million Jews living in the U.S.S.R. before the war, 2.5 million survived. Of the 850,000 Jews living in the Baltic countries, it is estimated that the number of survivors ranged from 450,000 to 650,000. Bulgaria held 400,000 to 430,000 surviving Jews, and in Hungary, 200,000. Of the prewar Jewish population of 2.8 million in Poland, only 12 percent, roughly 300,000, were still alive at war's end.

The initial vigorous denazification effort was barely visible to a combat regiment waiting to be redeployed to the United States. The counterintelligence corps, with support from U.S. combat forces, created civilian internment enclosures and aggressively went about the business of finding and arresting members of the Nazi Party who had held positions described in the *Arrest Handbook for Germany*. The handbook had been developed by the Americans and adopted by all Allied forces, and provided the defining authority for arresting and detaining Nazis—not by name but by position or rank in the party structure or the party's affiliated organizations. Identifying individuals to be brought to trial as war criminals was a quite separate exercise. Denazification and the preparations for war crimes trials were separate but at times overlapping efforts.

Germany was a defeated and occupied nation with a devastated landscape that had been quickly divided between communist Russia and the West. The Red Army was deployed along the militarily historical line of the Elbe River; Stalin, like Hitler, was confident that Western Europe was within his reach and was determined to build an empire extending to all of Eurasia. The West, under the reluctant leadership of the United States, did not yet fully understand the character and aims of the Soviet Union. Moreover, Stalin did not understand the character and potential power of a free world that was dedicated to freedom, democratic order, and international law.

Though the American public and a majority of the members of the U.S. Congress did not adequately understand this new reality, President Truman had learned just how fragile the Western alliance was at the first summit meeting held in Potsdam in late July and early August 1945. The Soviets had established a sphere of influence reaching westward to the Elbe. Moreover, in the midst of the Potsdam gathering the British had unceremoniously cast aside their great wartime leader, Winston Churchill. France was in disarray psychologically, militarily, and politically. Truman left Potsdam knowing that the United States faced awesome global responsibilities inextricably tied to a group of weakened European allies.

Americans and Germans had fought each other on land, at sea, and in the air, but they knew very little about each other during the early days of the Occupation. Aside from the symbolic American soldier sharing a chocolate bar with a hungry child, communications between the two peoples did not come easily. Thousands of German-speaking American Jews, many of whom had been refugees from Germany and Austria during the 1930s, returned to Europe to assist in every aspect of the Occupation. Although the German immigrant communities in America from the 1800s had been assimilated into English-speaking America, their sons and daughters were not much in evidence as linguists in Germany after World War II. While British and French officials in postwar Germany tended to be individuals with highly developed language skills with prewar personal associations to Germans, few Americans from the U.S. armed forces had undergone serious German language training and fewer still had been sent on multiyear tours of duty at the German language Kriegsakademie in Berlin.

Only a few American journalists had been on assignment in Hitler's Germany and a small number of American diplomats had developed close ties with German diplomats in a variety of prewar assignments, most notably those stationed at the U.S. Embassy in Moscow. Finally, American law firms, banks, and large corporations had extensive prewar connections with Germany's expanding presence in the world of international business, but because of the deindustrialization and de-cartelization aims of the U.S. government, these associations were rarely evident in the first years after the war. Yet, though the Americans came with an inherent disadvantage through lack of prewar personal ties to Germany, the British and French, who had such prewar connections, were often handicapped by the policies and machinations of their governments.

President Franklin Roosevelt had created the framework for the American postwar occupation by giving the Joint Chiefs of Staff responsibility for the first six months after the end of hostilities; he left open how and when the JCS role would end. This open question of withdrawal gave the secretary of war, the elderly Col. Henry Stimpson, a central role in occupation policy that was exercised initially by Assistant Secretary of War John J. McCloy. But at Yalta in February 1945 and at Potsdam in July and early August 1945, Allied summitry really set the stage for global developments for the rest of the century. With FDR's death in March 1945 and Winston Churchill being voted out of office in the midst of the Potsdam summit, significant change was taking place at the top.

An existing coordinating committee comprised of members from the departments of State, War, and Navy (and later Treasury and the Federal Economic Administration) quietly initiated unilateral planning for dealing with occupied and liberated areas after the end of hostilities. The committee assumed unconditional surrender by both Germany and Japan. The group working on Germany became known as "The Informal Planning Committee, Germany," which hammered out a policy for postwar Germany. In April 1945, the Joint Chiefs' order Number 1067 (classified top secret) became U.S. policy. Initially intended as a guideline for the occupation and decentralization of Germany's political structure in the early postwar period, the policy remained in effect far beyond that time. The guidelines called for the dissolution of the Nazi Party, the disbanding of German armed forces, and the arrest of war criminals. Although not formally developed in consultation with the British government, much of the order was apparent in the policies adopted by the Allied Expeditionary Force operating under the command of Gen. Dwight Eisenhower.

A revised version of JCS 1067 (still top secret), was issued in May 1945, and an unclassified version was issued in November 1945. JCS 1067 was to serve as guidance for the U.S. member of the Allied Control Council, for the U.S. Military Governor, and for the commander of the U.S. Forces–European Theater. By July General Eisenhower held all three of these positions simultaneously. Gen. Lucius Clay represented Eisenhower on the Allied Control Council in Berlin and was appointed to act as the deputy U.S. Military Governor—the role on which he quickly built his dominant position during the Occupation.

The U.S. military was as unprepared as the German people were for the social, political, and economic chaos of immediate postwar Germany. The Germans accepted the fact that the Treaty of Versailles and the subsequent limited occupation of the Rhineland after World War I had not worked. Unlike the British and French, Americans had limited colonial experience. By European standards the American inexperience in nation-building gave it little status among the more-experienced Europeans. The Americans had fought a revolutionary war against the British less than two hundred years earlier and had created a durable constitutional government with a powerful Bill of Rights, all of which Americans had come to take for granted. Though the character of the postwar alliance that eventually confronted and faced down the Russian-dominated communist empire took some time to evolve, nevertheless in the end the American-German relationship proved central in maintaining peace and stability in western Eurasia during the second half of the twentieth century.

UNTIL THE summer of 1945 I had gone along in life without ever taking any initiative to influence the course of my career. In my early days and during World War II I just accepted each day as it came. Even my June 1939 commission in the Regular Army had come as a result of no real initiative on my part, beyond four years of reserve officer training. The colonel who headed our ROTC unit had asked me to be interviewed by a traveling board of three Army officers, the most senior of whom was a cavalry major. I had no reason to think that my interview would lead to an Army commission. In the first days of June 1939 I was totally surprised when I received a Western Union telegram asking that I accept a commission as a second lieutenant in the cavalry of the U.S. Regular Army.

As a professional soldier I had taken each assignment and experience one after the other, always finding that I had the necessary education, training, and experience to successfully accomplish whatever I had been assigned to do and, in the process, had gained experience to accomplish whatever was required in the next assignment. Soldiering had been my career and life for six years; I thought of it as the profession of the rest of my working life. But that was before I looked more carefully at the world around me, the result of two great wars in the first half of the century. During my years in World War II the character of war had changed dramatically even as it was being conducted by what were considered the world's most civilized nations. I was shocked and appalled by the damage that saturation demolition and firebombing had done to countless great cities. Air power had not brought the Germans to a timely acceptance of defeat in the face of an escalating war against civilian populations. It appeared, however, that the added dimension of the atomic bomb had convinced the emperor of Japan to command his officers to surrender. Had we discovered a magic line separating man's perception of an old-fashioned conventional war and one that would be fought with nuclear weapons? Unconventional warfare was destined to pass through many phases in the second half of the twentieth century. More immediately at hand were the problems of recovery from the war that had just ended. The skills and experience I carried out of the war suddenly appeared not very relevant to the challenges that professional soldiers like me would face now that war had ended.

Midway through the summer of 1945 I saw a War Department circular offering a crash course in geopolitics at Columbia University aimed at preparing a number of officers in ranks from major to colonel for duties with U.S. major commands in occupied Europe and Asia. Seizing on the opportunity, I requested assignment to begin the course in early September. Finally, at age twenty-eight, I took the first self-motivated initiative that would change my life forever.

My hastily planned return to the United States gave me a few days for that long-awaited reunion with my wife and family, whom I had left in our hometown of Fargo, North Dakota, two years before. When I went to war Connie was pregnant with our second child and she and my young daughter, Michel Ann, spent the war years living close to both our families. She shared the war years with many other young wives of husbands from my ROTC class who served during the war. My son, Jimmy, was born in December 1943. I arrived in Fargo at two o'clock in the morning on a Northwest Airlines DC-3. Once home, I went into the nursery to see Jimmy. He stood up in his crib, looked at me, and then looked at a postwar head and shoulders portrait of me in uniform hanging on the wall that had been painted by a Lithuanian artist refugee living in Germany. Jimmy looked back at me—an up and down survey—and took one more look at the portrait. Then I heard him speak his first words: "He's got legs." Obviously I needed more time with my family.

The "retreading" program at Columbia and at several other universities was the idea of Secretary of the Navy James Forrestal. I and about thirty-five military officers from all branches of the service undertook the intense educational experience. The professors who lectured us left lasting impressions. We were, in fact, provided with a clearly marked chart for navigating the half-century that followed. The six-month program of classes from morning until evening included an extensive element of required reading. The principal textbook, *Foundations of International Power,* published by the Princeton University Press, is a collection of critically important essays and papers written by noted scholars and statesmen of the time.

Our mentor throughout the entire course was Prof. Grayson Kirk, a specialist in geopolitics who later followed Dwight D. Eisenhower as president of Columbia University. Professor Kirk met with us for one long afternoon session each week, during which he painted a panorama of a world in which the United States had discovered itself at the center without planning to be there. His subjects often related to current developments in a world of great change. The course focused only on Europe, where most of us would be sent immediately after we finished at Columbia. Dr. Carleton Huntley Hayes, recently back from his wartime assignment as ambassador to Spain, guided us to an understanding of the evolution of the European nation-state as an institution, as well as the lasting influence that the 1648 Treaty of Westphalia had had on all of Europe. Dr. Charles Cole, who later became the president of Dartmouth College, enlightened us on the French Revolution and traced France's survival through two world wars. Cole was the most lively, articulate, and entertaining of our professors, and he had a talent for pouring out an enormous amount of factual history in one short hour. Several professors lectured on the history of Russia. Six months after victory in Europe, by and large Russia was still viewed as our country's great ally, and at least one economics professor extolled the virtues and success story of Russia's industrial development under Joseph Stalin.

The Germany of 1945 was in a sense the centerpiece of the course. We heard little information about the history of Germany before the rise of Hitler. We were dealing with the contemporary situation in Germany. Our principal instructor on Germany was Franz Neumann, a professor of economics whose book, *Behemoth,* was published early in the war and later reissued with an update on the months of the late war. I thought then—and still think now—that *Behemoth* was a brilliant intellectual work. I remember little about Neumann's personality. He made no comment on his own background or wartime activity; not until much later did

I learn that he had been the principal architect of the U.S. denazification policy conducted in Germany. Neumann, who headed the Eastern European section of the OSS Research and Analysis office, was viewed as the ultimate authority on the Third Reich, the entire Nazi Party, and all of its affiliated parts. Also required course reading was *Germany Is Our Problem* by Secretary of Treasury Henry Morgenthau, which Neumann considered an entirely unacceptable and unrealistic approach on many different counts. Morgenthau's plan was to divide Germany into two essentially agrarian nations in the center of Europe with no industry. It was reported that Neumann and Morgenthau clashed while serving together on the working group committee that hammered out the basic U.S. policy for postwar Germany.

Within forty-eight hours after the end of our course at Columbia almost all of us were on an army transport ship headed back to Europe—my second troop transport trip to Europe in three years without my family, but this time it was to contribute to peace rather than to war.

2

Fremde Heere Ost—Prewar and Postwar

IN JULY 1945 when Reinhard Gehlen arrived at the Twelfth Army Group interrogation center at Wiesbaden, Germany, he and his surviving staff (and the carefully cached files on Soviet tactical and strategic military strength) constituted the only comprehensive information on Soviet military power held anywhere by anyone in the entire world. The United States and its Western allies had made no serious effort to gather intelligence on the Soviet forces; in fact the Soviets had forcefully prohibited American and British citizens living in the Soviet Union from doing so. At the start of the war against the Soviet Union in 1941 the responsibility of the German Army General Staff had been cut back and activity was limited to the eastern front. Chief of staff Gen. Franz Halder had moved to an isolated headquarters in east Prussia and taken most of his General Staff with him. Hitler's interest in intelligence on Soviet forces greatly increased when he personally assumed command of the war in the east in December 1941. He remained focused on the eastern front until the Allies went on the offensive, first with the November 1942 invasion of North Africa and later the landings in Sicily and Italy in 1943 and the major Normandy landing in 1944.

The estimates by the German Army General Staff intelligence organization Fremde Heere Ost (Foreign Armies East) about the Soviet armed forces in 1940 and early 1941 were subject to widespread criticism, probably a reflection of the euphoria among Hitler and his top German officers who believed the Soviets would be defeated in a matter of months. It was assumed that the Wehrmacht's victory in Western Europe could be replicated in the east. Rommel's initial success in reaching the Libyan border with Egypt and the Army's ability to finish the Balkans war and drive the British out of Greece led Hitler and most Wehrmacht officers in 1941 to favor attacking the Soviet Union. I firmly believe that most German officers saw Hitler's geopolitical ambitions to the east and in the Indian Ocean region as easily supportable, had they not been so integrally a part of his primary goal of destroying the Jewish population and subjugating the Slavic and ethnic groups of Asia Minor.

Reinhard Gehlen, who was appointed to head Fremde Heere Ost on 1 April 1942, came from a family of modest means. Born in Erfurt, Germany, in 1902, Gehlen's boyhood and early years followed a traditional conservative path. He never dwelled on those years and seemed always a very private person. We do know that during his school years in Breslau he was a serious student and took home good academic reports. At the age of eighteen he joined the Army as an officer candidate in the Third Artillery Regiment and was appointed an ensign in 1922. For the next few years Gehlen led a conventional military life in the Reichswehr, which led to promotions and entrance into training for the General Staff. He was promoted to lieutenant in December 1923, to first lieutenant in 1928, and served as adjutant of the First Detachment, Third Artillery Regiment. On 1 October 1933 Gehlen entered the staff college, then spent the third year of his training at the Kriegsakademie, which had reopened in 1935; he was among the academy's first graduates. Upon graduation Gehlen reached his first major goal: admission to the corps of officers who carried the cherished designation of "i.G.," which authorized them to wear uniform trousers having the red stripe down each side.

From 1935 to 1939 Gehlen was posted as a captain of the General Staff and stationed mainly in locations away from Berlin. His duties primarily concerned fortifications. In 1939, by then a major, Gehlen was assigned to a reserve infantry division that missed getting into combat during the brief assault on Poland of 1 September 1939. During the 1940 campaigns in Western Europe, Gehlen came to the attention of Gen. Franz Halder when he served as Halder's liaison officer to Gen. Walter Model and later to Gen. Heinz Guderian, who had made history in leading the armored blitzkrieg across France to the English Channel. From May to October of that year Gehlen served as Halder's adjutant before his assignment to the Eastern Group of the operations division of the Army General Staff. Gehlen's interest in the Soviet Union and his relationship with Adolf Heusinger began there, and later proved to be the most important professional association of his life.

Adolf Heusinger, then a colonel, was responsible for planning the largest offensive in the history of land warfare—Operation Barbarossa, the invasion of the Soviet Union along a twenty-five-hundred-mile front. Heusinger, born on 4 August 1897 in Holzminden on the Weser, was the son of a teacher and a product of evangelical religious influence dating back to the sixteenth century. In 1915, having completed primary and middle school, Heusinger became a volunteer in the Prussian Army and during World War I spent three years as a lieutenant in the Ninety-sixth Infantry Regiment, eventually fighting at Verdun and Flanders. In July 1917 Heusinger was severely wounded and became a British prisoner of war, where he learned English and studied Russian. In 1921 he was taken into the one-hundred-thousand-man German Army authorized by the Treaty of Versailles; until 1927 he served in the Fifteenth Infantry Regiment at Kassel as a company commander and battalion adjutant.

From 1927 until 1930 Heusinger underwent what at the time served as the training course for future General Staff officers: two years in a regional training program in Stuttgart followed by a year in the war ministry in Berlin. On 1 October 1932 Captain Heusinger was assigned to duty with the General Staff. In 1934 and 1935 he commanded a company in the Eighteenth Infantry Regiment at Paderborn as part of his General Staff training, followed by a short assignment on a division staff before being returned to Berlin in 1937, where he joined the operations division of the General Staff. At that point Heusinger became intimately involved in Ludwig Beck's opposition to Hitler's plans to take Germany into a new war by invading Czechoslovakia. Heusinger served under three successive General Staff chiefs: Ludwig Beck, Franz Halder, and Kurt Zeitzler. When Hitler ordered the Army to prepare for the attack on the Soviet Union on 18 December 1940 Heusinger, by then a full colonel and head of the Operations Division, became responsible for planning the offensive.

Reinhard Gehlen assumed the leadership of Fremde Heere Ost, his first intelligence assignment, though he had no relevant experience in either collecting or analyzing information on the Soviets. Until that time Fremde Heere Ost itself had left the collection of intelligence on Soviet forces entirely in the hands of the Abwehr (under Adm. Wilhelm Canaris) and the evolving Nazi Party in Amt VI (under Schellenberg). As an energetic, efficient, and well-trained General Staff officer Gehlen quickly organized information that was available from several sources: firsthand descriptions from Russian POWs, photographic intelligence from Goering's air force, expanding German intercepts of Soviet and Allied communications, and reports about the military espionage of the Abwehr's "Walli-I" (the code name of the intelligence collection unit that had conducted operations against Soviet forces on the eastern front from the first day of the war there).

Although he directed Fremde Heere Ost until close to the end of the war, Gehlen, contrary to a widely held opinion among Western writers, had little personal contact with Hitler. As he told me, he met with Hitler only four times during the war. The intelligence he produced was presented to the Army chief of staff and integrated into Hitler's operational briefings at the Wolfschanze, usually later the same day that it was collected. Normally Heusinger, as head of the operations division, accompanied the chief of staff and conducted the briefing. Heusinger, therefore, was quite familiar with Fremde Heere Ost and its performance until late in the war.

Within Fremde Heere Ost, Gehlen had a small circle of talented young General Staff officers that included Lt. Col. Heinz Herre, his deputy, Capt. Gerhard Wessel, the dominant figure in the production of intelligence reports, and a staff of only about thirty-five individuals. When Hitler eliminated the Abwehr in 1944, Gehlen improvised an ad hoc relationship with Hermann Baun, the head of Walli-I, to give himself protection from the influence of the RSHA (Nazi intelligence). Among the many personalities Gehlen dealt with during this time, Baun was the critical element of his Soviet intelligence-collection effort. Born in Odessa in southern Ukraine, Baun had grown up in a Russian culture and spent his entire life at the center of relations between Germany and Russia as they evolved after the Communist Revolution in 1917. The Abwehr, which conducted both intelligence and counterintelligence operations against the Soviets, remained independent of Fremde Heere Ost even though that branch of the German Army was a major consumer of Walli-I's information on Soviet forces.

By late 1943 Reinhard Gehlen, like many other German Army officers, had concluded that the total mobilization of the United States and its determination to defeat both Germany and Japan meant that the war could not be won. Germany's war against the Soviet Union had not gone as planned. Stalin saw Roosevelt and Churchill's Casablanca Agreement, to carry the war to unconditional surrender, and their commitment to meet his forces somewhere in the center of Germany, as a policy he could support. The Red Army force that was deployed on a line running north-south through Germany at the end of the war would give him half of Germany and probably all of Eastern Europe. If the Red Army were in control of central and eastern Europe, the strong Communist elements in Germany, France, and Italy could probably deliver all of Western Europe into Communist hands. Stalin did not believe the United States was prepared to install itself as a long-term significant power in Europe.

In the security of after-lunch walks in the Mauerwald, Gehlen shared his thoughts with his deputy, Gerhard Wessel. Gehlen assumed that after the unconditional surrender and occupation of Germany, Europe would be divided and relations between the Soviet Union and the West would rapidly deteriorate, leading to a Western defense alliance in which a new Germany would find its place as an ally of the West. Gehlen foresaw that Europe and probably the entire world would polarize into two ideologically incompatible camps, one led by the United States and the other by the Soviet Union. The Soviet Union would prove itself to be not only an unreliable ally but also a threat to much of the free world—and Fremde Heere Ost was one of the few assets a defeated Germany could offer to the United States to alleviate this threat.

After his initial failure to take Moscow in 1941, Hitler seized the opportunity that Pearl Harbor presented to give substance to the Berlin-Tokyo axis, and declared war on the United States just four days after the Japanese attack. A wave of optimism swept through Hitler's entourage after the news from many fronts took a turn for the better in the summer of 1942. For many this optimism was partially regained in the early campaigns of 1942 when Hitler's geopolitical aspirations led to his break with General Halder over the decision to go for control of Stalingrad and open a new front in the Caucasus. Hitler dismissed Halder over the issue and replaced him with Gen. Kurt Zeitzler.

Adolf Heusinger believed that as an institution the effectiveness of the German Army General Staff ended with Halder's dismissal, even though it continued to exist and maintain a degree of integrity until the end of the war. Its influence was already diminished after the Wehrmacht's high command joined Hitler on the eastern front, and finally vanished after the 20 July 1944 plot to kill Hitler. Quite aside from the details of the 20 July plot, on 29 July the Gestapo investigation delivered detailed files of an earlier abortive plan to overthrow Hitler in 1938.

Back in 1938 both the Army General Staff under Beck and the Abwehr under Canaris were at the height of their influence. Ludwig Beck, who was totally opposed to Hitler's plan to take Czechoslovakia and to conduct a war in general, was immediately fired and replaced by Halder. Halder turned to the Abwehr chief of staff, Gen. Hans Oster, to organize the planned coup to remove Hitler at the height of the Sudetenland Crisis in the late summer of 1938. The 1938 plot to overthrow Hitler was aborted when Neville Chamberlain met Hitler's demands on the Sudetenland. Beck, a member of the resistance until the 1944 attempt, was executed after the assassination attempt failed. Shocked by the extent of the belatedly revealed resistance effort of 1938, Hitler ordered the execution of all the surviving plotters. Canaris and Oster were brutally executed in the last weeks of the war; the war's end saved Halder from the same fate. Adolf Heusinger supported the efforts of Beck and Halder to remove Hitler in 1938 and late 1939. As the war dragged on, however, he became skeptical that a successful assassination of Hitler would lead to an accommodation with both the Soviets and the Allies.

Heusinger had been a witting member of the resistance under Beck; after moving to eastern front headquarters in east Prussia, both men continued to be informed but were less active than they had been earlier in Berlin. Neither was actively involved in the plot of 20 July, but Heusinger was prepared to use his position to support it after the fact. The bomb exploded at Heusinger's feet as he briefed Hitler. Wounded and arrested following the attempt, Heusinger was taken to the Prinz-Albrecht-Strasse prison in Berlin and interrogated there by the Gestapo.

While in prison Heusinger wrote a candid description of the conduct of the war in which Adolf Hitler was not portrayed as a military genius but rather as a military leader responsible for the needless deaths of hundreds of thousands of German soldiers. The report was delivered to Hitler, who sent him to his Rastenburg headquarters before his house arrest. In Rastenburg he was shown into a small room where Hitler's aide offered him a seat. When Hitler entered the room Heusinger stood up and found Hitler advancing to him with an outstretched hand. They sat down and talked. Hitler expressed regret that Heusinger had been exposed to the ordeal of arrest and interrogation; Heusinger agreed that it had indeed been an ordeal. Hitler then quietly and calmly told Heusinger that he had read his critique, and offered some disagreements and explanations for his military decisions, emphasizing that he had broad objectives and responsibilities that sometimes superceded military considerations. Heusinger remained firm in the positions he had taken in the paper and the meeting came quietly to an end. Hitler was no doubt ambivalent about Heusinger. He admired his earlier performances and assigned great significance to Heusinger's service in the infantry trench warfare of World War I. Hitler obviously had respect for this calm and intelligent staff officer and was having a problem in understanding how he had lost him to the opposition. Heusinger was returned to his family.

It is widely accepted that Reinhard Gehlen was not a member of the German resistance. Based on conversations I had with Gehlen much later about the internal resistance effort and the 20 July plot, I believe that he was psychologically unprepared to participate in a plot to assassinate or even to overthrow a head of state who was also his senior military commander. The fact that he was assigned to the department concerned with fortifications and he was not physically present among the Army's General Staff in his early years may have also contributed to this reluctance. Heusinger's close association with Ludwig Beck in 1937 had caused Heusinger to join the conspiracy. By late in 1943 Gehlen had made a decision to preserve Fremde Heere Ost and draw his closest associates into his own conspiracy to deliver the organization to the West, most likely the United States—an added reason for staying clear of the plot against Hitler. Gehlen and Heusinger went their separate ways for three years after the failed attempt.

Not until early April 1945, just before the end of the war, did Gehlen reveal his postwar plans to Hermann Baun. Baun, by nature a disorganized man governed more by political and ideological emotions than by the General Staff disciplines of logic, reason, or military principle, had made no plans for the postwar period. In great secrecy Gehlen met Baun in a hotel room in Bad Elster, where Baun agreed to collaborate in forming a German intelligence effort that eventually would be offered to the armed forces of the United States. Baun, Gehlen recognized, would be indispensable to his postwar operation since a continuing supply of intelligence would be essential to the ongoing analysis of the Soviet armed forces after the cease-fire. Baun assumed, correctly, that the Soviets would deny the Americans open access to Soviet forces in Germany and central Europe, and that the Americans would be slow to recognize the need for a U.S. espionage network operating against their Soviet ally in occupied areas. Gehlen was fully confident that he would have no difficulty in turning his collection operations, Baun's operation, against the comparatively easy target of Soviet occupation troops. The agreement between Gehlen and Baun contained few details and no written record. A discovered conspiracy of the sort developed at Bad Elster would almost certainly have brought summary justice and execution at the hands of the Sicherheitdienst, (SD, the security service of the Reich). Under such circumstances it would have been unwise to go beyond a broad and secret verbal agreement. Baun's people later called it a "50-50 deal," and Gehlen's supporters have never argued that it was anything else. Although no notes were taken at Bad Elster, the two agreed on at least one fact: the Gehlen group would use the code name "Fritz" and the Baun group would use "Otto." The names stuck and they referred to themselves as such when they were reunited almost six months later.

In the last days of the war Siegfried Graber, Baun's deputy, and Dr. Roman Schellenberg, a lawyer and friend of Baun who late in the war had become part of Baun's loyal entourage, gathered Baun and what remained of Walli-I in hand and maneuvered their way into the south Allgaeu near the French Zone. By accident they ended up in the hands of the French, but with the assistance of Graber's brother, a Catholic priest, were able to move into the U.S. Zone.

At the same time Gehlen met with Gen. August Winter, who was second in command to General Jodl in the operations staff of OKW and the senior OKW officer in southern Germany, to explain his plan and the status of Fremde Heere Ost. Winter saw that Gehlen's plan gave him an opportunity to move with Fremde Heere Ost into the Western camp. Winter was a Bavarian, a general of the Mountain Troops, and the most senior OKW officer accessible to Gehlen in the last days of the war. Winter later became a member of Gehlen's organization but was never given any key responsibilities and was somewhat shunned by Gehlen's inner circle and even more by Heusinger and his group. In my view August Winter was political baggage, but if Gehlen promised safe haven to Winter after the war, he clearly met his side of the bargain.

By early 1945 Gehlen's preparations were being completed. A month before the end of the war Hitler dismissed Gehlen for "defeatism in his reporting." Wessel was left to continue what remained of the Fremde Heere Ost operation. Gehlen, free of the demands of his position, used those last weeks to put his plan into action. Earlier the Germans had captured and passed on to Fremde Heere Ost a copy of the agreement reached in London on what was planned for the Soviet, U.S., and British occupation zones, and Gehlen was determined to see the end of the war from a vantage point inside the U.S. Zone. Fremde Heere Ost files were stored at a location in the Bavarian Alps. Gehlen's plan was for three small groups to hide out in the same area, maintaining radio communications until the eventual cease-fire stabilized the situation and he could make contact with a senior American officer and then move his associates into safe hands. Soviet forces were in control of Berlin, Prague, Budapest, and Vienna. In Germany, Soviet and U.S. forces met at a dividing line along the Elbe River and on 8 May 1945 the war in Europe ended with Germany's unconditional surrender.

Adolf Heusinger was living in Walkenried in the Harz Mountains when the cease-fire became effective. He and another senior German general who was in retreat from the western front surrendered to the American forces. In the late summer of 1945 Heusinger was discovered by Lt. Col. Orin James Hale, a professor of German history from the University of Virginia who was part of a small team headed by Dr. George Shuster that had been sent to Germany in the late summer of 1945 by the historical division of the Army to locate and interrogate particularly interesting German officers and officials. Hale had heard about Heusinger from Gen. Ernst Koestring, a German Soviet expert serving in Moscow as the German military attaché before the war. Koestring described Heusinger as an officer of unusual talent. Hale found him in the general POW enclosure, ignored and in somewhat dire circumstances. Hale was enormously impressed by Heusinger's almost total recall. Years later Hale recorded his own view that Heusinger was the single most impressive general or senior official that he interrogated during those several months in 1945. Hale and another American who was temporarily assigned to the Shuster team, Brigadier Gen. Ronald C. Brock, were so taken by Heusinger that they went to considerable effort to have letters and food packages delivered to Heusinger's family—a practice Hale continued until Heusinger was able to renew contact with his wife, Gerda, and daughters, Ruth and Ada. It was the beginning of a relationship that resumed when Hale was assigned to Munich in 1950 as the deputy to the American Commissioner George Shuster, and continued until Adolf Heusinger's death.

All did not go as planned for Gehlen and his comrades, who were hiding out in the ski lodge in the Elend Alm. The radio communications among the three groups had not worked (allegedly because of the mountainous environment) and in the end they surrendered separately and for a time lost integrity as an organized group. It was a nerve-wracking time, with Soviet liaison groups on the prowl searching for POWs of special interest. Gehlen, hiding out for almost two weeks after the cease-fire, descended from the Elend Alm to Fischhausen and surrendered to a local CIC detachment, which to Gehlen's huge disappointment did not take seriously his request to see a senior American officer. Eventually over a period of weeks Gehlen was passed up the line to the Seventh U.S. Army interrogation facility at Augsburg. Gen. Bill Quinn remembered Gehlen's name from Allen Dulles's reports just before the end of the war, and when he spotted Gehlen's name in a list of POWs he ordered him to be sent to the interrogation center in Wiesbaden. Though the British and Soviets were both interested in Gehlen, it was the first time the United States had heard of Gehlen's plan.

Gerhard Wessel and his group also left their mountain hideout to become POWs. Wessel was concerned about the danger of being handed over to the Russian liaison mission representatives that were beginning to appear in American POW camps bearing lists of their most wanted German officers, particularly German intelligence officers. By July a German-speaking American officer, a recent Jewish refugee from Germany who had been brought into Army intelligence, removed Wessel from a POW camp and headed westward to Wiesbaden, assuring Wessel that he would soon be with friends.

The pair soon met with Capt. John Boker, a German-speaking U.S. military intelligence officer from a Solingen steel cutlery family in New York that had maintained its ties in the Ruhr district while manufacturing quality cutlery in America. Boker was an impressive officer—tall, fit, poised, and with body language exuding self-confidence born of moderate wealth, a good education, and a successful family business. Boker enjoyed the widespread respect of his wartime peers and superiors, though he planned eventually to return to private life in Manhattan. It was Gehlen's good luck to meet Captain Boker, because Boker was one of the few U.S. military intelligence officers looking specifically for Germans with unique knowledge of the Soviet armed forces. Gehlen had finally met an American to whom he could candidly describe his plan to turn Fremde Heere Ost over to American intelligence. Over the course of several days Gehlen found Boker willing to listen to his proposal. Their meetings proved to be the most critical link in the chain of events that shaped the postwar life of Reinhard Gehlen. Gehlen, a relatively unknown German officer who had attained the equivalent rank of an American brigadier general, was a man with a mission: to put the General Staff's intelligence experiences in the Soviet Union at the disposal of the United States.

Captain Boker put his own reputation on the line when he recommended that Gen. Edwin L. Sibert, the G-2 of the newly formed USFET, make a limited decision to take Gehlen at his word. Boker suggested that Gehlen's group should be assembled in a place where they could be put to work and judged on the value of what they produced. The files that had been hidden at a location in the Bavarian Alps would be recovered and returned to the experts who had created them. General Sibert agreed. The decision to assemble and take a better look at one German general and his small intelligence staff did not seem to be a major decision—but it was almost certainly made without informing the Army G-2 in Washington or the OSS, which was well represented in Germany in the summer of 1945. In fact, General Sibert probably thought it was not a matter requiring prior approval of General Eisenhower, by then commander in chief of the USFET, or of his chief of staff, Walter Bedell Smith. At the end of the war no U.S. policy or plan existed to assemble or use the German Army General Staff Intelligence Department at the eastern front. Chief Justice William Jackson, temporarily a general and the designated U.S. chief prosecutor for the major war crimes trials, was looking for a way to indict and bring to trial the most senior officers of the Wehrmacht without regard to the fact that the automatic arrest categories did not extend to the Wehrmacht, including the Army General Staff. Members of Fremde Heere Ost were clearly not in the category of the Gestapo, the SD, or Walter Schellenberg's Amt VI of the Reichssicherheitshauptamt (RSHA) —all of which were instruments of the Nazi Party and indicted at Nuremberg as criminal organizations.

In early summer 1945 the Pentagon's G-2 received word from the British that Gehlen was in Wiesbaden. Unaware of Sibert's plan for Gehlen, the G-2 ordered that Gehlen and six of his experts be flown to Washington for extended interrogations under the direction of the Army's G-2. In addition to Gehlen were Col. Konrad Stephanus, Maj. Horst Hiemenz, Maj. Hans Hinrichs, Maj. Erich Friedrich, Maj. Albert Schoeller, and Capt. Herbert Fuener. John Boker escorted the group aboard the general's private plane to Fort Hunt, an interrogation facility outside of Washington, where they were initially treated quite harshly as normal POWs—kept apart and interrogated intensively. Boker was finally able to reunite the group in a single barracks and have some of the restrictions eased. When General Sibert visited the Pentagon a few months later he reported on the Fremde Heere Ost project, which by that time had been given the code name "Operation X." But Sibert's report did not change Gehlen's or his comrades' status, who were held at Fort Hunt for a full year. During that year they contributed to the publication of the first postwar Army G-2 handbook on Soviet armed forces. Contrary to several published histories, Gehlen's sojourn at Fort Hunt was unrelated to the intelligence project under way in Germany. Although Gehlen and his group were of interest to senior analysts and Soviet specialists in Washington, none of their discussions concerned a future German intelligence service. From Washington Gehlen was able to exert only minimal influence on the development of the Operation X project.

Perhaps the single most important accomplishment in that year was the contact Gehlen established with Capt. Eric Waldman from the Intelligence Division of the War Department General Staff. Waldman spent considerable time at the interrogation center, listening with interest to Gehlen's ideas. With support from

John Boker, Waldman was able to significantly improve the condition of the group's confinement, even arranging to take Gehlen on at least one trip into Washington. Boker then returned to civilian life.

Gehlen persuaded Waldman to add Heinz Herre to his small group at Fort Hunt and Herre was flown to Washington. At the end of the war Herre narrowly avoided the fate of Vlasov and his staff, all of whom were executed on reaching Prague after the Americans turned them over to the Russians. Herre, much wanted by the Russian liaison officers in the U.S. Zone in Germany, managed to lose himself in an American POW camp until he was routinely discharged. He simply returned to his family's home in Kruen in the Bavarian Alps.

Meanwhile, back in Germany Sibert began to assemble some of Gehlen's wartime comrades at the U.S. Detention and Interrogation Center (USDIC) facility in Oberursel near Frankfurt. A small staff, mainly German-speaking officers, carried out a systematic effort to locate and bring to Oberursel other Fremde Heere Ost members and to retrieve Gehlen's files in the Alps. Decades later Gerhard Wessel recalled the astonishingly friendly and cooperative attitude of these young U.S. officers who were mainly Jewish prewar refugees from Germany and Austria. The project was run from a compound—code named "Basket"—that had been created from four villas immediately adjacent to the USDIC, a thirty-minute drive from USFET headquarters in Frankfurt. Wessel and several others were moved from the center at Wiesbaden and established in the "Blue House" at the compound.

Although the USFET head of intelligence could have used an existing military intelligence unit to organize and direct the assembled German staff, he instead chose to assign Lt. Col. John Deane as project officer. A USFET G-2 officer who was a paratrooper with no intelligence background and did not speak German, Deane reported directly to General Sibert. Colonel W. R. Philp, the head of the detention center, knew of the operation but had no direct responsibility for it. Deane renamed the project "Operation Rusty," a name that came into wide use within the U.S. intelligence community in the two years that followed. The Germans began calling Operation Rusty "the Organization," or simply "the Org." Wessel's staff soon developed ties with analysts in USFET and required no staff supervision at Oberursel.

Inexplicably, Sibert appeared determined to keep the commander in chief of the 970th CIC unaware of the project. Even after assigning an added counterintelligence and internal security mission to Deane's operation in the U.S. Zone in early 1946, Sibert bypassed his own counterintelligence branches in the G-2 and the 970th. The added exclusion of the OSS from any role made both decisions cardinal mistakes and resulted in a conflict that put the counterintelligence corps into an adversarial role that continued for years. In the chaotic intelligence community in West Germany the U.S. 970th CIC and Operation Rusty were by far the two largest intelligence efforts.

In September 1945 the U.S. staff at Oberursel agreed that Hermann Baun's operation could become the espionage arm of Operation Rusty, and was therefore an important piece of the plan to assemble Gehlen's people. While Baun was happy to be rescued from a POW camp in southern Germany, he was nevertheless uncomfortable at the Blue House among both the American staff and the German General Staff officers. After a very short time Baun persuaded both Wessel and the U.S. staff that to be effective operationally he needed to be established at an outside location. He moved into a requisitioned and isolated hunting lodge owned by the Opel industrial family in the Taunus Mountains north of Frankfurt. The Germans called it simply the Jagdhaus (the hunt house). Once stationed there Baun began to address the task of organizing agents to collect information on the Soviet forces in East Germany. Baun was left almost wholly unsupervised and he made it quite clear that he did not consider the Blue House anything more than a customer for the information he planned to collect within the requirements developed by the German Blue House staff or by the U.S. staff.

At the Jagdhaus, Baun proved to be something of a magnet for Germans with special interests in Russia and the Soviet Union. Siegfried Graber, Baun's deputy during the last year of the war, was persuaded to rejoin Baun and played a critical role in the new operation. Another Abwehr officer recruited by Baun in the early months, Hans von Lossow, later played a major role as Gehlen's personal emissary in Bonn during the most critical days in 1950. He traveled all the way to the Jagdhaus from Brandenburg on a wagon drawn by his own four horses. In this early period von Lossow performed many useful functions for the growing operation. At Graber's request Baun also brought in Dr. Kurt Kohler, an Austrian and former Abwehr officer who had served in counterintelligence on the eastern front and who had been discreetly removed from a civilian internment enclosure outside of Salzburg. The Americans had quietly extracted many men like Kohler from American custody in Austria and put them to work in Baun's expanding secret service, some of whom simply remained in Austria as members of an Austrian operations base. Several Abwehr officers who had served on the eastern front joined many others who were simply experts on Russia looking for an immediate safe haven and three meals a day, including Herbert von Dirksen, former Ambassador to Moscow, London, and Tokyo, and Gustav Hilger, a German diplomat with long service in Moscow and numerous connections among the circle of U.S. Russian experts who had served in Moscow before the war. Rapidly the population at the Jagdhaus exceeded the lodge's capacity; the U.S. staff in Oberursel solved the problem by requisitioning a small hotel in the nearby resort village of Schmitten.

Baun had little personal contact with or influence in the Blue House even though he depended on it and the USDIC for material support. This proximity to power—General Eisenhower himself was commander in chief of USFET until November 1945—assured Operation X, including Baun's operation, access to American supplies for the specific purpose of supporting intelligence operations. The Baun operation, like all American intelligence groups operating in Germany, depended on these supplies to generate money from the black market. In his early months at the Jagdhaus, Baun had only one vehicle at his disposal, an ancient Mercedes that was kept running by his son, Rolf; the Blue House supplied all transportation between Oberursel and the Jagdhaus. But since there was almost no public transportation operating in Germany at the time, communicating with Baun's operation bases was the single most difficult problem he encountered.

Building a spy organization in Germany in early 1946 demanded the creation of a network of one-on-one relationships based on mutual trust and confidence. It also required individuals with experience and a special talent and passion for clandestine operations. Baun put out his network—under the auspices of the "Technical Intelligence Branch" (or "TIB")—in search of intelligence operators to establish small bases in the U.S. Zone that would dispatch agents into the Soviet Zone to recruit agents in place. There was no immediate need for Soviet spies within the Soviet occupation forces; the German staff in the Blue House mainly wanted to learn the Soviet order of battle. It was not a sophisticated espionage network.

Establishing a network of individual agents residing in the U.S. Zone demanded the requisitioning of individual German houses and establishing communications and supply lines from these to the Jagdhaus. Supervision and support was complicated by the totally chaotic circumstances in postwar Germany, but for the hundreds of unemployed German intelligence officers a job with U.S. intelligence was indeed a prize that offered status, some legal protection, and, above all, housing and a reliable supply of food and other items to sell on the black market.

The overwhelming number of Soviet security forces and East German communist police forces present in the Soviet Zones of Germany and Austria made it difficult for a visitor from West Germany to find, recruit, and communicate with agents. Successful resident agents, preferably operating from an observation post near a major railroad terminal or near a landing and takeoff pattern of a major military airfield, were expected to observe and report on Soviet military deployments and activities. Berlin, at the center of the Soviet Zone, had a great many communications links under development and immediately assumed importance in Baun's effort. By the late summer of 1946 the Baun organization, operating with limited support and essentially no control from any staff at Oberursel, consisted of a message center in Berlin and approximately 125 full-time agents dispersed throughout West Germany. Their efforts had delivered a total of roughly eight hundred reports to Wessel's staff, which were then delivered to USFET in Frankfurt for onward distribution to other U.S. customers in Europe and the United States.

One of Baun's circle at the Jagdhaus was Georgian Prince Kudacheff, a connection that had grown out of wartime Abwehr operations. The prince, interned by the counterintelligence unit, had met an Abwehr corporal named Alfred Bentzinger while being detained in Civilian Internment Camp No. 10 in southern Germany. Bentzinger was inclined to embellish and exaggerate his wartime service as an Abwehr noncommissioned officer, a tendency that had kept him classified as "definitely a security risk." Baun arranged for Prince Kudacheff's release from the internment camp and at Kudacheff's urging Lieutenant Colonel Deane officially intervened and Bentzinger was released. Little did Deane realize how much security he was putting at risk in making Bentzinger the head of Baun's counterintelligence effort. Bentzinger enjoyed a brief stay at the Jagdhaus before being assigned to develop and head a counterintelligence group called "Dienststelle 114" ("Workplace 114") in Karlsruhe, near his home in Mannheim. The quite irresponsible Bentzinger had a certain amount of native shrewdness, or what the Germans called "*bauernschlauheit*" (farmer's slyness), so the CIC monitored Bentzinger closely as he moved into the Karlsruhe operation.

The creation of a counterintelligence capability came in response to a USFET directive for Operation Rusty to develop the capability to monitor the activities of the Soviet liaison mission personnel in the U.S. Zone. Logically the monitoring activities should have been handled by the CIC, and the counterintelligence organization headed by Bentzinger later proved to be the greatest disservice Baun could have done to the absent Gehlen. Dienststelle 114, which was later designated "GV L," (General Vertretung, or General Agency L) became a recurring disaster for the organization. Most of Gehlen's later security problems found their origin in Dienststelle 114, and much of the blame should be placed on Baun. The evidence suggests that Wessel had not been consulted or informed on the Dienststelle 114 development; indeed, Deane and his staff more or less bought the idea floated by Baun that collection and evaluation were quite separate affairs.

Eventually Deane and the small American staff assigned to Operation Rusty began to distinguish between the Wessel and Baun groups, and recognized that the relationship between the two was a problem. Baun saw his intelligence-collection service as an operation that would support but not be subordinated to Wessel's group in Oberursel, and the American staff at Oberursel had contributed to Baun's independent attitude by facilitating his separate status at the Jagdhaus. While Wessel's staff at Fremde Heere Ost were living and working in daily contact with the small American staff in the Blue House, Baun remained aloof, high in the Jagdhaus, appearing as infrequently as possible. Baun was secretive and conspiratorial by nature, and he had no intention of working closely with either the Americans or those General Staff officers in the Blue House. It was becoming apparent that Fritz (the German General Staff) and Otto (the Abwehr) were separated by much more than different code names—Otto was out of sight in the Jagdhaus, Fritz was close to the center of power at the Blue House. Baun and his circle at the Jagdhaus assumed in error that Fritz (Gehlen's group) had achieved an agreement with high American officials in Washington. Baun's Otto group was obviously not in close touch with anybody of importance on the American side.

Moreover, Baun did not speak a word of English. At the Jagdhaus the isolated and ill-equipped Otto group felt little admiration or respect for the General Staff officers in Oberursel. Most of the officers who had served in Baun's Front Reconnaissance Unit in the war had come to them from front-line duty in a long war. Many had developed a disdain for high level staff officers that comes naturally to front-line soldiers of all armies. But with Baun's men that ill will went even further. In the business of running agents, they saw German General Staff officers as dilettantes.

In the late spring of 1946 Capt. Eric Waldman was sent to Frankfurt for ninety days of temporary duty as the advance man from the Pentagon to ensure a smooth arrival and reintegration of Reinhard Gehlen and his group into the USDIC. Waldman joined Jack Deane's staff at Oberursel and soon became the project's most actively involved U.S. staff member. Waldman came from a solidly Catholic Viennese family, though eventually he left Austria in September 1938 through the help of the Quakers. In January 1939 his father had been called in by the Gestapo and was never again seen alive. The father's ashes were sent to Waldman's mother and were buried in a Catholic cemetery in Vienna. Waldman's mother was killed in an air raid on Vienna—probably an American air raid. Waldman had never discussed his background with the Germans and they had never questioned him. Sibert, finding Waldman of immediate value, arranged to have his temporary duty orders changed to "PCS"—a "permanent change of station" from Washington, D.C., to Frankfurt, Germany, which permitted his wife, Jo, to join him.

In July 1946 the Gehlen group left Fort Hunt and returned to Germany. Gehlen and his family were established in the wholly unfamiliar surroundings in the Blue House and Oberursel. Working closely with Wessel, Gehlen assumed responsibility for the group but found that Hermann Baun had achieved considerable independence, insisting that he and Gehlen have separate but equal organizations within the larger intelligence project. Gehlen responded slowly, and ultimately developed a plan to gradually ease Baun out of a central position in his organization. To keep track of what was going on at the Jagdhaus, Gehlen appointed Hans-Juergen Dingler, a former colonel and personal relative, to the newly created job of chief of staff. After their return Gehlen could not find an appropriate role for Heinz Herre and subsequently sent him up to Baun's operation to develop a commercial cover. A significant role for Herre was not to begin until later.

Gehlen was soon confronted with a new crisis. General Sibert's tour was ending in August, and Gehlen still did not fully understand the American's plan to develop a new German intelligence service. On 30 August Sibert convened a meeting with Gehlen, Wessel, Baun, Deane, and Waldman to discuss the future of Operation Rusty. Gehlen began the meeting by reciting (from a prepared text) his intention to build a German intelligence service that would be supported by the Americans and later be transferred to a future democratic German government. Gehlen emphasized that the organization would remain German in character and under his direct leadership. For Gehlen it was urgent and essential that he obtain a commitment of support from General Sibert.

The general interrupted, saying that he had to cut the meeting short because of further arrangements necessary for his departure on 1 September. Without responding to Gehlen's statement General Sibert moved directly to discussing a plan of his own. During the year after his initial decision to assemble the Fremde Heere Ost group, General Sibert's own thinking on how the German intelligence operation at Oberursel might fit into the future of American intelligence had led him to reach a startling conclusion: the German organization would become an integral part of American intelligence!

Gehlen had somehow received advance warning of Sibert's idea, and had mentioned as such in his concluding remarks. He acknowledged that in the worst case event of a Soviet aggression against Western Europe, the entire German organization could be integrated into the U.S. intelligence community, while its members and their families would be evacuated to the United States, leaving only the operating elements of the German organization behind in Europe. Gehlen clearly based his planning on the assumption that a German government would emerge, one that was allied with the West. His organization would be an incipient official German service. The German record of the 30 August meeting does not reveal just how far Gehlen delved into his plan before General Sibert interrupted the presentation. But Sibert agreed to take an English translation of Gehlen's paper to study at a later time.

Sibert's proposal, that Gehlen's entire organization be integrated into a new American intelligence effort with the members of the organization and their families becoming American citizens, included some basic requirements. The Americans would have the right to inspect Otto, Baun's information collecting organization. Some members would remain assigned in Europe and be occupied there. Economic cover, which Baun was known to advocate, was good but there was the danger that the individual would become preoccupied with making money and neglect intelligence work; this must be eliminated. The organization must become an American organization and lose its clear German character. "[Such] is necessary," he said, "especially when you are entrusted with sensitive tasks, because of the suspicions of Americans—not me personally, because I know you. I must be able to guarantee that the organization works for and not against America. Acceptance of American citizenship [means] taking over all obligations of American citizens."

A new intelligence headquarters would be established somewhere in Europe and the agents' dependents would be moved to the United States as soon as their immigration affairs could be arranged. General Sibert asked when the organization would be prepared to move on his proposal. Gehlen appeared to be in a state of shock; Baun, looking for space, said that it would take perhaps two months. Sibert noted that when he reached Washington he would be participating in the restructuring of American intelligence. "You will hear from me within a few months. With immigration a consideration, it would be perhaps next spring before immigration difficulties could be overcome."

Despite what had transpired at this meeting, as the years passed Gehlen more than once affirmed that he had presented his plan and that Sibert had agreed to it. The paper Gehlen had prepared for that meeting offers the most complete and comprehensively stated version of his vision for the future. That evening Gehlen, Baun, and Wessel met and agreed on what Sibert had proposed. The following is Gehlen's summary of the plan:

A. The organization would become purely American.

B. Americans would have the right to inspect the organization.

C. The organization would become part of a future American intelligence, but as a free economic enterprise that does intelligence instead of an American organization of an official character with U.S. officials and employees. With these requirements, that are entirely clear and have been offered to us, one must become accustomed to them and accept them.

Baun commented disingenuously that it was obvious that he personally was in agreement with Gehlen's position but that he was skeptical that members of the organization he had created would go along with a purely American solution that does not remain international in character under the theme "Fight Against Bolshevism." Gehlen responded,

Your concerns may be justified, but it is decisive that we carry on the fight against Bolshevism and a part of that is the unconditional meeting of such American requirements. When Bolshevism will one time have been destroyed, there remains to be seen whether the intelligence work against Russia is in question and whether the subordinate organization can then cooperate or not. It is correct to think these matters through but it is decisive that today we accomplish our tasks. Our decision for the West and thus for America is uncompromising and we have thereby to do everything to support America—so long as personal honor is not disturbed. For the present we can only carry on the work here and we must press the American staff to be more efficient in getting our reporting more rapidly to the USFET. Then we must wait and see what we hear from General Sibert in the next months.

Later that same evening Captain Waldman met with Gehlen, thanked him for the briefing given General Sibert, and reported that General Sibert was convinced of the value of future reporting, even though time had not permitted Gehlen to present his report on the state of the Soviet military presence in East Germany. I believe that Waldman put on a positive spin when he relayed Sibert's reaction. Of primary importance to Gehlen, however, was General Sibert's clear commitment to the continuation of the operation. To nail this down and use it to his own advantage in dealing with the urgent problem of Baun, Gehlen proposed a weekly meeting regarding the Baun group between himself, Captain Waldman, and Lieutenant Colonel Deane, and a weekly meeting of Wessel's group and the order-of-battle experts from USFET. The search for alternative headquarters for the organization must be continued and developed with Colonel Deane's assistance; emergency mobilization planning and preparations should also continue.

On the following day, 31 August, Gehlen met with Baun and Wessel and reported on his talk with Waldman the previous night, including the planning for the evacuation of dependents to the United States that would proceed and the expeditious search for a new headquarters in Europe, possibly before the end of September. Gehlen, who was prepared to cooperate with the Americans rather than lose momentum on his plans for his organization, asked Baun for his opinion regarding Soviet short-term military intentions.

The meeting with General Sibert, followed by Eric Waldman's assurances the following day, were the most important developments in those early postwar years at Oberursel. The assurance from these two men gave Gehlen the first tangible evidence that U.S. support of his plan, flawed though it might be, would continue; after a year of experience with the group at Oberursel the senior American military intelligence officer in Europe had heard Gehlen reiterate his aims. Sibert in turn had given Gehlen unambiguous evidence that his successor, whoever that might be, would continue support of Operation Rusty. It was of no importance that Sibert had not and could not respond to the specific points of Gehlen's plan. Sibert's departure freed Gehlen from one other concern: as far as Gehlen knew, General Sibert had received no criticism from Eisenhower—who was known for his denunciation of German officers—for saving an element of the German General Staff, and for having done so without the knowledge of the commander in chief of USFET. Though he previously had gotten cool treatment in Washington, the same Eisenhower (who had taken a hard line on Germany and dismissed Patton for being too soft on denazification) had succeeded Marshall as head of the Joint Chiefs of Staff. Gehlen had always worried that Eisenhower would break with Patton and act even more abruptly with a less important general for coddling an element of the German General Staff at Oberursel.

I believe that Gehlen and General Sibert both assumed that his own ideas had been presented and the other had agreed. If circumstances back in the United States required it, Sibert could say that he had discussed the idea of integrating the German operation into American intelligence and that the Germans were making the necessary preparations. Sibert could infer he had agreement from the Germans in principle. Gehlen, on the other hand, could say that relations with General Sibert had gone a long distance—that Sibert had a high regard for the intelligence already produced and that he had Sibert's tacit agreement on his long-term vision and plans. The "gentleman's agreement" reached that day, as Gehlen often described it, became part of postwar history. Sibert and Gehlen came away with preconceived but very different ideas about what had transpired; they had talked past each other and each believed that the other had heard what he wanted him to hear. None of this, of course, was known to the rest of us in the Third Army stationed in Heidelberg just ninety kilometers away.

Gehlen continued to live at Oberursel for another year, fully preoccupied with familiarizing himself with Wessel's organization and nurturing his relationship with the Americans. He found it increasingly important to share his thoughts with Eric Waldman. Waldman had heard a report one day while he was at the PX in Munich that a compound in the village of Pullach would be available at the end of 1947; he took the initiative to obtain the G-2's support to consolidate and relocate the Fremde Heere Ost and Baun elements into one organization there. The move to Pullach proved to be a crucial event in the postwar history of German intelligence.

During this same period Gehlen moved to constrain Baun's influence by assigning three of his own associates to Otto. Yet Lt. Col. John Deane finally resolved the conflict between Gehlen and Baun by simply publishing a military order that made Gehlen "the German chief" with no reference to Baun and no distinction made between the intelligence-collection operations and the evaluation and analysis of that intelligence. Deane's formal military directive made it equally clear that he himself was still the American commanding officer. Under any other circumstances Gehlen would have been uncomfortable with Deane's resort to a military order to establish Gehlen's control of the German organization. Armed with the directive, however, Gehlen waited for the best moment to simply remove Baun from any and all responsibility for tactical collection.

I am convinced that General Sibert's ambitious plans to americanize Operation Rusty were entirely unrealistic and held no prospect for any genuine German or U.S. support. The few remaining German General Staff members, having made the transition from the Mauerwald to Pullach, would not have gone one large step further to life in postwar America. Bringing Werner von Braun to America to work on missiles was one thing; taking Gehlen, Wessel, Baun, and a large number of former General Staff officers and a number of old hands from the Abwehr to work as naturalized American citizens within the American intelligence corps would have been quite another. General Sibert's operation had garnered little support in Washington, though a meeting that Sibert attended in New York a few weeks after his return to the United States may have planted the seeds that germinated and flowered a few years later. Present at this providential meeting were Lt. Col. Deane, Allen Dulles (at the time a New York lawyer), Dulles's friend William Jackson (another lawyer interested in intelligence), Richard Helms, and Col. Donald Galloway, an Army officer on duty with the Central Intelligence Group. Dulles and Jackson, on behalf of the White House, were engaged in one of the innumerable postwar studies of the intelligence issue. The meeting was called to discuss the future of Operation Rusty, though today it is unclear who initiated the meeting. Sibert and Deane had the best opportunity to describe the German operation because of their close personal involvement. In reality the meeting may have had an impact on the thinking of both Dulles and Helms regarding an eventual relationship with Gehlen's organization.

The few OSS veterans who remained in Germany after Truman's deactivation of the OSS in September 1945 were clustered in the free section of Berlin and other parts of West Germany. By 1946 these strategic service units (SSUs) were subordinated to the Central Intelligence Group (CIG) that had been created as a temporary bridge between the OSS and the CIA. The Army G-2 had not consulted the OSS in creating what became Operation Rusty. During 1946, when its existence was made known to the SSU, a solid opposition to Sibert's operation developed, and repeated efforts by both the G-2 in Germany and officials in Washington to persuade the CIG to take over Operation Rusty were rejected. Under growing pressure from Washington, Gen. Hoyt Vandenberg, the head of the CIG, sent Lt. Col. Bill Quinn, who had been assigned to the intelligence group as head of the SSU, to Germany to assess the German station. These former OSS veterans consistently reacted negatively toward taking over any part of Operation Rusty.

In early 1947 a second effort was made to persuade the intelligence group to conduct a detailed assessment of Rusty, this time by an officer sent directly from headquarters, a German-speaking CIG officer by the name of Sam Bossard. After spending more than two months with Gehlen at Oberursel and with Baun at the

Jagdhaus, Bossard's report flew in the face of the prevailing attitude by recommending that the CIG take over Operation Rusty. The German station did not concur, but support for the Bossard report came from Richard Helms, the division chief, and Colonel Galloway, who had replaced Quinn. Adm. Roscoe H. Hillenkoetter, who had just replaced Vandenberg as head of the CIG, was not impressed. Hillenkoetter dismissed the report, and sent a memorandum to the secretaries of State, War, and Navy, as well as to the president's intelligence advisor, strongly recommending the liquidation of the entire Rusty operation. The result was more than Army G-2 Gen. Stephen Chamberlin had bargained for. Chamberlin informed Hillenkoetter he would not show the document to the secretary of war and requested that it be withdrawn. On 19 June, Hillenkoetter convened the principals in the intelligence community and agreed to withdraw his letter, but he warned the Army G-2 that the risks involved in supporting a revived German General Staff and its intelligence service was greater than the value of any intelligence the operation might produce. Gen. Robert L. Walsh, the new Army G-2 in Germany, was encountering numerous problems in relation to Operation Rusty, partly due to the currency reform that overnight had dramatically reduced the black market. Walsh urged Admiral Hillenkoetter to take one more look at Rusty.

Gehlen's relations with the Americans changed little after Sibert's departure in 1946. Eric Waldman provided what little continuity there was, and no significant change occurred in the level and character of the Army G-2 support. Gehlen had learned that Adolf Heusinger was well established as Halder's assistant at the Neustadt camp operated by the U.S. Army historical division. Though Gehlen and Heusinger had never become friends, Heusinger had been Gehlen's mentor and supporter during their time together in the General Staff.

In a letter dated 13 July 1947, which Heusinger sent to his wife Gerda, he told her that Gehlen had proposed they meet. By then Heusinger had concluded that the historical division of the U.S. Army was just that, an organization concentrating on Germany's history. It appeared to be neither involved nor interested in influencing Germany's future and offered neither contacts nor involvement in the new Germany that was surely but slowly taking form. Heusinger had heard something about Gehlen's development of a significant organization having considerable support from the U.S. Army; Gehlen's organization appeared to be involved in changes taking place in Germany and Europe of which Heusinger wanted to be a part. Additionally, Gehlen might offer Heusinger an American connection beyond those he had established in the activities of the historical division. Heusinger was gradually coming to the conclusion that the future of Germany and Europe lay in the hands of the Americans.

In September 1947 Gehlen and Waldman met Heusinger at a U.S. medical center in Marburg. During this discreet meeting Gehlen described the status of his operation and asked Heusinger to join him. Waldman sensed an element of tension, which he attributed to the reversal in implied ranks and status between the two. Waldman maintains that the meeting did not have the character of a negotiation about how their respective ideas on the future might be synthesized. Gehlen was simply offering employment to his former superior. Heusinger accepted and agreed to join Gehlen six months later. Waldman has speculated that human factors, such as an opportunity to reunite with his family, the prospect of an improved standard of living, and the uncertain conditions prevailing in Germany were all sufficient reasons for Heusinger's decision. Heusinger consciously understood that, contrary to the work taking place in Neustadt, Gehlen's effort was addressing the future.

This meeting preceded the Berlin blockade and subsequent airlift; the more punitive phase of the Occupation had ended in early 1947. Gen. Lucius Clay, commander in chief of USFET and acting military governor, had moved into a more positive posture regarding the economic and political prospects for a separate West Germany. The Occupation was experiencing a period of relative tranquillity, although the Allied agreements reached at Potsdam on ruling Germany were rapidly eroding. It is not surprising that the meeting between Heusinger and Gehlen was as low-key and nonsubstantive as Waldman describes it. Though they had gone separate ways after 20 July 1944 and had no contact in the interim, Gehlen and Heusinger had a mutual need for each other. An element of persistent uncertainty hung over Gehlen's relations with the Americans. Sibert had returned home a year earlier and nothing about his ideas or any influence he had in Washington had been heard of again. The CIG had been created in Washington and had sent Sam Bossard to Oberursel, but nothing had come of that either.

General Clay, who was known to be hostile to the entire USFET headquarters staff, particularly the G-2, had never shown the slightest interest in Gehlen and his project. Clay had taken a uniquely hostile position toward all former members of the German Army General Staff. Gehlen's plans to form an intelligence service that would be offered to a future government had not changed, but he had detected no real American interest in his idea. Gehlen saw in Adolf Heusinger a man of stature who would clearly contribute to the image Gehlen wanted to create.

In December the Operation Rusty project that had been so widely dispersed in the Frankfurt area was relocated to Pullach, a small, picturesque village sitting high on the left bank of the Isar River, roughly ten kilometers south of the center of the city of Munich. The first group from Oberursel moved into the compound on 6 December 1947, and from that time on the compound was referred to as "Nikolaus." Traditionally the German Santa Claus, Saint Nikolaus, makes a visit on that day to leave gifts for good children, or sticks and ashes for the not-so-good. Perhaps a surprised Saint Nikolaus was unsure what to leave in Pullach that night when he discovered the new occupants. Christmas 1947 was the first of what were destined to be many Christmas seasons spent in Pullach by German intelligence.

On a flat meadow between the villages of Pullach and Grosshesselohe the Nazi Party built a compound in the 1930s for the use of the party hierarchy such as Rudolph Hess and Martin Bormann, who at different times occupied the main house in the center of the small compound. The complex, no more than three city blocks long and two blocks wide, was commonly known to local Pullach residents as "Bormann Siedlung" ("Bormann Development"), and the main residence as "Haus Bormann."

The streets within the compound were lined by two-story houses, each surrounded by a small garden behind a wrought iron gate set in a two-meter-high masonry wall capped with unpainted natural limestone. The same type of masonry wall lined Heilmannstrasse along the eastern side of the compound, and had afforded some privacy and security to the elite Nazis in residence, but in no sense was it an isolated, fortress-like facility. In those early years the Nazi leaders apparently were satisfied with only limited privacy and did not find it necessary to deny the citizenry of Pullach and Grosshesselohe the use of the street running through the compound. The German troops that took possession of the facility very late in the war and the Americans who followed them had been less considerate. Guarded gates were installed at each end of Heilmannstrasse, closing it off from public use.

All the masonry walls and all the houses except one were covered with faded yellow stucco. The one exception, Haus Bormann, was an architecturally undistinguished three-story building that appeared to have at one time been painted white. By the time it was occupied by the Americans in the late 1940s Haus

Bormann was a graying structure. An oblong courtyard around the house was shared with two family-sized houses that were identical to all the others except for their direct access to the courtyard. From the front entrance of Haus Bormann was a small green park, beyond which one could see a long, single-story red brick building trimmed in white that looked more like Colonial Williamsburg than a conference facility where Adolf Hitler had shared his conspiracies with his fellow Nazi elite. The architectural character of this community center was presumably what caused it to be named "Colonial House" by the Americans. In Hitler's better days a flagpole in front of the Colonial House had flown the now-reviled swastika.

The destroyed stone sculpture above the front entrance door of Haus Bormann was the symbolic Nazi eagle clutching a swastika in one claw. The first American troops to occupy the building had enthusiastically but crudely chiseled away the lintel's main features and had renamed Haus Bormann the "White House"—partly because the house was the only one in the compound that appeared to have at one time been painted white, but also because the new name sounded more American.

The interior of the house, while neither ornate nor lavish in any sense, was on a modestly grander scale than the other individual houses in the compound. The front entrance led directly into a fairly spacious marble-floored foyer with a great marble fireplace and high ceiling. The foyer looked out the back of the house to a small garden. At the center of the garden was a lily pond holding several statuesque bronze nudes of Germanic womanhood, characteristic of Third Reich art. To the left of the foyer was a large music room with paneled wood carved in a musical motif. The Persian carpet, obviously made to fit the dimensions of the room, was still there, as was the Bechstein concert grand piano, still in excellent condition. To the right of the foyer a door opened into a dining room that could easily accommodate more than fifty guests. It too had wood carvings in the paneling. Unlike the music room, however, it was painted in a bright Bavarian style. Just inside the front door was a small reception hall leading into the foyer. In the hall a door to the left led to an office suite with a large reception area and, beyond that, to the office of the Nazi in residence—Rudolph Hess, Martin Bormann, or whoever was then the building's principal occupant.

Reinhard Gehlen established his office in one of the houses across the courtyard from the White House. In the early years the house had also served as the living quarters for his wife Herta and their four children—Katharina, Christoph, Marie-Therese, and Dorothee. The other house attached to the courtyard served as the office and living quarters of Horst Wendland, the last head of the Organization Division of the German Army General Staff, who emerged as the chief administrative head of the Gehlen Organization.

Only after the move from Oberursel did the G-2 in Frankfurt give the Gehlen Organization a military cover—the "7821 Composite Group." The mission of the 7821—which consisted of about ten officers and fifteen enlisted men—was limited to providing an administrative cover, a very desirable headquarters for Gehlen, the necessary interface with the U.S. military occupation force, and a mechanism for obtaining the full services and support of the Munich military post. Fortunately for Gehlen, the man in charge there was Colonel W. R. Philp, probably the most senior U.S. Army colonel in Europe and, even more important, an officer who had served with Clarence Huebner in the Big Red One in France during World War I. Huebner, the senior general stationed in Heidelberg, was a deputy to General Clay in Berlin. Philp drew on his status in the U.S. Army in Germany to dramatically increase the compound's supply of black market bagged coffee beans and cases of cigarettes, goods that were immediately moved out and into the black market to get essential financial support for the operation. Colonel Philp obviously made life in Pullach better for both the Americans and the Germans. He and his wife were comfortably established in the living quarters of the White House. In season, he and his friends were treated to highly organized hunting expeditions arranged by Bavarian officials responsible for the nearby forest and game preserves.

Gehlen's postwar objectives were quite clear: he wished to retain a relationship (meaning support) with the United States. He intended to develop the FHO into a national intelligence service supported by the Americans but possessing a German character that would be amenable to a future German government. He planned to move his organization as rapidly as possible into some defined legal status within a new German government. In the meantime he would limit U.S. access to information about his organization, its members, and its operations. That Gehlen thought that such terms would be acceptable to American intelligence authorities is quite remarkable, but ultimately he was able to accomplish the better part of it.

3

The U.S. Occupation of Germany

By December 1945 Gen. Lucius Clay had established the Office of Military Government of the United States (OMGUS) in Berlin and had gained de facto control over the military's government activities in all of U.S.–occupied Germany. Three months later the demobilization of troops was largely completed and the Third Army, with its headquarters in Heidelberg, occupied the entire U.S. Zone. By sheer force of his personality General Clay controlled the Occupation from 1945 until his departure in 1949. Clay was a distant and aloof figure running OMGUS from Berlin; the Third Army had only a limited role. USFET initially tried to manage both security and intelligence throughout the area of Germany occupied by U.S. forces, but failed to adequately communicate with the Third Army or OMGUS. For example, Third Army intelligence was never officially informed of the existence of Reinhard Gehlen and his group at Oberursel. But by early 1946, when almost all U.S. wartime troops had been deployed out of Europe, USFET was an almost hollow shell with few troops to command. Clay's influence continued to grow. And the Third Army's position, vis-à-vis both the USFET and OMGUS, was severely diminished until its complete inactivation in March 1947.

When I returned to Germany in March 1946, Gen. Lucien Truscott, then commander of the Third Army, requested that I bypass U.S. Army headquarters in Frankfurt and proceed directly to Bad Toelz to join his staff. I had served under General Truscott in several assignments in Italy and France. Two days later I met briefly with Truscott, who informed me of our impending move to Heidelberg. Once in Heidelberg the Third Army carried on with its poorly defined missions: housekeeping services to the shrinking combat-ready forces and, starting in the summer of 1946, for the growing communities of U.S. military and civilians and their dependents; the logistics support of the war crimes trials, including the International Military Tribunal at Nuremberg and the military courts at Dachau; and the principal operational mission to provide security for the U.S. presence in occupied Germany, though no security threats had developed. The Wehrmacht and Hitler's massive SS force had been dismantled before the Third Army had assumed its responsibilities in Heidelberg and, remarkably, both the Army and the SS had peacefully dispersed into the population.

General Truscott was recognized by his peers and by those who served under him as a superior combat commander with a distinguished war record. He had been given command of the Third Army when General Eisenhower relieved General Patton of his command for not being tough enough on the issue of Nazi influence within the Bavarian government. As Patton's successor, Truscott had personally assessed most of the problems facing the American occupation. After examining the situation in the DP camps, paying particular attention to the Jewish camps that were becoming way stations on the exodus from Eastern Europe, he had observed and deplored the actions of the Soviet repatriation mission that was operating under the Yalta agreement, understanding the Soviet belief that "forced repatriation would be tolerated and supported by the United States." Truscott developed his own ways of making life difficult for the Soviet repatriation missions. He had come to the rescue of the ill-prepared International Military Tribunal by establishing a special command to sort out its chaotic administrative circumstances in Nuremberg. Though he was unclear about his own responsibilities when it came to the actions of the U.S. military courts that were conducting trials of German war criminals at Dachau, he had attended an early trial and found the Army court making the best of a difficult task for which they were ill equipped. Truscott's comprehensive examination of his responsibilities for security matters in the U.S. Zone led his staff to produce the first and last complete compilation of all the policies and directives relating to security and counterintelligence in U.S.–occupied Germany. Security Memorandum Number One was distributed mainly to Third Army units, working-level CIC members, military government detachments, military intelligence teams, and officers who were running civilian internment enclosures—and not to top level officers of the USFET or OMGUS. Apparently Truscott was not clear where the Third Army stood in the hierarchies in Frankfurt and Berlin. He had assumed that all working-level troops dealing with security matters were (or should be) under his command; in any case he wanted to keep the troops in the field well informed.

Far more tangible than the paper trail of his security mission was Truscott's decision to combine the three armored cavalry regiments stationed along the eastern border of the U.S. Zone into what became known as the U.S. Constabulary—a force of thirty thousand men. Truscott, a cavalry officer, and the three regiments were the direct descendants of several of the last horse cavalry regiments in the Army and the Constabulary was built on cavalry traditions. Constabulary troops wore bright yellow scarves and special uniforms. By most postwar standards they were highly mobile and had a good communication network. The unit was organized, armed, and trained to deal with any serious threat short of a major military attack. The reality, of course, was that by early 1946 the U.S. Zone of Occupation was among the most peaceful and stable areas in Europe. The Soviets were becoming uncooperative but not militarily threatening, though developments in the Soviet Zone of Germany were beginning to take a worrisome course. No one estimated that the Soviets would permit their emerging communist client in East Germany to do anything foolish in the existing circumstances. But the creation of the Constabulary was a prudent step. Its existence contributed to the decision a year later to inactivate the Third Army and transfer its few remaining responsibilities to the Constabulary.

Almost without interruption since my first day of duty as an officer, I had been in command of troops either preparing for or actually in combat. Now, for the first time in my Army service career, I was assigned to intelligence as chief of the counterintelligence branch of the G-2. My primary duties included security, in a very broad sense: the movement of people into and out of the U.S. Zone, the reestablishment of communication and transportation links with adjacent areas, and monitoring the thousands of Germans and other nationals either being held, wanted as security threats, or in connection with the war crimes trials. In all of these I relied heavily on my knowledge of U.S. Occupation policy that I had acquired at Columbia University. At the same time I personally was attempting to comprehend and put in some perspective the unbelievable level of war damage on all sides and the tumult and chaos affecting the lives of millions of Europeans churning about in the wake of upheaval.

American intelligence officers could be found interrogating individuals everywhere—within the civilian internment enclosures, in POW camps, and in numerous other camps where those charged with war crimes or witnesses were being held. Specialized teams of intelligence officers were still interrogating German scientists and industrial engineers who had designed and built weapons of war; many of these scientists and engineers had been quickly spirited away to the United States. American intelligence officers were just beginning to track down and interrogate the Germans who had come out of the Soviet Union one way or another, and who were believed to have knowledge of our recent wartime ally and about which we seemed to know so little. A few American intelligence officers were engaged in espionage against Soviet forces in Berlin and elsewhere in East Germany. From the outset the Soviets and the Americans eyed each other with distrust, which led to the preliminary skirmishes of an intelligence war that grew considerably over the next four decades. Most counterintelligence specialists, however, were occupied in raking over the still-warm coals of wartime German espionage. Some small residual groups left over from the wartime OSS—which had been renamed the Strategic Services Unit (SSU)—were keeping a low profile in Germany while waiting for word on their future. Counterintelligence was big business in Germany—it reflected the political, social, and economic circumstances in Germany during the immediate postwar period, but a large part of what was going on in the occupied areas was arbitrarily labeled "security" or "counterintelligence."

The plethora of intelligence activities, many taking place just below the surface, could only be described as an "intelligence jungle." The U.S. Zone, like all of occupied Germany, was swarming with intelligence and counterintelligence officers from all four of the occupying powers and a great many other nations as well. Thousands of police, security, and intelligence officers left over from the Third Reich were intensively searching for safe employment with an American intelligence employer, while at the same time avoiding capture by the security forces of the occupying powers. In the U.S. Zone most former SS members were living "black" (covertly)—unregistered and facing problems in just surviving.

Even after a full postwar year had passed the conditions in Germany continued to worsen because of the millions of refugees arriving from the East and the several million discharged German POWs in the Western zones coming home. Most of the communication and transportation infrastructure in the country was still in ruins. Nevertheless, a certain relationship between the German people and the occupiers had taken place. The immediate postwar policies of the Americans on such matters as demilitarization, denazification, and war crimes trials enlivened private discussions among everyday Germans. U.S. policies were quite well understood. Many German families had at least one family member or knew someone being held in a civilian internment enclosure for reasons connected to denazification or war crimes trials. A far greater number of those families had lost men and breadwinners who had disappeared into Soviet POW camps. Economic conditions in the U.S. Zone, while better than in the Soviet and French Zones, were providing the less competitive members of German society with an inadequate diet.

Most human activity that was not related to the daily business of survival had come to a halt. The U.S. and British Zones had become a refuge for millions of Germans and other nationals who had fled westward before the Soviet counteroffensive in 1944 and 1945. After Potsdam yet another partition of Poland contributed to a second wave of German refugees pouring into Germany; most of whom kept moving westward until reaching the American and British Zones. The economic impact of these massive population movements was becoming fully apparent only with the onset of the winter of 1946–47.

That winter, the coldest that people could remember, almost paralyzed life in central Europe. A sustained frigid wind out of the north froze over the rivers, and coal barges stopped moving. Gathering branches and twigs from the forests, piling them on bicycles, then pushing them through the snow by women and children seemed to be a national occupation. Germany was a devastated, cold, and hungry land. Entire cities became almost uninhabitable. Even urban areas that had escaped the bombing and survived with buildings still standing had large sectors that almost always went without heat or light.

Feeding the American occupation troops in Germany was simply a continuation of the supply system of the war. In the first months after the end of the war Americans ate ample meals at Army messes supplied by the massive logistical system that had moved American forces forward to the far corners of a world at war. By late in the summer of 1945 the Army had established a network of small stores at which certain incidentals—toiletries, cigarettes, candy, and some items of clothing —could be purchased only by Americans stationed in Germany. By early 1946 the post exchange had become the retail outlet for a vast purchasing, distribution, and sales system run by the U.S. Army. One could buy everything from a Burberry tailored suit made in London (thirty U.S. dollars) to one of the new stripped-down Volkswagens (selling for seven hundred dollars). Access to goods was tightly controlled and only holders of PX cards could buy. To get the coveted Volkswagen one's name was added to a long waiting list.

The total population of American, German, and displaced persons (DPs) sharing German soil was divided into three economic classes. The Americans, for the most part, lived well and had everything to make life comfortable and uncomplicated. The DPs fared less well but were gathered into DP camps where care and supplies were administered by the large number of relief agencies accredited by the U.S. occupation forces, including the United Nations Rescue and Relief Agency

(UNRRA). Though most of these agencies had some authority to acquire supplies from the U.S. Army, their civilian representatives learned that wearing uniforms that looked like U.S. Army uniforms gave them a certain degree of mobility, including access to American mess facilities and clubs. Appearing to be part of the U.S. Army also ensured a certain level of deference by the Germans. Civilians in uniform typically wore shoulder patches but no military insignia.

The third and largest class of people were the resident Germans, who traded with the DPs and the American servicemen and civilians, including their dependents. An Army wife with enough cartons of cigarettes could go a long way toward satisfying her desire to own Dresden china or Nymphenburg porcelain. As a result, a GI could establish himself quite comfortably in a home away from home. In the summer of 1946 one of the hit songs among the troops stationed around Heidelberg and Frankfurt was "I'm Cracking Up from Shacking Up in Schwabisch-Gemund."

The U.S. Military Government was having great trouble in maintaining a diet of 1,550 calories among the German population; in 1946 the level had declined to closer to 1,000 calories, and had caused General Clay intense concern. (In fact, thousands of Germans were living on 800 calories a day.) The active competition among our Western European allies for access to both American dollars and American wheat had generated considerable disagreement with Clay's high priority in seeing that the people of a defeated nation were adequately fed. Pockets of disadvantaged Germans were unable to compete in the struggle for survival within a chaotic economy. For the old, the sick, and the poor life was very difficult.

In a broad sense this commingled population was economically divided into American "haves" and German "have-nots," and a massive black market economy developed. The Reichsmark that was in circulation in Germany at the end of the war quickly lost value and was replaced by a deutsche mark (DM) that circulated in all four zones. As of December 1945 scrip, the American military currency, and U.S. Army Quartermaster and PX supplies were legally available to Americans and others officially accredited to U.S. forces in Germany only. The "hot" items were cigarettes, coffee, and the most concentrated food items like cans of ham that contained some fat, an item lacking in the postwar German diet of ersatz sausage, potatoes, and cabbage. By late 1946 all of Germany, not just the U.S. Zone, was one big black market. Scrip, which was periodically reissued to control its accumulation by large black market operators, was used until the currency reform in 1948 made the strong DM fully convertible to dollars.

The black market also supplied the network for getting ahold of those important five-gallon cans of American gasoline for the rare German that still had some kind of an automobile powered by a gasoline engine. Late in the war many vehicles had been converted to ingenious systems burning coal, charcoal, or wood, though by war's end most of these had stopped running. Germany's public transportation system was largely in ruins. Nothing had a higher priority by both the occupying powers and the Germans than getting some trains back into operation. In the intelligence black market, however, nothing was more prized than a working vehicle with gasoline.

The occupiers led a comparatively comfortable life. A new word, "requisitioned," had entered the German vocabulary—it meant that the occupier had taken possession. In the first days after the cease-fire an American soldier or officer could simply move into a house or building and tell the German occupants to leave. Under the edict of the Four Powers Act any property that had been owned by the German government or the Nazi Party became property of the occupying powers. It was widely understood by Americans and Germans alike that requisitioned property eventually would be returned to the rightful owner, though no one knew just how or when this return was to occur. Many an evacuated German had pragmatically attempted to establish and maintain a connection with his house's American occupier in order to keep an eye on his property. Many of these connections developed into lasting relationships.

The better houses requisitioned by Americans often had old but functional central heating systems fired by coal furnaces. By late 1946 the Army had organized its administration and support functions under the military posts run by German staffs, who kept requisitioned houses supplied with coal and electricity. Coal was regularly delivered by truck and hauled by hand into the cellar. An assigned military post worker would come by several times a day to keep the furnace stoked and the house warm. Typically the commander of an Army unit accredited to a military post could obtain requisitioned housing and be assured of routine services without regard to the use made of the house. It was absolutely uncomplicated for Major X of Unit Y to get a house. No one raised any question if the German maintenance staff later discovered that the house was then occupied by secretive Germans who went about their business. If any problems arose the German occupants would simply inform Major X, and he would sort it out with the military post. Many of the more privileged Germans working for CIC and the USFET operation at Oberursel got through that terrible winter of 1946–47 this way.

A few weeks after our arrival in Heidelberg, General Truscott developed health problems that led to his retirement. Truscott was replaced by Lt. Gen. Geoffrey Keyes, a wholly professional soldier with a sustained intellectual and official interest in what was going on in occupied Germany. Keyes realized that the Third Army had a limited role and he showed none of General Clay's determined ambition to assertively expand his role, his authority, or his responsibilities. In Heidelberg the war that had seemed so abstract in 1939 was now behind us. We in the famous Third Army that Gen. George Patton had led across France into Germany were ready to leave our mark on the defeated German nation. But in many ways the Third Army was less preoccupied with the Occupation than with the need to begin rebuilding a disciplined and professional armed force. Keyes's judgments on day-to-day issues of the Occupation were sound, but it was clear his capabilities exceeded the demands of his assignment.

During the first full year after the war no American dependents lived in the occupied countries. The first families arrived in Germany soon after the beginning of June 1946. Americans of my age who had served in the armed forces through most of World War II had experienced wartime family separations—military schools, long maneuvers, housing shortages, pregnancies of young wives, and, finally, going off to the war. It was a familiar pattern for all of the United States in those years. The railroad station in Heidelberg in June 1946 had become a nightly party with welcome signs, a Third Army buffet, and band music to greet the special trains bringing dependents from the port of Bremerhaven.

My family—wife Connie, daughter Michel Ann, and son Jimmy—were among the recent arrivals. Connie grew up just a few blocks down the street from me in Fargo. After high school we had gone happily on through college, confident of our future together. We had married just as I, a young student and cavalry officer, was ordered to the cavalry school at Fort Riley, Kansas, in 1940. Connie had taken to life as an Army wife as a duck takes to water. But for her the war years with two small children had been difficult. We used the year in Heidelberg to put our lives and family back together. I was assigned a requisitioned house on the slope of a wooded hill a half-mile upstream from the center of the old town and a few hundred yards beyond the castle and the neighboring Schloss Hotel (where Mark Twain had stayed while writing his book, *Innocents Abroad*). The requisition was, like so many of those occupied by Americans in Germany, a congenial compromise arrangement with mutual advantages.

The man of the house was a missing POW reported as "unlocated, somewhere in Russia." Gabriele, his wife and the mother of two children roughly the same age as ours, was a tall, gaunt woman who looked after the house. Gabriele's mother, a small but vigorous grandmother to everyone, lived in another house nearby. Gabriele had a younger sister of perhaps twenty years old who was waiting to resume her university studies; she lived with her mother and helped out. The steeply rising wooded area above our home, which never felt the sun, was a fern-covered wonderland and a veritable mushroom farm. Twice a week Gabriele took the four small children out as foragers and gathered a huge supply of mushrooms. She taught the children which were edible and which were not, though always reserved right of refusal. Thus we became a family.

By the summer of 1946 the widening cracks in the wartime alliance had made it quite clear that we were living in a dramatically changing world. The professional officers in the military services had not grasped the enormous changes that had taken place in the character of the war that had occurred between 1 September 1939 and final victory in Japan in August 1945. The ground under the feet of our professional military leaders was being shaken by geopolitical tremors that threatened to divide the world into two camps—one rapidly forming around Soviet military power and entrenched in central and eastern Europe, and the other a faltering version of the Western alliance that had joined the Russians in defeating the Germany created by Adolf Hitler and the Nazi Party. The predominant trend in American thinking was that the United States, holding an atomic bomb monopoly and a strategically capable air force, could disarm any foe provided it maintained enough military presence in Europe and Asia. It was not a return to the isolationism of the period between World War I and World War II, but rather a poorly defined assumption that economic aid and technical assistance, combined with a stronger United Nations and a world monetary structure defined at Breton Woods, would constitute an alternative to military alliances and large deployments of U.S. forces in Asia and Europe. (Such strategic thinking did not take into account the Middle East, where the British Empire was in decline.) Mainstream U.S. geopolitical thinking did not include a long-term major military presence for securing, as an integrated area, the Atlantic basin, including Western Europe and the maritime approaches to the Middle East; even less commitment was made to an American sphere of influence in Asia, centering on Japan.

This prevailing thought led to a rapid demobilization of U.S. conventional combat forces out of Germany and Austria in Western Europe and from South Korea in Asia. Stalin believed that this combination—vulnerabilities in Europe, revived isolationism in the United States, and a perceived strengthening of communism in Western Europe—almost assured the extension of Soviet hegemony in Eastern Europe, Germany, and Austria. Then through the threatening power of the Red Army and the communist parties in Germany, France, and Italy the Soviets could bring Western Europe into its sphere of influence.

Two of my closest associates in the Third Army G-2, Col. John Gloriod and Maj. Dewitt Armstrong, were quietly expanding U.S. operations against the Soviet Union. Their work was hampered by the presence of a Russian liaison team obviously engaged in tracking down wanted Soviets for forced repatriation. But the Soviet liaison mission also afforded U.S. access to a number of Russians, directly and through their sometimes more pro-American Eastern European colleagues. One troublesome recollection I have of my time in Heidelberg was a visit by two SSU officers seeking assistance at the last minute to liberate a Russian agent who was already in Soviet custody and on a train due to leave with a large group of forced repatriates. I was powerless to do anything about it. The issue of what to do about Soviet defectors was one that would not go away, since at the time it was U.S. policy to make no intelligence use of Soviet defectors. The low point in American handling of this problem came when we were governed by something called the "McNarney-Sokolovsky Agreement," a remnant of the Yalta agreement, by which both sides agreed to return defectors.

During our off hours Gloriod, Armstrong, and I would sit around the bar in the Europa Hotel and have long conversations about these questions. How did five years of war affect the future of U.S. armed forces? What was left of the wartime alliance that at Yalta, San Francisco, and Potsdam had seemed so promising? Could the Russians truly be our ally, or were they already emerging as a new enemy? What would be the weapons of another war? We had moved from the horse to the tracked and heavily armored vehicle, the tank, but what about the atomic bomb? We had all seen the great German cities ravaged by Allied fire bombing and the destructive character of Hitler's V-bombs in the Netherlands and the UK. None of these enormously destructive weapons had carried the awesome power of an atomic warhead. Combining all of the facts into an equation for strategic defense of the United States was going to be difficult. Yet even against the backdrop of these discussions I found a singleness of purpose among fellow officers. Weapons may change and strategic alliances may shift, but the U.S. Army would carry on, its standards and values unchanged.

Although the Third Army had no major mission beyond general security, life at Third Army headquarters was never dull. We felt the ripple effects of events occurring elsewhere. We entertained liaison missions from practically every nation of Western and Eastern Europe that had any status as a wartime friend or ally of the occupying powers. We knew it was prudent to assume that all of these missions had assignments to collect intelligence information on American activities. The Americans, after avoiding involvement in Europe in the 1930s, had come to Europe late in the war but had stayed on after it was over. Most Europeans were uncertain about American longer-range intentions concerning Europe. They had heard reports of an impressive isolationist faction in the U.S. Congress, but the Truman administration was demonstrating a willingness to remain engaged in the containment of Soviet expansionism, later called "the Truman Doctrine." Members of these many liaison missions had the privilege of using our open officers' mess facilities, clubs, and the PX. They were all having a great time. The Russians obviously had not yet gotten some of the Eastern Europeans under control. Some of them acted independently of the Russians and had not yet accepted the Soviet yoke. The head of the Czech liaison group, for example, was openly hostile to the Russians.

The punitive occupation of Germany, as a defeated enemy of the United States, was over by 15 March 1947, when the Third Army was inactivated and General Clay was appointed military governor. By then the United States recognized the Soviet Union for what it was. After attending a meeting of the Foreign Ministers Council in Moscow in March 1947, Ambassador Robert Murphy noted that "the Iron Curtain had come clanging down." A shaken Secretary of State George Marshall returned from the Moscow meeting and, using different words than Murphy, gave the American people the same message.

General Clay would probably have concluded that he had accomplished everything he could have and gone home. By his own choosing he stayed in Berlin as commander in chief of the USFET and military governor of Germany, where he spent the remaining second half of his four years dealing with the Berlin Blockade and everything that surrounded it. When JCS 1067 was withdrawn in July 1947, an unannounced end and subtle shift to the rebuilding of Germany began. A kind of stalemate developed between old and new forces regarding U.S.–German policy, and the punishment of Germany as a defeated enemy had ended. Clay stayed in Berlin with OMGUS alongside Murphy's imposing State Department staff, which was still dedicated to the widely accepted idea that an occupied Germany should be made a responsibility of the State Department. Clay continued as the wholly dominant figure in the U.S. occupation of Germany until his departure in 1949.

4

The Move to Vienna

WHEN THE Third Army was inactivated in March 1947, General Keyes was transferred from Heidelberg to Vienna, where he replaced Gen. Mark Clark as high commissioner and commander of the U.S. Forces–Austria (USFA). The USFA contingent was an offspring of the Allied force stationed in the Mediterranean theater which had crossed the Alps into Austria at war's end; in contrast, USFET was the creation of Generals Eisenhower and Bradley, coming out of England across France and the Rhine. The divided authority between USFET in Frankfurt and OMGUS in Berlin that had hampered the Occupation in Germany had no counterpart in Austria. Neither Eisenhower nor Joseph T. McNarney exercised any authority or influence in Austria. Mark Clark had kept his role clear as the U.S. supreme military and political figure in Austria. In 1947, when Clay replaced McNarney as commander in chief of USFET, Clark attempted to have General Keyes assigned as a subordinate to him, but the War Department summarily dismissed the idea. Keyes had clear and undivided authority in Austria and exercised it from Vienna, within the presence of an almost sovereign Austrian government and a working occupation arrangement among the French, British, Soviets, and Americans.

Austria assumed that its posture of neutrality would help it avoid integration into the Soviet system of satellites that was taking hold in the neighboring states of Hungary and Czechoslovakia and in Poland and the Baltic states. A certain amount of ambiguity and lack of recognition about Soviet behavior existed in Vienna that was not at all evident in Berlin. While Austria had been reorganized under Four Power occupation, unlike Germany it was left with a somewhat sovereign and largely intact government.

By agreement with the War Department, General Keyes took his G-2, Col. Charles P. Bixel, and a number of other officers (including myself) with him to Austria. We found that both the Austrians and the occupation forces had a much different life there than the people living in Germany. Austria was both "liberated" and "occupied." In Vienna, in the provinces, and in towns and villages the Austrian government was fully functional. The war had ended before Austria experienced much damage to its cities and villages. Parts of Vienna had been damaged in the fighting when the Soviet forces reached the outskirts of the city, but compared to most German cities it had not experienced either heavy fighting or sustained bombing by the British and American air corps.

Vienna was a city far less divided than Berlin. A *kommandatura* in District One, staffed by the Four Powers officers, ruled the city. The headquarters of the Soviet forces in Austria lay outside of the city in Baden; USFA headquarters was centered in the Allianz Bank building near the center of Vienna in the U.S. sector; the French occupied a large building in downtown Vienna; and the British installed themselves in grand style at Schoenbrunn Palace in their sector of the city. Most of the Red Army that had been stationed in Austria at the end of the war had simply found more permanent quarters and stayed. In addition to being occupied by representatives of the Four Powers, the city also was a place of romance, haunting zither music, espionage, and drug dealers.

It quickly became apparent to those of us accompanying General Keyes that General Clark's G-2 counterintelligence unit had evolved into a vigorous and productive organization that had served diverse needs in 1945 and 1946. Under Clark, activities at both the staff and operational levels cut across the dividing lines separating intelligence collection, intelligence analysis, counterintelligence, and other conventional intelligence functions. In the years immediately after World War II it would have been more accurate to describe the Army's counterintelligence unit as the catchall branch. In the occupied and liberated areas the CI branch was generally given tasks that fit no place else, partly due to the assumption that the only intelligence threats to our national interests had been destroyed with the defeat of Germany and Japan. In addition, senior commanders in occupied areas were assigned a plethora of new tasks that only remotely related to security. As they became aware of possible Soviet espionage against the United States, the hierarchy was faced with the decision to change its efforts from sorting out the histories of hostile services of World War II to instead focus on counterintelligence operations against Soviet intelligence. The change did not happen overnight, but I think it took hold in Vienna before it did in Frankfurt and Berlin simply because General Eisenhower and General Clay were among the last U.S. generals in Europe to write off the Soviet Union as an ally. USFET G-2 seemed reluctant to sign on to an active counterintelligence mission against Soviet officers serving in various capacities in the U.S. Zone. U.S. intelligence policies in Germany and Austria were decidedly different, as illustrated by the lax treatment the Soviets enjoyed at Nuremberg where they were able to recruit two members of the U.S. staff by the names of Kurt Ponger and Otto Verber. These two civilian employees of USFA were eventually identified as Soviet spies and arrested by the CIC in Vienna.

In an effort to organize a better intelligence group, Colonel Bixel organized several of the branches of the G-2 staff under a single staff officer. In this ad hoc intelligence experiment I became head of all U.S. intelligence operational activity in Austria, except for the small Central Intelligence Group (CIG), the precursor to the CIA. The CIG's Vienna station, under State Department cover, proved to be fully cooperative. My job was to "sort things out" and address the changing intelligence requirements that were gradually becoming apparent in Austria and the surrounding areas of Eastern Europe as the Soviet Union expanded its sphere of influence. With a foothold in Berlin, Prague, and Vienna, the Soviets seemed to have decided that Germany, Czechoslovakia, and Austria were within their reach.

Maj. Dewitt Armstrong, with whom I worked closely in Heidelberg, was also transferred to the G-2 Intelligence Branch in Austria, but quickly became my principal collaborator in developing a plan to carry out the task I received from Colonel Bixel. Bixel's decision to put much of the activity under a single officer gave us a unique opportunity to experiment with a consciously organized intelligence effort within Austria, which at the time was a well-defined area under a single U.S. authority (General Keyes was both high commissioner and commander in chief of USFA). Having come from Germany where the U.S. intelligence effort had been totally divided and uncoordinated, a centralized system seemed to be the obvious way to go. We were aware that the intelligence failure at Pearl Harbor had produced a move in Congress to centralize U.S. intelligence functions at the national level. Intelligence opportunities in Austria posed a unique situation in the postwar world.

Armstrong and I spent every available moment talking with the key players in the U.S. intelligence community. The support of the Army's CIC in Austria was crucial to the success of our plan. The 430th CIC was a large organization with regional detachments in Salzburg, Linz, and Vienna, headed by John Burkel in

Salzburg and Tom Lucid in Linz. From our first day the 430th CIC, a major coun-terintelligence player, was solidly behind our effort. The 430th's commander, Col. Floyd Snowden, had his office a short block away from our offices in the Allianz Bank building. We became partners.

Within a few days Armstrong and I had drafted a brief plan for a centralized effort to organize the large number of intelligence projects (both big and small) into a more conventional and manageable organization. Fortunately we saw little evi-dence of competition within the intelligence community. Colonel Bixel presented our plan to General Keyes, who promptly approved it. We assembled all of the principals from the operations level and several analysts from Vienna for a single, twelve-hour conference hosted by John Burkel and the regional CIC staff in Salzburg. We convened in a large villa outside Salzburg that had been owned by Hitler's for-eign minister, von Ribbentrop. Von Ribbentrop achieved fame by negotiating the Molotov-Ribbentrop Agreement that made Germany and the Soviet Union tem-porary allies from August 1939 until June 1941, when Hitler launched an all-out war against the Soviet Union. The spacious villa provided exactly the right atmosphere for our gathering. In a single all-day session we managed to reaffirm, modify, or in some cases reorder every operational mission in progress. It was a dramatic first step, enough to get the full attention of everyone involved, and it gave everyone a better understanding of the whole of our task as well as of each of its parts. The chief of staff and the senior intelligence staff officer from the U.S. Army command in Salzburg—a severely downsized division that had ended the war in Austria—were there. With the prior approval of General Keyes and Colonel Bixel we used the occasion to report that the high commissioner was petitioning the Austrian government to assume responsibility for completion of the denazification process in that country, a development precipitated by an incident that occurred shortly after we arrived in Vienna.

While the policy of "automatic arrest and detention" of Nazis that applied to Germany was also in use in Austria, General Clark had not followed General Clay's example in turning denazification over to the government there. Approximately nine thousand Austrian Nazis had been locked up in an internment camp near Salzburg at the end of the war. To get the attention of the new high commissioner the inmates of the camp rioted and, after commandeering a U.S. Army truck to smash through a flimsy high wire fence, they ended the riot, filed back into the camp, and asked for some official indication of the plan for their ultimate disposition. Because I had dealt with the civilian internment enclosures in Germany, General Keyes and Colonel Bixel handed the job to me. At the request of General Keyes, Austrian chancellor Leopold Figl assigned Max Pammer, a senior official in the Interior Ministry, to work with us. Pammer and I got along well and reached an agreement that the disposition of the inmates could be carried out within existing Austrian postwar laws on Nazis, its penal system, and its own courts. Those who had not been identified with any specific war crime were released and the rest were transferred to penal facilities nearest to their prewar place of residence, where they became the responsibility of the Austrian government. It was the pragmatic solution. At the same time I learned that the British authorities, under political pressure from London, were likewise making the interned Nazis the political responsibility of the Austrians.

A day or two after the Salzburg meeting I met with the CIG station chief, Al Ulmer, and his deputy, John "Jocko" Richardson, at the U.S. Embassy. Once they learned of our plans and request for their cooperation, they expressed enthusiasm for the concept and described the character and scope of their existing operational efforts. It was a good beginning.

A visible surge of intelligence activity occurred in Vienna, including our coverage of the economic and political activities of the Soviets in the Eastern European satellites and on Soviet policy to expand its influence within Austria itself. Coordinating and supporting the energized intelligence community in Austria was possible largely because we centralized our efforts (an essential element in the defector program that had developed and was the source of continuing confrontations with Soviet counterintelligence).

In 1947, when the masquerade that the Soviet Union was an ally collapsed, U.S. knowledge of the Soviet armed forces was significantly better than it might have been because of two decisions leading up to then. The first, made by USFET in 1945, was to preserve and use intelligence experts who had served in the German Army General Staff on the eastern front under Reinhard Gehlen. The second, made by Mark Clark, was to permit the USFA intelligence unit to accept, exploit, and resettle at locations outside of Europe all knowledgeable Soviet defectors from within the Soviet forces stationed in Austria (a policy continued by General Keyes). At that time the only policies regarding Soviet defectors was the Yalta Agreement's mention of the "forced repatriation of Soviet citizens" and the alleged "McNarney-Sokolovsky Agreement" that any defector from either Soviet or American forces would be returned to his home country. During my time in Vienna the Soviets did register official protests over some individual defector cases, but Soviet officials were uncomfortable with publicizing defections. U.S. sensitivity to Soviet complaints had sharply declined after the Council of Foreign Ministers meeting in Moscow in March 1947; after the council met in London in December 1947 the United States made no pretext of adherence to forced repatriation.

Early on we found that U.S. intelligence officials in Austria had been doing a brisk business in removing selected Soviet defectors from Vienna for prolonged debriefings in the U.S. Zone. Dewitt Armstrong began to focus on the potential these defectors presented as a source of intelligence on the Soviet Army. Soon many of our military intelligence reports were being sent to Washington, Frankfurt, and London. The G-2 in Washington began taking note of the reports coming from Austria. In a twelve-month period the USFA intelligence group was in clandestine contact with a total of over one hundred Soviet soldiers and officers, some of them simply deserters living "black" in Vienna or in the Soviet Zone. Between thirty and forty of these were in fact defectors who had come directly into our custody to be evacuated to the U.S. Zone in western Austria for extensive interrogation at special facilities before their resettlement somewhere outside of Austria.

The particulars involved in handling a defector, in devising a safe cover for removal to the U.S. Zone in the face of intense Soviet efforts to disrupt our operations anywhere along the way, and the direction and control of defector operations were all major management problems. Neither fell neatly into the intelligence or the counterintelligence branches. I brought in Maj. James Milano from Salzburg to be my overall chief of operations to deal with the defector problem. Milano, who had come up through Italy during the war, had boundless energy and enthusiasm and was well liked and respected. Like so many others from my time in Vienna, Jim Milano became a lifelong friend.

We soon learned that the 430th CIC had a whole array of Vatican connections that were useful to the USFA G-2. Catholic refugees in postwar Austria were willing surrogates in supporting the U.S. intelligence network's operations against Soviet communism. Relationships had in fact been formed between the Fifth Army in Italy and the Vatican. Without the Vatican connection and the help of numerous Croatian priests (who, for their own reasons, were active in Catholic international welfare and resettlement organizations), USFA could not have resettled the large number of Soviet defectors being removed from Vienna. Obviously some quid pro quos also were involved. One took place quite late in 1947 when two Catholic priests appeared at my home at 17 Lannerstrasse. After confirming my identity one of the priests handed me a sealed envelope which, they said, contained check stubs for several trunks that were in the baggage room of the railroad station in Innsbruck. These trunks, they told me, contained the priceless stamp collection of the Catholic Church in Hungary. They were concerned about the safety of the trunks and they had no practical way to safely move them to the Vatican. Help was urgently needed. Their superiors had instructed them to deliver the envelope to me and ask for my help. We recovered the trunks and sent them on, intact, to Rome.

The political tactics of the Soviet Union in taking control of the Eastern European nations "liberated" by the Red Army became perfectly apparent to us in Vienna. First they established a communist party. At the beginning certain concessions were made to local anticommunist forces, such as permitting a wide variety of anticommunist political entities, many of them new and conservative political parties, to form popular front regimes with the conservative parties on the right. During the first few years after the end of the war Moscow, through the force of the Red Army and the local communist parties, one by one isolated and attacked the political entities furthest to the right. We saw firsthand evidence of the strategy—called "salami tactics" —with the arrival of the political refugees from the "last slice on the right" of a failing coalition regime in a neighboring country.

One by one all the Eastern European and Balkan countries were coming under the control of communist regimes put in power by a Soviet Union that had not demobilized the Red Army at the end of the war. Contemporary information about these countries became a valued commodity. Each month a steady stream of displaced noncommunist leaders arrived in Vienna, usually by crossing the border into Austria in the trunk of a car or traveling on foot across the still unevenly policed borders of Austria's neighbors. Accommodating and interrogating these victims was a major activity for CIC and in some cases the CIG station, which provided a safe haven to wartime OSS agents coming across the border. Cooperation with Austrian authorities was expanding, even though resettlement of political refugees was a major and sometimes dangerous task for the Austrian government. In 1947 the Soviets were playing rough in Vienna; shootings and kidnappings by the Soviets and their surrogates regularly occurred.

The largest intelligence gap in Vienna was regarding economics. The primary purpose of the Soviet presence in Germany, Austria, and Eastern Europe was to gain control of economic assets before deciding which of those assets should be torn down and transported to the Soviet Union and which should be left in place under Soviet control. The Soviets insisted that all German assets in Austria be identified and transferred to the U.S.S.R. as reparations. We learned from a high level Soviet source in Vienna that the Soviets planned to leave all productive physical assets in place, anticipating that all of Austria, wedged in between Czechoslovakia and Hungary, would eventually fall into a Soviet economic sphere of influence.

To deal with the economic intelligence question we solicited the help of Eleanor Dulles, the economic attaché at the U.S. embassy in Vienna and the sister of John Foster and Allen Dulles. We stayed in contact with the CIG station, which was still in touch with some of the assets of the OSS in Eastern Europe. We learned that a large number of nongovernmental organizations—CARE, UNRRA, Jewish welfare agencies, and the Catholic Church—had considerable mobility moving in and out of areas of Eastern Europe where the Soviets had not yet closed all the doors. Using these well-informed organizations for intelligence purposes was not yet an issue.

Kenneth Hanson, one of my young analysts who later became one of John Kennedy's bright young men in the New Frontier, took the lead in evaluating and reporting economic intelligence. He developed a good personal and working relationship with Eleanor Dulles, an experienced individual who had arrived in Austria soon after General Clark had established his position in Vienna. Dulles understood better than any of us how large a role economics played in the formulation of Soviet policy. The Council of Foreign Ministers was still meeting every three months with a long "to do" list covering all the major problems left by the war. The meetings had become a platform for Soviet propaganda and aggressive diplomatic initiatives. Hanson, Dulles, and the CIG station chief pulled together an intelligence analysis on Soviet interests, objectives, plans, and intentions in Austria. Meanwhile, Generals Clark, Clay, and Keyes joined Secretary of State George Marshall in Moscow, where it became clear that significant disagreements existed over the growing gap between the Soviet Union and the West. John Foster Dulles, recognized as the principal foreign policy advisor to Republican presidential candidate Thomas Dewey, was part of the delegation attending the Moscow foreign ministers meeting. Eleanor, who had become an active and enthusiastic participant in our activity, communicated regularly with John Foster on the subject of U.S. relations with the Soviet Union. Our study on Soviet maneuverings in the Austrian economy was well received, which led to a decision to update the study for the next council meeting in London. In conversations with Al Ulmer and Eleanor Dulles some days after the end of the Moscow meeting we agreed that our next report would include even more sensitive material from a CIG source in the small Soviet policy-planning group in Austria.

We left the interpretation of Austrian political developments entirely to the U.S. minister in his role as political advisor to the high commissioner and to Henry Pleasants, a G-2 officer on Keyes's staff. Pleasants, a prewar journalist and music critic, was a German order of battle expert in the Fifth Army who after the war had arrived in Vienna with General Clark and became a close observer of Austrian politics. General Clark also established his own direct connection to Austrian Chancellor Figl by assigning Pleasants to the task. Henry enjoyed two distinct advantages: First, he and his wife Virginia lived in a villa on Peter Jordan-Strasse, next door to Chancellor Figl. Second, he and Virginia occupied an important role in the music world, he being an established writer and critic and she an accomplished and performing classical pianist. As an employee of the Office of War Information, Virginia was one of the first American women to arrive in Vienna after the war. She and Henry, in addition to being active in USFA, lived an almost separate existence during Vienna's revival as one of the world's great music centers, including its famous symphony orchestra, state opera, and several theaters producing the light operettas for which Vienna had long been renowned. The Pleasants made a recognized contribution to Vienna's revival as a city of great music. They also enjoyed well-established relationships with the staff of the embassy, including Eleanor Dulles and the CIG station officers. These relationships, well established before my own arrival in Vienna, were helpful in gaining embassy cooperation in our experiment in centralized intelligence.

My connection to Henry developed during our preparations of the *Weeka,* a weekly report required from every foreign post of the State Department and the Pentagon. The *Weeka* had a prescribed form of political, economic, and military sections, and a fourth called "psychological" intelligence. Our main focus was the Soviet Union, including its expanding influence in the Eastern European countries, though we eventually narrowed our focus to only Austria and its closest neighbors, Hungary and Czechoslovakia. We developed a list of Soviet actions that might indicate plans for Austria as a prospective satellite of the U.S.S.R. Accurate intelligence on even minor Soviet initiatives in Austria often permitted countermoves by the United States, usually in coordination with the British.

Our experiment in creating a centralized U.S. intelligence effort in Austria was done without consulting the Pentagon. During those early years after the end of the war the Army G-2, the director of naval intelligence, and, after the creation of the CIA, the director of central intelligence were all far too preoccupied with the struggle over the restructuring of national intelligence to be involved in what was going on in intelligence in the major commands overseas. No one in Washington except the Joint Chiefs of Staff intervened in command decisions made in Tokyo, Frankfurt, or Vienna.

5

The Jewish Factor in Germany and Austria

ALTHOUGH AMERICAN troops had overrun many concentration camps in the last days of the war, the character and dimension of Hitler's "Final Solution" was not well known to Americans in the Occupation; the term Holocaust was not yet in use. The contributions of thousands of Americans of Jewish heritage who had been born somewhere in Europe and found their way to the United States in the 1930s and early 1940s was a major factor in the success of the Occupation. Without their assistance the United States could not have accomplished what it did in the decade after the war. Jewish Americans contributed to a wide variety of occupation programs, particularly those requiring knowledge of the German language. They served in the military government, in the CIC, in military intelligence, in the CIG (and later the CIA), in the entire system of newly established courts (including the International Military Tribunal), and in dozens of other activities that involved significant interaction with the Germans. All of these activities depended on the well-educated and highly motivated former European Jewish refugees, most of whom wanted to repay the United States for the safe haven it had given them. This vital segment of the U.S. occupation force rarely demonstrated a revengeful attitude. Most displayed a strong cultural affinity for the German-speaking areas of central Europe.

By the summer of 1946 the Palestine question had become an identified issue influencing the movement of Jewish DPs into and through Western Europe. The British were not necessarily less humanitarian than the Americans, but they were attempting to stem the tide of Jews moving toward and into Palestine. The British also were facing problems within their own ranks. A Palestine brigade of the British Army had fought with courage and loyalty in the war, while the Germans were courting the Grand Mufti of Palestine. After the war, however, the sympathies of many in the brigade had shifted to support the Zionist goal of creating a Jewish state. The brigade had been part of the British occupation forces in northwest Europe at the end of the war; it was no secret that the preferred route to Palestine was through northern Germany and the ports of northwest Europe.

Late in 1946, British brigadier general J. H. Morgan, head of UNRRA, publicly claimed that the movement of Jews out of Eastern Europe was an organized affair. He was promptly fired and replaced by a former mayor of New York City, Fiorello LaGuardia, who had gained fame by reading the funny papers over the local New York radio station when the newspapers were on strike. An American named Cohen Meyer replaced the UNRRA representative in Western Europe, Jack Whiting.

In the late summer of 1946 the U.S. Constabulary guarding the checkpoints along the eastern border of the U.S. Zone in Germany reported large groups of Jewish refugees arriving by trains from Czechoslovakia and other locations in the Soviet Zone. The Constabulary asked for policy guidance. Washington replied that the United States would pursue its traditional policy of granting political asylum to individuals and small groups but would require documentation and prior clearance for organized large groups. At a morning staff meeting at the Third Army head-quarters I asked what distinguished a "small group" from an "organized movement," and learned that anything less than one hundred individuals would be considered a small group. We instructed the Constabulary to admit individuals and any group of up to ninety-nine; one hundred or more would be considered an organized large movement. A day or so later the Constabulary reported that all groups of Jewish refugees were arriving accompanied by an American Jewish organization representative, each with a manifest listing ninety-nine or fewer refugees seeking asylum.

An unwritten rule prevailed among Americans in Europe to give Jewish agencies tacit approval and all kinds of support in looking after Jewish refugees and, to the distress of the British, turning a blind eye toward the efforts of the militant groups Stern Gang and Irgun Zwai Leumi to maintain the kinetic energy of the Jewish exodus toward Palestine. Recognizing this postwar phenomenon, Jewish leaders in the United States found the "Gentiles Only" signs disappearing and the Jewish vote in the big cities of the United States achieving a whole new level of influence on the White House and the U.S. Congress. It was clear to all of us that the movement out of Eastern Europe was an organized effort. But it was difficult for American officials in Germany and Austria to assess whether it was the communists pushing the Jewish people out of Eastern Europe or if it was the world Jewish organizations pulling them out to put pressure on Palestine. The Soviet Union denied that it was organizing the movement, but it was among the first to recognize the new state of Israel when it was founded. The Soviets then systematically exploited the Arab-Israeli conflict to expand their influence in the Middle East.

The British Army moved the Palestine Brigade from northwest Europe to northern Italy; as a result, Vienna immediately became the major staging area for Jewish refugees arriving from all over Eastern Europe on their way through the Brenner Pass and the northern Italian ports to Palestine. The influence of the Jewish factor in Vienna in 1947 and early 1948 was far greater and immediately more apparent than it was in Germany for two reasons: Vienna had become the principal collecting point for the continuing mass movement of Jews out of Eastern Europe and the Balkans, the populations comprising the mainstream exodus to Palestine; and Austria had been "liberated" although still "occupied." In fact, it took a trained eye to detect any evidence that Vienna had ever embraced the Nazis at all, and no trace of anti-Semitism could be found throughout Austria. Vienna was enjoying a degree of cultural, intellectual, and political freedom and revival that was not apparent anywhere in Germany. Life in Vienna was simply more pleasant than life in Germany.

The Jewish refugee camp in Vienna, the Rothschild Kaserne, was almost a city within a city that tolerated no interference from anyone. The size of several city blocks and surrounded by high masonry walls, the camp administered itself and controlled all movement in and out. This arrangement seemed to be acceptable to USFA and the high commissioner's staff. Any observer easily understood that each day hundreds of people were moving into and out of the Rothschild compound in an organized fashion. The operation, run by leaders of organizations such as the Stern Gang and Irgun Zwai Leumi, were leading the exodus and the fight against the British in Palestine. (Decades later many of these same organizers provided the tough and enduring leadership of the state of Israel.) Thousands departed from Vienna by truck and rail and arrived in the U.S. and French Zones. Additionally, hundreds of individual Jewish refugees traveled to Western Europe, the UK, Canada, and, more than anywhere else, to Italy as a way station to Palestine. The United States was the preferred destination alternative to Palestine. But the organized effort intended to send as many refugees as possible to Palestine.

The French, the British, and the Russian intelligence services were all involved in supporting, opposing, or just trying to monitor the whole affair. The British, of course, wanted to slow the movement of Jewish refugees toward Palestine. In 1947 the Palestinian leaders were not at all sure where the United States stood in regard to the Palestine question. We Americans, presumed to be on the inside track about such information, found it difficult to know what was really going on inside the Rothschild Kascrne. I asked two American Jews on my intelligence staff to obtain a better picture of the situation there and to determine the extent to which the exodus was operating as an organized movement, with or without the support of the Soviet Union.

Our first comprehensive intelligence report on the matter revealed that almost 90 percent of the population in the huge compound in April 1947 were Polish; by July the compound's population consisted almost entirely of people from the Balkans. Obviously, at least at this point in time, few Jewish refugees from the Soviet Union were passing through Vienna. Though our reports on organized population movements through the Brenner Pass and ship movements out of Italy left no doubt that the movement was organized and disciplined, we found no evidence that the Soviets or Soviet intelligence units were involved in either supporting or opposing the exodus. Our prepared report was the only major study undertaken but apparently it was read with great interest in Washington. Undoubtedly we could never have produced such an intelligence study without the unique contributions by members of my staff who had been able to establish connections and access to leaders of the Jewish refugee organizations.

The amount of intelligence activity occurring in and around Vienna in 1947 was incredible. The Soviet Union, well along the way to imposing communist regimes on all the Eastern European countries and in the Balkans, had caused several recently dispossessed leaders to take refuge in Vienna. The struggle over Palestine was being waged between the British and the clandestine arms of the Zionist movement. At times the "games" in Vienna got fairly rough. A steady flow of traffic in clandestine movements of political and intelligence personalities took place in and out of Four-Power Vienna, which was surrounded by the Soviet Zone. Shootouts, occasional kidnappings of Austrian politicians, the arrests of agents, and occasional mysterious murders were typical (and were captured well in the movies "Four Men in a Jeep" and "The Third Man"). To a surprising degree the clandestine war was somehow linked to the flow of Jewish refugees—perhaps the early birth pangs of the coming state of Israel.

6

My Decision to Join the CIA

CREATING THE Central Intelligence Agency was a landmark improvement in our national security system. My experiences in Vienna, after spending almost a year in Germany, had convinced me that intelligence could play a new and bigger role in the conduct of U.S. defense and foreign policy—a role perhaps equal to that of the American armed services. In the two years between the demise of the OSS and the creation of the CIA, the men and women who had kept the idea of centralized national intelligence alive had learned to live and operate under temporary agreements and circumstances. The National Security Act of 1947 unified the military services, including a new and separate U.S. Air Force, into the Department of Defense; the act also created the Central Intelligence Agency and a National Security Council to assist the president in the management of foreign relations.

I returned to the United States in January 1948 with a feeling of uncertainty about the future. My year in Vienna had eliminated any doubts I had that the emerging phenomenon of a heavily armed Soviet Bloc posed a formidable strategic threat to the stability and security of Western Europe and other regions on the periphery of the expanded Soviet sphere of influence. I could not conceive of the idea that, considering its enormous losses in World War II, the Soviet Union would initiate another major war. The United States and her allies regarded the U.S. monopoly of the atomic bomb a powerful deterrent. We in Vienna had not considered the possibility that the

Soviets would develop their own atomic bomb, nor that a successful espionage effort in Britain and the United States would accelerate its development.

I cautiously began to explore the idea of joining the CIA as an option for my future. In Germany I had known several SSU officers, but mostly in casual social circumstances only. On one occasion I had met and briefly spoken with a visiting former OSS officer from Washington, Richard Helms. In contrast to my time in Germany, in Austria I had worked closely and productively with the high-quality officers in the CIG in the U.S. embassy, many of whom later appeared in the leadership cadre of the new CIA. En route to Washington after landing in New York, at Eleanor Dulles's urging I called on John Foster Dulles in his office at 48 Wall Street. At the time Dulles was acting as a foreign policy advisor to Thomas Dewey, the front-runner in the 1948 race for the presidency. At the end of our conversation on the situation in Europe he called his younger brother Allen into his office. I spent another hour with him. Allen showed an interest in the situation in Europe as we had seen it from Vienna. In answering my question about his future involvement in intelligence, he told me that he had returned to the practice of law. I told him that I had orders to report to the Army General Staff operations staff. In retrospect I think that neither Allen Dulles nor I were quite as certain as we let on about having no interest in intertwining our futures with intelligence.

While on my way to Fort Knox to attend the advanced armor refresher course, I met with Dick Helms in Washington and expressed my appreciation for the cooperation I had received from Al Ulmer's CIG team in Vienna. When Helms learned of my satisfaction with what we were accomplishing in Austria, he simply said that if I ever decided to make a career of intelligence, he would help in any way possible. But I was headed for Knox and planned to be assigned to the operations staff in the Pentagon by summer, a stint that would include three academic years at Princeton to obtain a Ph.D. Helms laughingly replied that "the CIA could not compete with that."

My family and I reported to Fort Knox and were assigned quarters in a single-story wartime temporary building. We had two bedrooms, a bath, and a kitchen. Each bedroom held two metal folding cots, each with a mattress, pillow, and two sets of army-issue sheets and olive drab woolen blankets. In the kitchen was a refrigerator and a gas stove, a small folding wooden table, four metal chairs, and enough plates, glasses, pans, and utensils to meet our needs. We were back in the U.S. Army and, to our surprise, found it reassuring to be there.

I soon discovered that my classes at Knox included quite a large number of my contemporaries who had begun their careers in 1939 as officers in the cavalry.

During the war years they had served in Europe or the Pacific. Most were career officers, that is, Regular Army, and were settling into the typical career patterns taking form after the demobilization of World War II had been completed. Many had served with the famous armored divisions and armored cavalry regiments that swept across Europe after the infantry, the engineers, and the airborne forces had cracked the German defenses at Normandy. The course at Fort Knox was designed to give these battle-experienced officers an appraisal of the lessons learned, projections on what the next generation of tanks would look like, and ideas that were evolving on the role of armor in future wars. While we had research projects to work on, most of our time was spent cruising about in tanks, firing slightly larger tank guns than we had known in the war, tearing down and learning the intricacies of a tank transmission, and listening to the Armored School's current theories.

While at Fort Knox I finally reached the agonizing decision to end my career in the U.S. Army in exchange for the prospect of an uncertain career in the new CIA. My wife Connie seemed equally supportive of either choice. I made my decision very much alone, and no one in the CIA made a hard sell to recruit me or promised anything about the future except that a career in intelligence would be a great challenge and cause. There is not the slightest doubt in my mind that my decision to end my Army career and join the CIA was the direct consequence of the unique combination of events and influences of my life—the war years, the changing character of war including the introduction of the atomic bomb, my time at Columbia, and my two years of intelligence work in Germany and Austria. I had gained a wide horizon against which to examine the future. I decided that within this changed world a career with the CIA might give me the opportunity to make a real difference. Ending my military career was nevertheless a very difficult decision; soldiering at my age and during the World War II years had been a meaningful and rewarding experience. I was a profoundly patriotic young American vaguely conscious that a unique role and responsibility had been thrust upon the United States.

In the three years after the end of the war I was still unable to perceive what the character of war in the atomic age would be like. The bombing of Hiroshima and Nagasaki made a huge impact on me. Once we contemplated the full implications of the atomic bombs that had been dropped on Japan and what lay ahead in an era of nuclear weapons, I believed that mankind would be unable to tolerate even the idea of a general nuclear war. An enormous and undefined constraint would rest on the head of any nation capable of starting a nuclear war. Yet if nuclear arsenals remained in the hands of nation-states of diverse size and character, we would have no alternative but to maintain military superiority, including nuclear offensive and defensive weapons. Intelligence, in many guises, could become a major instrument for detecting threats and deterring nations from starting a nuclear war. This underlying opinion has strongly influenced my professional actions and thinking over the past half century during which we have experienced numerous crises and limited wars but no second use of nuclear weapons. In 1947 and 1948 we were just beginning to see the first limited wars, mainly "wars of national liberation" against colonialism, that later proliferated and flourished in most regions of the world for several decades after the end of World War II. In Greece, Turkey, and Iran we were experimenting with the process of giving military aid and assistance as a way of encouraging client states to contribute to the containment of early communist pressures orchestrated by the Soviet Union.

When I informed Dick Helms of my decision to join the agency he introduced me to Col. Don Galloway, an army officer serving temporary duty as head of the Operations Directorate of the CIA. On Galloway's desk I could see what appeared to be at least part of my Army file. After getting the stock answers explaining my decision, Colonel Galloway rose, shook my hand, and said, "You are a damned fool to be leaving your Army career, but we are glad to have you." Neither Helms nor I thought the statement required a comment and we departed.

A few days later I officially joined the CIA and began my orientation in a temporary building in Foggy Bottom near the Senate beer brewery. Connie and my two children had left to stay with our families in Fargo, and were preparing to join me in time for our ship's departure from New York to Europe. Then tragedy struck. On 11 June 1948 Dick Helms's secretary, Elizabeth Dunlevy, called me to take a telephone call from Helms's office. An Iowa state trooper informed me that Connie and my sister's young fiancé, who was helping to drive Connie from Fargo to Washington to meet me a few days prior to sailing, had been killed in a car accident in eastern Iowa. My world was shattered. Within an hour I was flying to Iowa, deeply depressed and with no concept of my future without Connie. The idea that her death was an unforeseen consequence of my decision to alter the pattern of my life only added to my sorrow.

After the funeral and several painful weeks in Fargo, I considered quitting my job with the CIA and finding a simpler life in North Dakota among friends and family. My mother, a widow and a great woman of solid Midwestern stock, persuaded me to return to Washington. She broke up her own home and accompanied my two small children, my grieving sister, and me to Germany, where she got all of us through a very difficult year. We sailed out of New York at the end of August on the *New Amsterdam*, bound for an assignment in Munich.

My initial task in Munich was to establish a center for intelligence operations to produce information on the Soviet Union—a nation about which Americans were almost totally uninformed. In my absence the decision about my assignment had been made by Dick Helms, the head of Foreign Division M (Middle Europe), and Harry Rositzke, who was forming a new Soviet division to concentrate solely on our wartime ally. (The division responsible for the Soviet Union had not yet been established.) It was a challenging mission of the kind that had attracted me to join the CIA in the first place. Aside from assigning a half dozen officers, most of whom had Russian language abilities, to join me in Munich, the German station in Karlsruhe had done nothing else in establishing the proposed center in Munich. I was starting from square one.

7

An Unexpected Change of Mission

THE OPERATIONS base in Munich was located in a modern and reasonably large house in the Schwabing district on the northern edge of the city's Englischergarten. Within days of my arrival in Munich four or five Russian-speaking American case officers, a deputy from Karlsruhe, two young administrative support staffers, and an experienced secretary from OSS joined me. The operations officers began their work with a preliminary examination of the large community of displaced persons of Soviet and Eastern European origin. This group of DPs was one of the main reasons for locating our operations in Munich. Within weeks we had an inventory of all Eastern European émigrés living in Munich after World War II.

Many Eastern European refugees had cooperated with the Nazis during the German advance deep into Russia and had fled westward ahead of advancing Soviet forces late in the war. Several hundred thousand of the German refugees had simply been turned out of their homes as a result of the gains and losses of territory during the course of the war. Stalin had come away from Yalta asserting that Churchill and Roosevelt were guaranteeing the "humane transfer" of the German population out of the territory east of the Oder-Neisse line—these German territories were going to a newly partitioned Poland. Ethnic Germans from Russia, the Balkans, and the Baltic countries had swelled the steady stream of German refugees. The enclave around Koeningsberg in East Prussia had been a loose piece of change left on the geopolitical poker table that Stalin had simply picked up and pocketed, renaming it Kaliningrad. The more accurate term of "ethnic cleansing" had not yet replaced "humane population transfers." An estimated eleven million ethnic Germans were transferred into the occupied zones of postwar Germany; a majority of these had simply pushed westward, escaping from the Soviets between the Elbe and the Oder-Neisse line.

For other reasons Munich, a comparatively undestroyed major city in the U.S. Zone, was the preferred place not only for the CIA, but also for Radio Free Europe and Radio Liberation—both of which were later identified as separately run CIA operations. Munich had become the center for the threatening cold war and was crawling with intelligence officers and agents of many nationalities. By September 1948 U.S. intelligence in occupied Germany was preoccupied with building new organizations and still sorting out people and situations left over from the war. It had not yet settled down to the serious business of long-term intelligence operations in the strategic confrontation already under way after the communist coups in Prague in February 1948 and the soon-to-follow Berlin blockade. The United States had ended World War II with no realistic appreciation of the Soviet intelligence effort being directed against it.

Around the middle of October I attended my first CIA monthly meeting, an evening session run by the station chief in Karlsruhe, Gordon Stewart. Most of those attending were former OSS officers, including Dana Durand, Peter Sichel, Tom Polgar from Berlin, Charles Katek (who headed an operational effort targeted solely on Czechoslovakia), and Henry Hecksher from the station. Stewart informed us that Colonel Galloway was arriving from headquarters the next day, and Galloway wanted the station to conduct an investigation of a German intelligence group that had its headquarters in the village of Pullach near Munich. The DCI had agreed that the CIA would assess the Army's operation with the possibility of taking it over. The information was all new to me, since there had been no mention of Operation Rusty during my few weeks in Washington.

None of the officers present at the meeting demonstrated any interest in the assignment. They believed the CIA should not get involved, based on Rusty's origin in the German General Staff and its reputation among CIA officers for insecure operational practices and the questionable value of its intelligence production. Dana Durand, the Berlin base chief and obviously qualified for the task of investigating Rusty, made it clear that he did not want the job, offering the gratuitous opinion that it was a job that would not enhance anyone's career. He suggested the issue could be dodged by proposing that I, already resident in Munich on a Soviet division mission, could visit Rusty in my spare time and prepare a report for Admiral Hillenkoetter. I only had a vague knowledge of Rusty's activity from my days in the Third Army and was not aware that the operation had moved from Oberursel to Pullach. I did what I could to remain aloof from the discussion since it was not related to my Soviet mission—or so I thought.

The following morning I departed from Karlsruhe for Munich, confident that I would not be involved in the Rusty investigation. It is an understatement to say I was surprised when I received a cable from the CIA director on 27 October requesting that I make a four-week investigation of the operation in addition to my Soviet assignment. The mission described in the cable was clear and incredibly explicit: "To recommend at the end of four weeks of investigation whether the German organization should be liquidated or continue to receive support from the U.S. and, if the latter, whether the CIA should assume responsibility from the Army G-2." I had every reason to ask that I not be given this task. I was new to the CIA, and still quite downhearted, trying to adjust to the loss of my wife and the mother of my two small children. I was not an OSS veteran with a background in German operations. I had been asked to investigate a German intelligence organization about which I had been given virtually no background information. I surmised that in its three-year postwar history the operation had become highly controversial at high levels in Washington and within the CIA station in Germany. I had left Washington with a challenging assignment focused on the Soviet Union, not Germany. I had never even met the director who was asking me to undertake a complicated mission that almost certainly put at risk the interests of the CIA, the Army, and possibly the broader interests of the United States.

Yet I found the proposed mission distinctly intriguing. Confident that my wartime experiences, my studies at Columbia, and my two years just completed in Germany and Austria had given me some understanding of the moral, legal, and political issues involved, it occurred to me that we were living in times of great change in which the mission in Pullach might reveal potentially useful information on what remained of the last German Army General Staff. What would its role and influence be in the new Germany that was taking shape in discussions among the Allied high commissioners?

After receiving the cable I expected to hear from both Stewart and Richard Helms's division in Washington, to get both background data on Rusty and some indication of their preferences in the matter. I heard nothing. In the fortnight after receiving my orders from Washington it gradually seemed there was something strange about the whole affair, something involving the Army, the CIA, and

Rusty. My impression was strengthened just prior to my visit to Pullach when Col. Robert A. Schow, the Army G-2 in Heidelberg, blandly told me in the presence of Gordon Stewart that G-2 had no files on Rusty beyond those maintained by the Army staff in Pullach. I had the distinct sense that I was being manipulated and almost certainly deceived; both the CIA station chief and the Army G-2 were telling me that they had no useful information on Rusty. What had they been doing in their last three years in Germany? A very strange affair indeed!

My initial reaction of surprise and resentment that I was being sent to Pullach totally unbriefed gradually developed into a belief that there was some advantage to taking on this task without guidance. The less I knew the better. I made a conscious decision to undertake the proposed investigation and to do so on what seemed to be agreed terms by the CIA and the Army G-2: no briefing and no hint of the CIA's or the G-2's preference regarding the results. There might be an advantage to going to Pullach unencumbered with biased opinions on the issues that obviously had created disagreements at high levels in Washington.

FLASHBACK TO NUREMBERG

Just two years before my initial visit to Pullach I attended the verdict session of the International Military Tribunal in Nuremberg as representative of the commander of the Third Army. With regard to the German military the tribunal had sentenced Generals Keitel and Jodl to death and Admirals Doenitz and Raeder to long prison sentences. Goering cheated the hangman by committing suicide.

For trial purposes the tribunal had created an artificial German organization, the "General Staff and High Command," and attempted to indict it as a criminal organization, including specifically the 130 most-senior generals and admirals serving in the three branches of the Wehrmacht. The group included the commanders and chiefs of staff of the German Army, Air Force, and Navy, as well as major field commanders of the three branches. Officers who had occupied any one of those positions between 1938 and the end of the war had been identified. The same tribunal, after creating the "General Staff and High Command," ruled that it was not truly an organization and, on this technical point, did not declare it a criminal organization. In accompanying legal commentary the tribunal assigned great guilt and responsibility for war crimes and crimes against humanity to these officers, but drew a line and assigned no guilt to any command or staff members at any lower level. The tribunal's ambiguous decision left to the individual occupying power the option of determining which of the 130 officers should be brought to trial. An erratic pattern of trial emerged, and only some of the 130 were subsequently indicted of individual war crimes.

After listening attentively to the tribunal's judgment on 1 October 1946 I left Nuremberg with two questions: (1) What in the history and character of this group of 130 senior officers had led to the tribunal's harsh and definitive treatment, and (2) What in the history and character of the rest of the Wehrmacht, including the officers of the famed German General Staff, had caused the tribunal to so pointedly exonerate those members from organizational guilt and responsibility? While General Clay's law of 5 March had made General Staff officers, as a category, war criminals subject to mandatory trials by German denazification courts, the tribunal had declared its disinterest in rank and file General Staff officers and had in effect exonerated them from indictment and trial as war criminals. When I left Germany for Vienna in early 1947, I assumed that the tribunal judgment would prevail. But Clay simply left the contradiction to the German courts. In 1948 when I went to Pullach I was particularly concerned that I might find some of the 130 most senior Wehrmacht officers working in Operation Rusty. I also did not know how the German courts were dealing with General Staff officers under the terms of Clay's law, but I had heard of no General Staff officer serving any sentence under it. The explicitly stated opinion of the tribunal disclaiming any interest in General Staff officers clearly undermined Clay's initiative, which had been promulgated seven months before the end of the primary Nuremberg trial. Much later I heard an experienced German lawyer explain that the German authorities had not made an issue of it with Clay but had pragmatically permitted the courts to interpret Clay's law in light of the earlier judgment of a superior court (the tribunal).

WHAT I FOUND IN PULLACH

Although the Army G-2 had made arrangements for me to meet the German staff in Pullach, none of the officers took part in the briefings that followed. Before meeting with Reinhard Gehlen I carefully worked out in my own mind how I would approach the task: I would request a full briefing on the size and character of the German organization, including a list of the real and cover names of its members; I would ask Gehlen for a full description of the assignments he had received from the USFET and USEUCOM, and his own assessment of the organization's performance; and early on I would try to spend as much time as possible with the intelligence production staff, including the experienced analysts from the original Fremde Heere Ost and the resident liaison officers from G-2 and A-2, who had been described to us by Colonel Schow as a useful and substantive communication link at the working level.

After my general briefing about the organization and my meeting with the production staff, I planned to address the important question of operations: espionage, counterintelligence, and numerous related concerns. I knew that the time needed to accomplish the task, including time for travel to outside bases, would easily consume the four weeks allotted by the CIA. But I was determined to get answers from Gehlen regarding political questions dating back to the Nuremberg trial and to the history of the General Staff out of which Fremde Heere Ost and Reinhard Gehlen had come.

Before my investigation ended I wanted fairly specific answers to four key questions: Were any former Nazi Party members in the organization? Were any of them war criminals? Did it include any of the former 130 senior officers described in the Nuremberg indictment as the "General Staff and High Command"? And, how did Gehlen and his key aides view the history and character of the German Army General Staff vis-à-vis their organization? This last question was important because I had inferred during my CIA discussions that the General Staff element in the German organization constituted some kind of risk to the United States. I also knew that the American press, public, and Congress would have their own ideas about preserving any part of the German Army that had overrun most of Europe and taken the lives of thousands of young Americans. I knew, of course, that I would find a cadre of the Army General Staff in Pullach, remnants of Fremde Heere Ost. I hoped that I would find none of the senior officers described at Nuremberg.

My mission was limited. Essentially I was to recommend whether Rusty was to be liquidated or preserved and, if preserved, whether the CIA should assume control of it or leave it within the purview of the Army. Neither Gehlen nor the U.S. staff would be informed of the nature or specifics of my mission—I was just another official from the Pentagon making a four-week visit. I realized also that Reinhard Gehlen would not believe this for one minute.

I drove into the Pullach compound on 18 November and parked my old black Chevrolet in the cobblestone courtyard opposite the "White House." I noted the

Stars and Stripes flying on a lone flagpole above a stretch of green lawn beyond the courtyard. I paused momentarily to consider the symbolic significance of our flag flying over this particular place. My first meeting with Gehlen took place on the front steps of the White House at the center of the small compound, once the abode of the Nazi Party. "I am Doktor Schneider," he informed me. I replied, "I am Marshall, James Marshall." It was 9:00 a.m.. During my eight years in Pullach I used the name Kent J. Marshall in signing all documents and in all contacts within the German organization, though most Americans and Germans in Pullach knew me by my middle name, James or Jim. Gehlen never permitted himself that degree of informality. He referred to me as "Herr Marshall" until his death almost thirty years later. And I always, out of habit, addressed him as "Herr Doktor."

Doktor Schneider was a man of average stature, lean and trim in appearance, with a small, neatly trimmed mustache and closely cut brown hair. He had a clear, almost translucent complexion with the skin below his noticeably blue eyes stretched tightly over moderately high cheekbones. At that first meeting he wore a dark gray-green business suit with a shirt and necktie. He was accompanied by one of his senior aides, a slightly taller and pleasant-looking man who spoke fluent British-accented English. Doktor Schneider waved me in through the door into the large wood-paneled room to the left, the former music salon. Besides a small bar in one corner and a coffee table with four chairs, a Bechstein concert grand piano was the only furniture in the room.

After we were seated a woman served us coffee. Gehlen offered a cigar, which I declined, and then asked if I minded if he smoked. I smiled and said, "of course not." He took a small instrument out of his pocket and clipped the end of a cigar, which he then lit and puffed on several times. He then leaned back, obviously ready to talk. I noticed he put three teaspoons of sugar into his coffee (which I later learned was part of a routine he never varied).

I briefly reported my background, though he knew exactly who I was and that I had been a U.S. Army intelligence officer who had served in Germany and Austria as recently as 1947 and early 1948. He knew that I had come from the CIA, but seemed unsure of the purpose of my visit. I acknowledged that I had only recently joined the CIA, which explained why I did not know Sam Bossard, the counterintelligence group officer who had spent a long period with Gehlen's own group in 1947 when they were still located at Oberursel. Gehlen indicated that he hoped my investigation would lead to a change to his work being sponsored by the CIA instead of the Army. He gave me his undivided attention but clearly was uncertain about the CIA's intentions, as well he should have been. He was beset by problems and assumed the CIA would assist him in resolving some of them, including a financial crisis produced by early uncontrolled growth and the currency reforms of June 1948. Gehlen was desperate for an association with the new CIA although his expectations were, I found, somewhat unrealistic.

During our initial meeting I told Gehlen that I wanted to know the identities of every member in and the structure of his organization, and a full description of his operations. He told me that he wanted to preserve the integrity and separateness of the German organization. I responded that I had no problem at all with keeping the organization separate as long as we Americans were adequately informed. I further suggested that his objectives, as he described them, were not necessarily in conflict with the CIA's objectives, but they might become so if we were not kept informed. At these words I detected the first tension in Gehlen's reaction. After an obvious pause, during which he puffed on his cigar and emptied his cup, he leaned back and explained to me his basic philosophy in maintaining the integrity and German character of his organization: a German organization was more likely to gain support and acceptance from a new German government. I think Gehlen's inclination to be secretive with the Americans about his organization was a major error. When we reached what seemed to be an impasse on agreeing that he would provide essential information, I closed my briefcase and threatened to terminate my visit. Gehlen backed off and reverted to a compromise on these issues that was acceptable, under the circumstances. However, the issue was never entirely resolved; I do not think Gehlen had thought through the issue of whether or not to adopt a trusting and candid relationship with the CIA. I believe Gehlen was by nature private, even secretive, more so than most of his inner circle of associates. Beyond his personal traits it was probably a matter of principle to him that the creation of "his" national intelligence service justified limiting information to a foreign intelligence service, even though we were standing in a nation that had unconditionally surrendered to an occupying power. On the issue of war criminals Gehlen told me that it was his policy to employ no war criminals; during that visit I observed none. Nor did I find any immediately definable Nazis. The gap between the Nazi Party and the last prevailing Army General Staff had become fairly wide by the beginning of the war in 1939. But, and even more significant to me, I found no member of the "General Staff and High Command."

I met Adolf Heusinger on the second day of my visit to Pullach. Heinz Herre, who arranged the meeting (as he did most of my interviews) escorted me to a building with a small, weathered sign that identified it as the one-time SS barracks Number 103. We were met at the door by a man of average stature whom Herre introduced as "Doktor Horn," the head of the evaluations staff. Horn was lean and fit, perhaps in his late forties or early fifties. This pleasant man, I thought, could be a professor. Standing beside him was a taller, younger, erect, and reserved man whom he identified as his deputy, "Herr Wieland." The two men—actually Adolf Heusinger and Gerhard Wessel—eventually played important roles in the eventful decade that lay ahead.

Heusinger was wearing a warm, grayish green sweater which ironically had been made in America. As I made my rounds in Pullach during the weeks that followed, I noted that a number of the Germans working in the still unheated building were wearing some of those thousands of sweaters knitted by patriotic American grandmothers "to keep our boys at the front warm." The American soldiers, for whom these were intended, had long since departed to resume civilian lives in the United States. An enterprising American supply sergeant in Pullach had discovered the sweaters in surplus stores at the Munich quartermaster's warehouse, and they had obviously become a welcome item of clothing in the cold buildings. Salvaged German and American military clothing was in evidence throughout the compound. We were already into the late autumn and the central heating system had not yet been activated for the winter, and coal in Germany was still in short supply. Fuel oil was not to be found.

Adolf Heusinger, soft-spoken and quite articulate in a nearly unaccented English, was relaxed and self-confident working in wholly unpretentious circumstances in Building 103. I had no knowledge of his identity and background until I was briefed by Herre later that day. I never would have imagined on that November day that this scholarly man would within a decade head the new German armed forces and serve beside American forces in a Western alliance. He was surrounded by people who obviously had great respect for him and knew what they were doing. The evaluation staff was the first major group I visited on my initial trip to Pullach—Gehlen was obviously putting his best foot forward.

During the four weeks after my arrival I met with Gehlen almost daily. One or two of his staff usually accompanied him, most often Heinz Herre, who appeared to be Gehlen's alter ego. After observing the scope and complexity of the subject I was ordered to investigate in a short four weeks, I bowed to necessity and brought my deputy, Jay Carlton, to Pullach, and put him into contact with several elements of the German staff with whom I would not have time to meet. Jay was a bright and outgoing Bostonian who performed well and added to the scope of our knowledge. I also relied greatly on Eric Waldman, who possessed an impressive understanding of the entire operation—including Gehlen's aims and expectations —along with a remarkably objective attitude regarding the former German officers in Pullach. Waldman was my only instantly available window into the German organization. He accompanied me on visits to several of the operating bases and provided background information on the principals directing each. He was the only member of the U.S. staff who seemed to be well informed on the activities, structure, and personalities of the organization. Beyond that, he seemed to have established a rapport with Gehlen and a friendship with Heinz Herre. I relentlessly peppered Waldman with questions about what he knew and impressions he had formed, and learned that he had made it clear to Gehlen we would not tolerate any member of the Nazi Party in the Pullach compound, and had in fact found none. Waldman believed that Gehlen had drawn a firm line, ruling out any wanted or suspected war criminals in his organization. But some borderline cases worked in peripheral areas of the organization. I made an effort to recruit Waldman into the CIA, but he preferred to return to an academic life once his service was over. Eric viewed our experience in Pullach as living history; once it was over he became a professor of history at Marquette University and later taught for many years at the University of Calgary. We have been lifelong friends.

During the course of my investigation I visited the A-2, Brig. Gen. "Pappy" Lewis, in Wiesbaden to study the intercept operation being run by Gehlen's station at nearby Schloss Kransberg. General Lewis had made a local deal with Captain Redden, an American officer from Pullach residing in the Frankfurt area who was responsible for monitoring Operation Dustbin, the code name for the intercept operation. Redden and I observed perhaps ten experienced German operators wearing headsets and hunched over individual radio receivers as they monitored Soviet air and ground voice communications. Redden told me that much of the equipment had been informally provided by the Americans in Wiesbaden in exchange for the delivery of near real-time traffic reports and analysis from the site. Through the reports the U.S. Air Force A-2 learned whether the Soviet MIGs were up or down, and what fields they were using. I think this visit prompted me to recommend that the United States set aside its debate on the future of Operation Rusty until it was more fully defined or the Berlin Crisis was resolved. The raw traffic from the operation had assumed unique value to General LeMay when he sent hundreds of planes through the air corridor into Berlin after the Soviet blockade of the city. The Soviet blockade was meant to force the United States and the West out of Berlin as a first step in extending Soviet hegemony over Western Europe. A February 1948 coup in Prague had consolidated Soviet control of the Eastern European countries. In March, General Clay in Berlin had shaken up Washington with a cabled opinion that the loss of Berlin would lead to a discrediting of the United States and the loss of all of Europe to the Soviet Union. Clay considered a Soviet military action possible. President Truman had solidly supported Clay's proposal of an airlift. The Germans in Berlin had responded courageously and a West German government was evolving in the three Western zones. The airlift had been the collective answer of President Truman, General Clay, Britain's tough foreign minister Ernest Bevin, and General LeMay. The Soviet Air Force had a large number of MIGs that they kept moving around airfields in the Soviet Zone. If they had wanted to take the risks and escalate the Berlin Crisis into a real shooting war, the fleet of lumbering cargo planes stationed in the corridor would have been the most accessible targets. Locating and counting MIGs on the ground in Soviet airfields in East Germany had for months been a primary mission of Gehlen's agents. Only the intercept operators at Dustbin could provide real-time reporting of MIG activity, so without hesitation I recommended continuation of the project via the most direct secure communications available.

At the end of four bewildering weeks of briefings, conversations with the German staff members, and almost daily meetings with Gehlen, I had answered enough of the questions in my own mind to recommend that U.S. support continue and that the CIA assume responsibility for oversight. In Pullach I had found a centralized German intelligence service, a staff of roughly three hundred persons working in the compound (many living in cramped conditions), and an American presence that did little more than provide a military cover and logistical support. I also found what I concluded were a significant number of German Army General Staff officers who had been isolated on the eastern front throughout the duration of the war with the Soviet Union. All the key people in the Gehlen Organization were either Army General Staff or Abwehr, all of whom had come out of the war and the Nuremberg Trials with reasonably clean slates. None had been identified in the *Automatic Arrest Categories,* the booklet given to U.S. and British troops entering Germany late in the war. Neither group had been labeled as criminal or indicted by the tribunal. The Abwehr under Admiral Canaris and the Army General Staff assembled by General Beck between 1934 and late 1938 had formed the core of the resistance effort within the Wehrmacht. When Hitler abruptly eliminated the Abwehr in February 1944 the competing influences of the Wehrmacht and the RSHA caused Abwehr officers to lead a precarious life in the last year of the war. Sorting out surviving Abwehr officers at the end of the war was not an easy task.

At the end of those four weeks in late 1948 I was persuaded that the former German Army General Staff officers in Pullach constituted no risk to the United States. I had been influenced by what I had learned from the main trial at Nuremberg, from my own first impressions after meeting perhaps twenty of the men, and on the knowledge and opinions of Eric Waldman, who had been with the Gehlen group since 1945. Nevertheless, I was quite aware that the information gathered in a four-week investigation was limited.

I sent a long cabled report on the organization to Washington a week before Christmas. I recommended that the Gehlen Organization continue to receive support, but initially only at the existing level of Army intelligence. I proposed that responsibility for the mission should be assumed by the CIA, and a professional staff should be assigned to work with and study it for a year or two before making a decision on any further American connections. In the cable I adopted the name "the Gehlen Organization" and dropped the use of Operation Rusty, since Reinhard Gehlen, "Doktor Schneider," was the dominant figure in the operation.

My decision was easy to reach. The United States was involved in a dangerous phase of challenging the blockade using the gigantic Berlin airlift. I had personally observed that the Gehlen Organization was providing the high quality and real-time intelligence of Soviet air activity in East Germany. Considering the circumstances I wondered why the United States was even considering drastic action on the Gehlen Organization. Also, it seemed to me that in the context of changing policy on Germany, politically the United States had passed the point of no return in forming a West German state, a factor the CIA would have to take into consideration in shaping a plan for the ultimate disposition of the Gehlen Organization. I consciously avoided any effort to sort out my own assessment of Gehlen as an individual beyond the fact that he was the dominant figure in Pullach and at times could be difficult. I believed that the long-term interests of the United States were best served in accepting Gehlen's position on preserving the German character and the integrity of his organization. In the changing situation in Europe it made sense. Yet I also concluded that for the time being the CIA should withhold its opinion on his plans to transform his organization into a new official German government intelligence service.

More than fifty years after sending my recommendations to Washington I learned that Admiral Hillenkoetter, the DCI who sent me to Pullach, had several months earlier in 1947 proposed in writing to the highest levels in Washington that the Army's German operation be liquidated. When the Army G-2, who was intent on shifting the operation over to the CIA, objected to the drastic proposal, the admiral had expressed his opinion that preserving any element of the German General Staff posed a security risk to the United States. He believed that the risk outweighed the value of any intelligence the organization was producing. The Army's opinion had produced a minor crisis that exerted new pressures on Admiral Hillenkoetter to take another look at the controversial operation. This series of events had led to my somewhat strange mission to Pullach. I remain grateful to Dick Helms and others who did not complicate my assignment by giving me this background information. Even had I had it, the information would not have influenced my recommendation—reason, common sense, and historical evidence were on my side.

The reality was that by the autumn of 1948 Gehlen was beset with problems that would have overwhelmed a less persistent man; his organization's growth had been largely uncontrolled during the tumultuous time in Germany in 1945 and 1946. Gehlen's residence in the United States during this critical period had given Hermann Baun an opportunity to expand the organization while Army support, in the form of German currency, U.S. black market commodities, and travel documents continued. It took Gehlen much of the year after his return to Germany to regain some control. Once he moved to Pullach, Gehlen took a calculated risk, relying on institutional black marketing to recruit new staff members to meet the specific requirements caused by the changing character of the organization. The currency reform in June 1948 caught Gehlen extremely overextended. Conflicts over funding and management problems in the American military staff headquarters had fueled Army efforts to transfer the Gehlen group to the CIG, and after September 1947 to the new CIA. By late 1948 Gehlen was keeping an eye on the first moves by the West toward forming a new West German government, all the while considering the possible advantages of having the new CIA as his American sponsor. When General Clay delayed the organization's actual transfer to the CIA, financial conflicts between the Army and Gehlen increased. By the autumn of 1948 currency reform had made his financial situation desperate. Furthermore, he had no real agreement or understanding with any U.S. official concerning his organization despite numerous earlier efforts to enlist the support of General Sibert in August 1946. In spite of these problems Gehlen showed no tendency to lower his sights and cut his losses. He was determined to preserve the group's character and organizational integrity.

My recommendations to CIA headquarters were approved and I was asked to head the CIA staff assigned to Pullach. Assuming oversight of the operation was to many CIA officers a decision that put the agency and U.S. interests at risk. Ultimately it constituted a landmark change in my own career. I viewed my assignment as a logical consequence of the exploratory mission I had accepted earlier. My job as chief of the Soviet Operations Base in Munich was turned over to Charles Katek, who had moved to Germany after the coup in Czechoslovakia. General Clay, who was preoccupied with the airlift, delayed the turnover date set for 1 January 1949 until July. I welcomed the delay. I simply established a small office near the entrance to the compound and became better acquainted with the German staff and the American Army cover unit, the 7821 Composite Group, that I was to inherit.

As head of the CIA's Pullach Operations Base my mission was to become better informed about the Gehlen Organization while developing plans for the CIA to assume responsibility for it when the time came. During these six months I carefully avoided involvement in Gehlen's working relationship with Colonel Philp, the commanding officer of the 7821 Composite Group. In the face of a financial crisis and support being limited to $125,000 dollars a month, Gehlen succored Colonel Philp to use his rank and relationship with General Huebner to gain some relief by significantly increasing the supply of goods from the quartermaster and the PX that continued to bring comparatively high DM prices in the black market.

During most of that time my CIA staff was limited to one person, a former OSS secretary and administrative assistant named Irene Terhaar. Irene had come from the German community of New Ulm, Minnesota; she possessed a sophisticated understanding of our situation and mission. I established a small office away from the White House and kept my work quite separate from Colonel Philp's. Heinz Herre was our main contact, and he was in and out of our office at least once a day. Gehlen, almost always accompanied by Herre, became a more frequent visitor as well. May and June produced a virtual avalanche of senior U.S. military officers, all of whom were curious to see what went on in Pullach before the keys were passed to the CIA.

As we approached July I shouldered myself into a large and easily accessible office in the White House, which at one time had been the second-story bedroom of Martin Bormann. Supervision of the Gehlen Organization was turned over to the CIA on 1 July 1949, the same day as John J. McCloy replaced Lucius Clay as Germany's military governor. To the casual observer in the village or from inside the compound, nothing changed. Local U.S. military authorities accepted without question that I was simply replacing Colonel Philp as the officer in charge. To strengthen our military cover in the face of growing press interest in the Pullach operation, I resumed an active military status in dealing with the military community in Munich and other unwitting U.S. military personnel. Gradually more American civilians came in and went out of the compound as the U.S. Army continued to demobilize.

8

The CIA and the Gehlen Organization
Settle into Pullach

AFTER ASSUMING control at Pullach, my learning curve on the organization and on Gehlen himself turned quite sharply upward as the CIA sent additional competent staff. The staff included veterans of OSS such as Fred Stalder, Toivo Rosvall, and Andre Rittner, all of whom spoke German. Gradually during the ensuing year I engaged several former colleagues, mainly from my Vienna days, such as Tom Lucid, an experienced counterintelligence officer stationed in Linz, Bill Graver, a U.S. Air Force intelligence officer, and later Henry Pleasants, my good friend who was the high commissioner's personal liaison officer to Austrian chancellor Figl. Each became intimately involved in developing the Gehlen Organization. Most of the rest of the staff came from Washington, mainly young intelligence officers on their first assignments after being recently recruited into the new CIA. Some had wartime experience but outside the OSS. They were a well-trained, talented, and enthusiastic group.

Gehlen and his colleagues were anxious to learn who I was and what credentials I had to head the group so vital to their future. From day one it was clear that Gehlen's immediate staff members were assigned the task of digging into my background. How old, Gehlen wanted to know, was Kent J. Marshall? What experience has he had? Are we being taken seriously? Is sending this young man a brush-off? Aware of their curiosity I made a conscious decision early in 1949 to candidly and openly reveal my background to Gehlen and those around him. I had no reason not to do so, and thought it might offset any disadvantage caused by being years younger than most of these Germans. Reinhard Gehlen was forty-six when I met him, fifteen years older than I, and Heusinger was twenty years my senior. Gerhard Wessel was one of the few that appeared closer to my age. I used several casual conversations to describe my childhood in North Dakota farm communities that had been settled by nineteenth-century immigrants from Scandinavia and Germany. I noted that in contrast to many members of the German organization, I had in my background a complete absence of aristocracy, wealth, or family-based social status. I described life as a young cavalry officer at an old frontier American cavalry post in the Black Hills of South Dakota, attending the cavalry school at Fort Riley in Kansas, and my service in a cavalry command as a young major and lieutenant colonel on the Mexican border. I made a point of discussing attendance at the Command and General Staff School at Fort Leavenworth, and a variety of wartime staff and command experiences that geographically led through North Africa, Italy, France, and Germany (placing some emphasis on my experience as a member of the operations staff during the planning held in Naples for the invasion of southern France). Heusinger, I found, seemed to find the planning of the amphibious invasion of particular interest since he had worked on Sea Lion, the German invasion across the English Channel that never occurred. One of Gehlen's senior staff members, Conrad Kuehlein, and I discovered that we had intermittently been stationed in the same Alsatian village that had several times changed hands between German and American attacking forces in the last winter of the war. They learned I had visited the command post of the First German Army in the last days of the war to arrange surrender procedures. The Army commander in Pullach, Gen. Hermann Foertsch, had himself been sent to a major surrender ceremony with a group of senior U.S. generals and I had dealt with his staff. To add perspective I touched on my Army intelligence experiences in Heidelberg and Vienna after the cram course in geopolitics at Columbia University. Over the course of numerous personal conversations my background was conveyed to the Germans and I thought they contributed to an expanding rapport between us. Many of these former German officers could relate to my experiences but most of them had not expected a CIA representative to have them.

Nearly all of the Germans and a few of the Americans working in the compound also lived there; families with children were much in evidence. Others of the American staff lived in nearby villages. Gehlen and his senior staff, and their wives (many of whom also worked there), all impressed us as being unusually intelligent and well educated. In personal characteristics, apparent values, and thoughts about the future of Germany and Europe these former General Staff officers did not seem to me significantly different from my contemporaries in the U.S. Army. Our work and social existence became entirely integrated. For security reasons our contacts with the villagers of Pullach were prohibited.

The CIA staff spent practically no time with the American community in Munich as the city slowly rebuilt itself. The nearby Alps offered us fabulous skiing and trekking opportunities, a welcome diversion from life and work in the small compound. These were always combined German-American outings. Among most in the compound there was no trace of military protocol or reference to former rank and title, and those few who attempted to preserve any semblance of bygone days were usually ridiculed. Dress was mainly determined by availability as most everyone settled into what was their first full winter in Pullach. A few of the more affluent Bavarians appeared in grays and greens of the reopened Loden-Frey Department Store in Munich; all the other men and women wore sweaters, jackets, and other items of clothing probably secured from surplus military supplies.

Relationships between the Germans and the Americans at "Nikolaus" (the nickname for the compound) existed on two levels: officially it was based on the reality that the German intelligence service was to be scrutinized, assessed, and utilized, but unofficially it reflected the fact that we three hundred individuals had many common cultural, religious, and social attitudes. Because both Americans and Germans avoided involvement in Munich, they tended to face inward in their day-to-day lives in Pullach. Surprisingly, language was not much of a barrier. Many of the Germans spoke excellent English; most of the Americans had a working knowledge of German, and some were fluent in the language.

Virtually everyone in the compound used an alias in their contacts within the organization, including the field elements. For eight years I was Kent James Marshall, which for almost everyone became simply "Jim." I do not know whether this elaborate system of aliases succeeded in confusing the Soviet and East German intelligence services but, especially considering the frequent substitutions for compromised aliases, we managed to confuse ourselves. It is a fact that even amid the growing press coverage about the Gehlen Organization and the compound in the later years I never was identified by name. The children in the compound took the lead in ignoring political and social reasons for separation. A one-room school for the kindergarten and lower grades had no barriers. All of the children in attendance, German and American, used the working aliases of their parents. Many years later my daughter Ann humorously observed that until she was fourteen years old she thought all children had two names.

By 1948 it was perfectly clear that the German government being sponsored by the three Western Allies was taking shape. Gehlen assuredly was hitching his hopes for his organization more on the prospect of a future German government than on the CIA, which was unresponsive in resolving either his financial problems or his legal and political status vis-à-vis the new government. The organization Gehlen envisioned in 1945, out of a resurrected Fremde Heere Ost, by late 1949 had become a more sophisticated concept of a highly centralized and in the long run largely civilian national intelligence service that would be subordinated to the chancellor and serve the foreign intelligence needs of the entire government. While the service was very much in the mold of the CIA, I do not think that Gehlen used the CIA as a model but rather studied the intelligence experiences in World War II and drew many of the same conclusions that Washington had drawn in creating the CIA. Gehlen's own experiences in Fremde Heere Ost, the production and evaluation of intelligence, was the central influence on his thinking. Gehlen's ideas about operations, espionage, counterintelligence, covert action, and communication intelligence were less well developed, although he presumed the service would have an appropriate role in each.

Gehlen had clearly moved on to a two-track strategy that explained the presence of the larger and more diversified staff coming out of the last days of the German General Staff in the Mauerwald. The former generals Heusinger, Gehlen, Hermann Foertsch, and Horst von Mellenthin, supported by a strong cast of other former General Staff officers, became the inside team that consciously gave considerable attention to strategic affairs. In these matters Heusinger was the dominant figure.

Less than five years after the war ended this group of former officers inside the Gehlen Organization had developed a wide area of agreement on the answers to three critical questions about the future of Germany: Along what lines should Germany's armed forces develop? What kind of a national intelligence service would best serve Germany's needs? How should Germany contribute to the security and defense of Western Europe? For Gehlen, Heusinger, and their comrades the overriding question was simply how these ideas would play in Washington, London, Paris, and, most important of all, in the new German capital in Bonn.

Gehlen never took the initiative in discussing Heusinger's role with me, beyond his capability as a very qualified expert on Soviet armed forces who added weight to the intelligence judgments coming out of Pullach. It was clear from the outset that the operation at Pullach was larger and far more complex than I had expected. His small "inner circle" remained central figures in German intelligence in the years after the founding of the official German intelligence service and Germany's entrance into NATO. Members of the inner circle (in the order that I met them) were Heinz Herre, Gerhard Wessel, Horst Wendland, and Conrad Kuehlein; Gehlen and Heusinger, the

95

two central figures, began their close association in October 1940. The two were never personally close, but had come to have great mutual respect. Temperamentally they had quite different personalities, and the quiet, intellectual Heusinger found Gehlen almost too efficient, too ambitious, and too "grasping" in his style.

Heinz Herre, our key man in Gehlen's inner circle, was the one who, when the going got tough, was able to deal with both sides, keep communications open, and lead the search for compromises. When Herre returned from the United States in 1946 after his time at Fort Hunt, he plunged into learning everything he could about American culture. He became an expert on American baseball and off the top of his head could quote batting averages and league standings—then carried on a continuing exchange on the subject, particularly with the American GIs in the compound. No one else invested as much time and energy as Herre did in maintaining contact with the Americans.

Regardless of his job description during those eight years in Pullach, Heinz Herre was the ever-present figure at Reinhard Gehlen's side. Certainly on anything and everything relating to the Americans, Herre was the dominant influence. Herre was the ultimate alter ego. Gehlen depended on Herre to find answers to the hour-to-hour and day-to-day problems that appeared across the board, including personnel decisions, operational matters, and the whole range of politically sensitive issues with Bonn and the Allies. But I never heard Gehlen refer to Herre as his deputy. In a sense Herre was probably too close and too much inside Gehlen's own view of himself. Herre always knew the situation and could find solutions to problems that he felt Gehlen would accept. Because he was so highly sensitized to Gehlen's personality and thoughts and so intimately and openly in contact with the Americans, Gehlen appeared to be both dependent and at times resentful of Herre's role.

Gerhard Wessel, a young General Staff captain when Gehlen took over Fremde Heere Ost, was one of Gehlen's most competent men. However, during the war on the eastern front Gehlen unofficially appointed Herre instead of Wessel as his deputy. Herre outranked Wessel and had more experience in Soviet affairs. This competition between Herre and Wessel remained apparent in later years in Pullach. Gerhard Wessel pursued a career in which he remained loyal to Gehlen but aloof. He never involved himself in Gehlen's political maneuverings with Bonn. In my early years at Pullach I could see that Wessel was very much his own man, quietly working loyally and closely with Heusinger on the evaluation staff. He moved to Paris in 1952 as a principal associate of Hans Speidel, who at the time was the top German military representative dealing with the Allies. Wessel did not return to Pullach until 1968, when he ended a tour as the German representative on the NATO Military Committee. He came back to be Gehlen's successor as president of the official German intelligence service, the BND. Of the many working in the inner circle, from beginning to end Wessel had the most consistent, detached, and balanced view of Gehlen and Gehlen's work. Wessel was the only one of the inner circle who retained control of his own career.

Conrad Kuehlein, a young General Staff colonel who was Franz Halder's senior adjutant during the early years of the war on the eastern front, for a time was assigned to the Fremde Heere Ost staff to gain intelligence experience. Later Halder retrieved him to serve a second tour as Halder's senior adjutant. Kuehlein was working in a field organization when Gehlen moved him to Pullach to work under Walter Schenk, the head of the operations staff, and eventually replace him. Though he exuded a warmer and more outgoing personality, Kuehlein like Wessel remained aloof from Gehlen's political maneuverings. Most Americans were very comfortable dealing with Kuehlein; he and I were particularly close. Conrad was one of my most frequent mountain climbing companions, where our security often depended on a fifty-foot nylon rope connecting us.

Horst Wendland, head of the organization's Department of the Army General Staff late in the war, shared with all of these officers some eastern front experiences and like the others found his way to Pullach. Within months after assuming the top administrative position in Pullach, Wendland had earned the trust and confidence of everyone of both nationalities living in the compound. Gehlen formally gave him the title of deputy, then left him reasonably free to administer the German staff that was running the compound and the field units. Wendland did not insert himself into operations or into the maze of political activities in which Gehlen, von Mellenthin, Heusinger, and Foertsch were involved.

No list of the significant personalities in this story would be complete without the name Eberhard Blum, who in a sense was almost of the next generation. Blum was Gehlen's special assistant during my last year or two in Pullach, and he played an important role transitioning the Gehlen Organization into the BND. Later, as the BND chief in Washington for an uninterrupted twelve years, Blum gave a somewhat different character to the German delegation there. Blum had served at some time on the eastern front but never in Fremde Heere Ost or at the headquarters in the Mauerwald. Nor was he a member of the General Staff. He brought a more relaxed approach to relations between Germany and the United States for almost two decades. Blum was recalled from Washington in 1978 to replace Wessel as president of the BND. What distinguished Blum from all the others was that he obviously came from a civilian background with strong British and West European cultural ties.

Although he had served as a lieutenant and led a platoon of horse cavalry across the western German border in 1940, one could detect in his personality or demeanor no trace of the influence of the Army or its General Staff.

Gehlen's immediate staff included Annelore Krueger who, more than any other former General Staff officers, had the distinction of continuously working for Gehlen once she joined him in the women's detachment of the German Army at Fremde Heere Ost. Krueger was his constant administrative assistant, holding in her hands the official strings of his remarkable and diverse life. I always assumed she more than anyone else knew all the secrets.

Sometime during our first year the few CIA members I had assembled in Nikolaus became conscious that Gehlen's Organization had a greater preponderance of General Staff officers than I had observed in late 1948—and the number was expanding. Including those in the inner circle, we figured about thirty to forty held key positions, partly due to the triumvirate of Adolf Heusinger, Hans Speidel, and Hermann Foertsch. Heusinger's purpose and objective were entirely different from Gehlen's: to shape the development of a new German armed forces, or, as he chose to call it, "remilitarization." By accepting a senior position in the Gehlen Organization, Heusinger had gained the advantages of a base of operation; material support, security, and cover; access to intelligence information; and, no small factor, connection to the Americans. The Heusinger circle met a number of times with Gehlen in late 1948 and 1949, finally reaching an agreement to work together to achieve their separate but related objectives. Close coordination was ensured by Heusinger's status as head of the evaluation staff, which produced the finished intelligence that bore the Gehlen label.

It was largely an accident of history that made the Gehlen Organization such a significant repository of former General Staff officers in the decade after World War II. The impact of the creation of a democratic German government in Bonn in 1949, compounded by the war in Korea, certainly contributed to the rising expectation that both a German intelligence service and a German armed force would appear. The long and unanticipated delay in the actual formation of both, one in 1956 and the other in 1957, meant that a large number of General Staff men stayed in the Gehlen Organization to retain some status. That Gehlen was able to reorganize and expand after moving to Pullach made it possible to accommodate these men. Gerhard Wessel and Conrad Kuehlein told me about this in the early 1990s, but back then the reason was less clear. I found no evidence that either the CIA or Army intelligence understood this dichotomy.

At times between 1948 and 1951 Gehlen on occasion told one or more of his inner circle that in his absence Heusinger was to be regarded as the senior person in charge. In reality Heusinger never involved himself in the organization, its operations, or its short- or long-term management—but his image as head of the evaluations staff added to the organization's prestige.

Former Lt. Gen. Hans Speidel was an old comrade of Adolf Heusinger. They had intermittently served together, had taken their three years of General Staff training at the same time, and had both been jailed by the Gestapo and charged with involvement in the 20 July 1944 plot to assassinate Hitler. Almost any list of German generals with a future in the new Germany would likely have Hans Speidel and usually Adolf Heusinger near the top. By 1948 Speidel was living quietly in Freudenstadt as a part-time college professor in Tuebingen in Baden-Wuerttemberg. Speidel occasionally gave lectures on wartime lessons to Swiss military officers, and was maintaining extensive contacts with French military and civilian officials. He, more than Heusinger or Foertsch, was in a position to maintain a wide array of political contacts in the Baden-Wuerttemberg region. In 1948 he was already in contact with the prominent leader of the Christian Democratic Union, Konrad Adenauer, and was well thought of by senior members of the German Socialist Party. In December 1948 Adenauer had met with Speidel and even this limited interest in a German general had provoked criticism from some of General Clay's staff, who quite correctly pointed out that because of Allied High Commission Law Number 16, it was illegal for Adenauer as a member of the *Parlamentarisch Rat* to be meeting with a German general. In the summer of 1949 Speidel had called on Adenauer to offer his opinion that when he became chancellor, Adenauer would be unable to avoid the issue of Germany's defense. Adenauer had listened politely but offered no reaction. Nevertheless, the Heusinger triumvirate assumed that Adenauer would sooner or later be asked to participate in talks with the Allies concerning a German role in the defense of Western Europe. They further assumed that when such a meeting occurred, the chancellor would be seeking advice. Adolf Heusinger considered Hans Speidel the person to whom Adenauer would most likely turn for such advice. Speidel was never identified as a member of the Gehlen Organization. He probably did not meet Gehlen more than once or twice in the critical period of 1948 to 1951, and the Gehlen Organization went out of its way to respect his independent status.

Lt. Gen. Hermann Foertsch, the commander of the First German Army at the end of the war, acted on behalf of the absent commanding general of Army Group G in its surrender to American general Jacob Devers, commander of the U.S. Sixth Army Group. General Foertsch had the reputation of being among the most intellectual of the German generals, an accomplished writer, and an admired commander of troops in combat. Gen. Franz Halder, looking at the prospect of a new German Army in 1950, expressed his opinion that Hermann Foertsch was the most experienced and capable field commander to preside at the rebuilding of the German armed forces. Foertsch's commanding presence was that of a reserved, taciturn man, tall with an angular build. In practice Foertsch was halfway in and halfway out of Nikolaus. He lived and worked in a house near the Nymphenburg Palace, close to the Munich exit of the autobahn that ran from Stuttgart to Karlsruhe. Foertsch's function was related almost wholly to remilitarization, but his writing talent turned out to be a mixed blessing in postwar Germany. As a young officer Foertsch had been selected by his superiors to write, under his own name, a chapter in a large, full-color coffee table–type book about Adolf Hitler. The chapter, titled "Adolf Hitler und Deutsches Soldatentum," was an uncritical account of Hitler's earliest relationship with the military. Foertsch also had been chief of staff of the Army Group in the Balkans in 1941, where internal partisan warfare had played a large role in creating circumstances in which the Germans resorted to harsh measures. Foertsch had been charged with war crimes related to partisan warfare and had been a defendant in the Balkans trial. He was acquitted.

One of Foertsch's jobs was to influence German officers to support President Theodor Heuss and Chancellor Adenauer's request that officers avoid any activity that might convey the impression of a German initiative in addressing the question of Germany's role in Western defense. Foertsch produced a monthly newsletter, *Orientierungen* ("Orientations"), that initially was distributed to staff members only. Soon, however, the newsletter was being distributed to a growing mailing list of former officers that Foertsch had developed with the help of Horst von Mellenthin. One Saturday an American sergeant working in the air section of the evaluation staff discovered that the newsletter was being printed using the equipment and supplies of the evaluation staff. The following Monday morning Gehlen visited me and assured me that the activity was inappropriate within Nikolaus, and would not be repeated. I assumed that the production of *Orientierungen* would continue somewhere outside of Nikolaus, and accepted Gehlen's assertions and later arranged to get a copy of future editions of *Orientierungen* for myself. (In some matters I felt it was better to be informed than self-righteous.) I did understand the basic purpose of the newsletter since it generally set out interpretations of contemporary events that were not in conflict with American interests. Life in Pullach was never uncomplicated.

Another activity taking place in Pullach but more or less off to the side was known as Special Connections, run by former general of artillery Horst von Mellenthin. Just before the war von Mellenthin had headed a department of the General

Staff that controlled the entire organization of military attachés, an experience that was obviously useful and relevant to his job within the Gehlen Organization. Von Mellenthin was a sophisticated, intelligent man, worldly in his outlook and endowed with a sense of humor in viewing his own work. Von Mellenthin was living near the Chiemsee, just off the Munich-Salzburg autobahn, doing press analyses while waiting for something more tangible to appear. I do not recall ever hearing just who recruited him into the group. In March 1949 he appeared in Nikolaus with the task of organizing and systematically developing the Special Connections unit. In American terms Special Connections was a lobbying organization designed to win friends and influence people. This task, because of its sensitivity and importance, made von Mellenthin a member of the inner circle and someone who became quite effective in exerting influence on Reinhard Gehlen.

The Special Connections staff looked out over the entire horizon of postwar German society, including the emerging structures of the state and federal governments, Germany's slowly reviving industry, the political parties, and the churches. Von Mellenthin's task was to grease the skids to bring the Gehlen intelligence organization into a smooth arrival in Bonn. His small group of sophisticated leg men, four to six in number, were very specifically targeted to work on individuals in postwar German society who were in a position to support either the desired legalization of the Gehlen Organization or the remilitarization of Germany along the lines foreseen by Heusinger, Speidel, and Foertsch. Of course none of this had anything to do with the production of current intelligence on the Soviet armed forces—but it did have a great deal to do with the respective objectives of Gehlen and Heusinger in making the right connections in Bonn. Von Mellenthin obviously served two masters but seemed to enjoy the challenge of doing so. Early on I identified von Mellenthin's group as one nerve center that merited our attention and made the case with Gehlen that it was as much in his interest as it was in ours to have a member of my staff intimately involved with von Mellenthin's work. I suggested that I had the perfect candidate, my friend Henry Pleasants, who was a music critic by profession and who had been a wartime German order-of-battle expert with the U.S. Fifth Army in Italy. Pleasants had spent time in Hungary, Austria, and Germany before the war, was fluent in German, and had established effective ties with both the conservative Peoples Party and the Austrian socialists during his tour in postwar Vienna. I told Gehlen that Henry was still in Vienna serving as the high commissioner's liaison to the Austrian chancellor, a fact that no doubt impressed him. After listening to my description of Henry, Gehlen took a long puff of his cigar, leaned back in his chair in my office, lifted his hands, palms upward in a characteristic gesture signaling agreement, and said "Why not." It had become a familiar gesture indicating that we had just made a deal. Shortly afterward I traveled to Vienna, had lunch with Henry and Virginia Pleasants, and proposed that they join us in Pullach. They agreed and Henry was soon working in Pullach.

Henry Pleasants and Horst von Mellenthin were an instant success story. Gehlen lived up to his part of the bargain and gave the Pleasants–von Mellenthin team every support. In the months that followed I was impressed at how often von Mellenthin found it in his own interest to include Henry and, when appropriate, Virginia, in meetings with his Special Connections operatives. A year or two later, after the important decisions of 1950, Henry left Pullach to become chief of the CIA station in Switzerland, and later moved to Bonn where for another eight years he remained deeply involved in the expanding relations of the Federal Republic with the United States. During his years in Bonn Henry became a friend and associate of Ambassador David Bruce, who described Henry as the "only professional music critic that successfully used the CIA as a cover for thirty years."

Gehlen, Foertsch, Heusinger, and von Mellenthin functioned as a very loosely organized committee that gave guidance and advice to Special Connections. Von Mellenthin carefully canvassed the entire membership of the Gehlen Organization for old family, professional, and personal contacts who could be used in the initial approach to any prospective Special Connections candidate. Gehlen did, I believe, keep a fairly close rein on von Mellenthin's operation, which sometimes touched on his own ventures to develop connections quite separately. In his expanding contacts with Americans von Mellenthin worked hard at developing a more relaxed and egalitarian image. Eventually he became, at least in name, one of Gehlen's several deputies. Special Connections was an indispensable asset during this period in which contacts to Bonn, to the state governments, and to major institutions were being established and nurtured.

I also discovered, once we settled into the Pullach scene, that the U.S. Office of Naval Intelligence (ONI) was in touch with several former German admirals. Unlike the U.S. Army G-2 in Heidelberg, or the U.S. Air Force A-2 in Wiesbaden, ONI did not maintain a resident liaison officer in Pullach. Cdr. Val Rychly, the head of ONI in Munich, was in fact the Navy's liaison to the Gehlen Organization and an active contact between it and senior U.S. Navy officers, including several chiefs of naval operations who had visited Munich.

I knew Val Rychly well. He was a Czech-American from Chicago, a child prodigy violinist taken by his father to study in Prague. When he was still very young Val was forced to give up his father's dream of his becoming a great concert violinist because of nerve damage in his left hand from over-practicing. Eventually he played violin in Wayne King's famed orchestra in the United States during the 1930s and 1940s. In 1946 and 1947 he had been active in ONI operations in Czechoslovakia and the Balkans. Rychly periodically appeared in my office in Vienna to fill me in on his observations and to share his perceptions of what was happening in the countries where he was active. Initially he had been based in Prague but later went to Belgrade. By the time I arrived in Munich in late 1948 Rychly was established as the ONI representative there.

By 1949 Rychly was maintaining close personal ties with a number of former German Navy officers, including the former admirals Wagner, Ruge, and Heye, who were associated with a Navy historical project that Capt. Arthur H. "Speedy" Graubart had organized in Berlin after the war. Before the war Graubart had been the U.S. Navy attaché in Berlin. One day Rychly brought Graubart to my office in Pullach to ask that the former German admirals with whom Rychly was in contact be put in touch with the Gehlen Organization. I suspected the Navy may have been having a dispute about the project involving the former admirals, though the group did in fact become a major influence in Heusinger's remilitarization effort. The Gehlen Organization enjoyed good relations with former German Navy intelligence personalities during the years prior to the founding of the BND.

Rychly met with Gehlen directly, but always discreetly. It was apparent that Gehlen was quite enthusiastic about the opportunities he had been given to meet with a variety of senior flag officers and occasional members of the U.S. Congress, all arranged by Rychly. Rychly was also in regular contact on Soviet naval matters with several experts in Heusinger's evaluations staff, having obviously extended contact directly to Heusinger. One day Heusinger simply disappeared from Pullach for almost a week. When he returned he gave me a glowing account of his experience as a guest of the captain of one of the large carriers participating in a U.S. Sixth Fleet training maneuver in the Mediterranean. Heusinger was deeply impressed by the appearance and performance of the pilots and crews of the carrier. He added that Commander Rychly had arranged and escorted him on his visit to the Sixth Fleet, for which he was deeply appreciative. For a future top officer in the Bundeswehr this had been an important experience.

Rychly combined a low-key connection with the German naval analysts within Heusinger's staff with routine ONI activities, and maintained an active relationship with the group of former German admirals as well. Rychly can be credited with an important contribution in the history of the transition of the German Navy from an enemy to a member of the Allied fleet. Like other elements of the transition, this

U.S.–German connection had been controversial at some levels of the ONI and frequently put Rychly at odds with his colleagues, most of whom were not involved in his operation.

One of Gehlen's major aims was to bring together the diverse elements of the German Army and Navy communications intercept organizations that existed during the war. We brought in Alan Conway out of the world of signals intelligence in World War II and who was at the time stationed with the CIA in Frankfurt. Conway became an important presence in Pullach on all matters dealing with communications intelligence. In terms of policy and security, communications was a sensitive area and one in which Conway was in close ongoing contact with elements of the U.S. intelligence community. Gehlen was quite successful in intelligence prior to becoming head of the BND. Just shortly before Bonn achieved sovereignty Gehlen escorted Conway and me to a site where his staff demonstrated a device, developed by the Germans probably with the help of the Swiss, that had the capability to produce cryptographic systems.

Two separate and distinct CIA policies existed in regard to liaison operations with the Gehlen Organization. I agreed with them both. The CIA's Operations Directorate, for reasons of security, fenced off the Pullach operation and imposed limits on visits to Pullach by its operationally active members. In contrast, the Intelligence Directorate of the CIA encouraged an active dialogue with Heusinger's staff of analysts and experts in numerous fields. The CIA deputy director for intelligence, Robert Amory, visited with Gehlen and Heusinger at Pullach and expressed to me his desire to establish a staff representative under me who would perform a task similar to that of the liaison officers from the intelligence staffs of the U.S. military commands in Europe. I supported Amory's proposal as a step toward a better assessment of the character and capabilities of the Gehlen Organization. Although we had not attempted to define our longer-term thinking on Gehlen's aspirations, by late 1949 it was perfectly clear that a long-term relationship between the United States and postwar Germany would develop. A pattern of visits to Pullach by senior analysts from the Intelligence Directorate ensued. An individual of Bob Amory's intellectual talent and wide range of knowledge of current world affairs gave Heusinger and his staff, most of whom were fluent in English, an unusual opportunity to expand the dialogue on both the question of Soviet capabilities and intentions and the thinking of senior American officers on the problems of defending Europe. But Heusinger also showed interest in the views held by visitors from Washington regarding the new National Security Act of 1947, including the role of the National Security Council and the Central Intelligence Agency. Heusinger was even more interested in the comments of informed visitors concerning the creation of the U.S. Air Force as a separate branch of the military services, and the impact of the unification of the armed services within the Department of Defense. At some point the German staff translated the entire National Security Act of 1947 into German, and it became an important reference document in the library of the Gehlen Organization. The evaluations staff and Bob Amory's overt CIA analysts developed and maintained a positive, less-sensitive, but durable relationship with German intelligence, which carried over into the liaison connection in Washington after the formation of the BND.

Contrary to a widely held perception, none of the 130 senior officers identified in the "General Staff and High Command" at Nuremberg were ever members of the Gehlen Organization, an exclusion supported by both Gehlen and Heusinger. A small number of former generals resided at Pullach but every case was explained by special circumstances. Gen. Alfred Kretschmer, for example, had been the military attaché in Tokyo and came to Pullach on the recommendation of Douglas MacArthur's intelligence chief, Gen. Charles A. Willoughby. General Willoughby had come to know Kretschmer in Japan when Kretschmer revealed his role in the Richard Sorge case and was debriefed on other Japanese-German matters of interest to MacArthur and to Washington. Kretschmer had cropped white hair and a scar on one cheek, which many automatically assumed was the result of a duel in his youth. He appeared to be every inch the movie version of a stereotyped Prussian officer. The scar was in fact the result of a wound received in World War I. Kretschmer held a number of different jobs during those years, part of Gehlen's stable of spare senior officers who were rotated through a variety of assignments. He was not close to Gehlen or a member of the "club," but got along well with the Americans. He was a reasonably useful generalist and brought an element of diversity to the staff. Kretschmer appeared to play no role in Heusinger's plans, and was kept at some distance from Gehlen's machinations in Bonn as well.

Gen. Hans Doerr, the wartime German military attaché in Madrid, simply stayed there at the end of the war and eventually became the first chief of station of the postwar German intelligence service. I never doubted that he was useful to Gehlen. For us Spain was a place that had some chance of staying strategically out of reach of a Soviet offensive into Western Europe, and seemed prepared to offer our illegal German service safe haven on its own credentials.

General Koestring was prewar Germany's military attaché in Moscow, and was Germany's premier expert on the Soviet military before the war. I suppose that Koestring was a Special Connection. I heard about him often but met him only once or twice in the company of Heinz Herre, who obviously revered the elderly

Koestring. In CIA terminology we would have called Koestring a "cleared outside consultant" on Soviet affairs. He had dedicated his life to acquiring fluency in the Russian language and a knowledge of Russia and, as it evolved, of the Soviet Union. He was one of that group of Russian experts at the embassy in Moscow that had extensive overlapping associations with the Moscow-based American diplomats and attachés. Once Hitler began the attack on Russia, Koestring left Moscow and served on Franz Halder's staff as an expert on Russian questions. He had been wholly aligned with the element in the German Army that had contemplated the liberation of the anti-Stalin Russians. Gehlen's contact with General Koestring after the war was mainly at the hands of Heinz Herre, who had served with Koestring in Moscow. Koestring had supported the general concept of the "freiwillige" ("volunteers"), and specifically had supported the attempt to build the Vlasov Army of which Herre had been the German chief of staff at the end of the war. Koestring, an admirer of Adolf Heusinger, was the man who in the summer of 1945 told Army historian Orin Hale to search out Heusinger as the most intelligent of the German generals.

Gen. Wolfgang Langkau appeared in Pullach during 1950 when Gehlen's connections and activities in Bonn were expanding and had become too complex for Gehlen to handle by himself. If there was any former officer in Pullach whom I would describe as a "friend" of Reinhard Gehlen, it was General Langkau. Their association appeared to go back into their early military careers. Langkau was not a member of the General Staff, nor had he shared the war years on the eastern front, but he became a member of Gehlen's personal staff that was not involved in any way with the rest of the organization. In his first year in Nikolaus Langkau was, more than anything else, Gehlen's confidant on political matters. Eventually the intelligence activities of Langkau became known as "doktor operations" (the equivalent of "Eyes Only Gehlen"). Gehlen kept him at arm's length from the Americans. We knew Langkau by sight and only exchanged conversations with him in casual encounters.

One former general living in Pullach—August Winter—was not so innocent. August Winter was an enigma to me and most likely the organization's only true example of "Hitler's generals." He was a pompous figure disrespected and disliked by the majority of the Germans in Nikolaus, and he made no identifiably useful contribution to the Gehlen Organization. Winter had come straight out of Keitel's OKW, probably part of Gehlen's cover and insurance program at the end of the war when things still looked very uncertain. As the senior OKW general stationed in southern Germany very late in the war, Winter gave Gehlen something resembling authority to proceed with his plans for turning Fremde Heere Ost over to the Americans. This,

I was told, was August Winter's ticket to a free ride in the Gehlen Organization after its relocation to Pullach. I never heard any suggestion that Winter was closely linked to the activities of OKW that took Keitel and Jodl into the dock at Nuremberg. Winter never had a real function in the organization and was never accepted in the Mauerwald circle. I never saw any evidence that Heusinger and Foertsch gave any recognition to his presence, but they made no issue of it either. As far as I could observe he played no role whatsoever in shaping the remilitarization of Germany. August Winter was carried over into the BND and remained with it until his retirement many years later.

9

The Survivors and the Nonsurvivors

under Gehlen

IN THE LATE months of 1949 the strategic thinking of Heusinger, Speidel, and Foertsch converged rapidly into a commitment to an Atlantic strategy based on integrated NATO forces—with full U.S. participation—headquartered in Europe. The only problem with the plan was that the United States had not adopted such a policy. Washington remained hopeful (in some quarters even optimistic) that Western European unity would develop into a European defense force under a "United States of Europe" model that would be a separate force subordinated to a NATO alliance in times of crisis or war.

Gehlen found it unnecessary for achieving his purposes to go as far as the three generals had in favoring a NATO command dominated by the United States. His objective was to form a national intelligence service responsible to a German government. Gehlen assumed that the German Federal Republic would become sovereign and a member of a Western alliance, unconvinced that a Western European defense plan would work. From the outset he was opposed to integrating German intelligence into any international military staff, whether European or dominated by NATO.

Reinhard Gehlen and Adolf Heusinger viewed their agreed objectives—intelligence and remilitarization—as achievable within the developing geopolitical climate surrounding Germany. In my conversations with them, however, I detected a subtle difference in their respective views beginning to take shape as 1949 came to a close. Two separate visions of the future of Europe emerged. Gehlen favored Adenauer's view of a small, democratic, predominantly Catholic but strongly Christian Western Europe built around de Gaulle's France and de Gasperi's Italy. Reinhard Gehlen, like Adenauer, was a German nationalist in the same way that de Gaulle was a French nationalist after World War II. In 1948 and 1949 Gehlen gave high priority to establishing liaison relations with the French, the Swiss, the Vatican, and Spain. After 1943 Gehlen assumed that the Soviet Union and the West would arrive at a strategic stalemate in Europe. The United States would tend toward isolationism but would maintain the alliance with Britain that had been formed during the war. The other vision of Europe's future was built on a study of its past by Heusinger and his evolving think tank centered in the Pullach compound. Heusinger was a convinced Atlanticist and saw Germany as a member of an alliance based on NATO and a U.S.-led military defense alliance encompassing the North Atlantic, Western Europe, and the Mediterranean. Gehlen was skeptical of a genuine British commitment to a Western European community and was equally skeptical that the French would be willing to revert to the wartime relationship in which, until the last months of the war, they had barely been counted as a member.

REINHARD GEHLEN'S PERSONALITY

From the beginning I knew I was dealing with a difficult personality. Time and many conversations with Gehlen and those around him led me to develop my own profile of the man. Without question he was intelligent, but he was no intellectual. He had a high standard of morality with Christian beliefs that were evident and reinforced by his wife Herta and their family. But he did not indulge in philosophical and abstract discussions of politics and morality. He was most accurately described by a close associate as *"immer sachlich"*—one who gets right to the point. He was pragmatic and interested in the facts.

The image of Gehlen presented in postwar history suffers from the fact that he seemed to have left no record of his views on national socialism. He rarely touched on the subject in our conversations. He did not identify with the resistance, and saw it as a flawed scheme and unlikely to achieve its stated purpose. He had little in common with the 20 July circle that became prominent in Bonn in the early 1940s. Gehlen had embarked on his own conspiracy, one that assumed the war would run its course and end much as it did.

One of his close associates described Gehlen as lacking in charisma but talented at creating esprit within his organization. I observed that Gehlen had an aversion to involvement in difficult management problems but at the same time he would not delegate to a deputy. He surrounded himself with a variety of individuals, whom he assigned to different tasks that interested him. This management style was equally apparent in his use of older, unemployed associates to study management problems on which he was unprepared to act. He seemed uncomfortable with wide public exposure or unnecessary contact with employees, and used security as a reason for avoiding numerous contacts. He rarely made visits to field organizations. At times he demonstrated flawed judgment. He was known to select people who posed visible security and political risks for tasks he needed to get done at the moment.

I think that Gehlen, an obscure one-star general in the last year of the war, had a touch of insecurity and a need for recognition that persisted and could be seen in both of his later books. He seemed to enjoy the sudden fame of "the Gehlen Organization" while cultivating the image of a man of mystery under dark glasses, a snap-brim hat, and an aura of secrecy regarding his movements. Gehlen was by nature a deeply suspicious individual. As he aged he had a tendency to become almost paranoiac in suspecting people of communist connections and political views that did not adhere to his own conservative political outlook. He was very suspicious of the motives of the Social Democratic government led by Willy Brandt that moved openly and aggressively into the Ostpolitik and opened communications with East Germany, Poland, and the Soviet Union itself. Moved by his suspicions, Gehlen ventured into sensitive domestic politics to a degree that was extremely controversial.

Those of us who saw a lot of Gehlen never thought of him as a "man of mystery" or the "spy of the century," which was the public's perception. But he did have a consummate fascination for political matters, whether in Bonn or within the intricacies of elaborate counterespionage operations against communist regimes. Like many intelligence officers of his era, Gehlen had developed a theory that political action operations could be successfully played out in the milieu of counterespionage.

Gehlen's relations with his immediate associates were not close. The word "friend" was not a part of his vocabulary. I never heard him speak of any of those who shared the war and postwar experiences with him as anything but "*kollegen*" or "*mitarbeitern*"—colleagues or coworkers. But I think he regarded Eric Waldman and probably John Boker as friends, possibly because they were Americans and outside of his professional world. Gehlen and I were in continuous contact. There was never any disagreement between us on the larger purpose that had brought us together. Mostly we agreed on the direction we were going but, particularly in the first two difficult years, we had differences of opinion on how to get there. Our relations were always civil, correct, and impersonal. Neither of us ever raised our voices, used profanity, or walked out of a meeting. When we differed on something of importance we each stated our position and then began the search for a compromise, an exercise in which our associates were often involved.

Gehlen was uniquely qualified to play his part in history. His war experiences had expanded his mind to think of the world in geopolitical terms. He was the one person who saw Fremde Heere Ost as a card that could be played as the first step toward building a bridge to the West in an anti-Bolshevist alliance defending Western Europe. I can attribute to no other former German officer the vision, the determination, or the practical political skill that he demonstrated in sticking to his guns in that turbulent decade that began in the last days of the war. But there were limitations on his ability to play out his role.

Gehlen was a German nationalist and, after the war, a Gaullist. He attached great importance to the existence and preservation of Germany as a European nation-state. He consistently told the Americans on whom he relied for support that the integrity and German character of his organization must be preserved if he were to steer a course toward its destination in a restored German nation allied with the West.

ADOLF HEUSINGER'S ROLE

Some days after the CIA takeover in Pullach I made a critical comment to Gehlen that my group had observed the arrival of many new Germans and found most of them former officers, many without intelligence experience. A day or two later, no doubt having been prompted by Gehlen, Heusinger invited me to join him for a glass of wine after dinner. This began a series of more relaxed meetings with Heusinger that gave me important insight into what was going on.

I learned that Heusinger's presence in Nikolaus had a purpose quite separate to his position as head of the evaluations staff. One day I asked Heusinger why he did not use a more explicit and less cumbersome word than "remilitarization." The term was long and somewhat ambiguous in meaning, and had a negative political connotation in postwar Germany. Why didn't he simply call it "re-arming"? Heusinger said he did not think that my suggestion was much of an improvement, and, besides, it was the Americans who had coined demilitarization as a word in the German vocabulary. Reversing the process logically became remilitarization. Yet the task that the German people and government faced went far beyond the normal problems of creating and maintaining armed forces. The German public, including former members of the Wehrmacht, had been exposed to an intense program of demilitarization that had been spelled out in punitive terms in JCS 1067 and the documents of

Yalta, Potsdam, the Allied Control Council, and the Military Government directives. Beyond this, he said, were the war crimes trials. For better or worse, the German Federal Republic had inherited the legacy of Nuremberg. The task facing a new German government preparing to contribute armed forces to Western defense would be complicated and difficult. The Soviets would leave no stone unturned to block Germany's entrance into a Western alliance. Remilitarization would require a change in public opinion, in the attitudes of the occupying powers, and in the rebuilding of a whole new national security edifice in Germany. "Remilitarization" seemed to encompass the whole array of problems to be faced.

Heusinger, Speidel, and Foertsch were simply attempting to think their way through the process of forming an entirely new national defense system that would serve the new government in Bonn, be supported by the German people, and be accepted by the Western Allies. Heusinger acknowledged that no one had asked the three generals to do this contingency thinking and planning, but there were both security and political problems to be faced in continuing to do so without at least tacit approval of an occupying power. The Gehlen Organization offered a secure, politically protected, and administratively supported base. When he and Gehlen had agreed on his joining it in early 1948, Gehlen's organization had been an operation of the U.S. Army in Germany. Heusinger expected that he would be put in touch with a senior American officer, someone with whom he could discuss the separate activities he was pursuing with Speidel and Foertsch. Then the CIA entered the picture. In some ways the transfer of responsibility to the CIA might prove, he thought, to be an advantage. Initially remilitarization would be an entirely political matter and thus the responsibility of the civilian high commissioner in Bonn. Heusinger assumed that I would appropriately inform U.S. authorities about his activities. At this juncture there had been no contact with Adenauer.

In our many conversations Heusinger expanded his description of how the thinking of the three generals had developed from 1945 through 1947. Because of his long experience as head of the operations division of the Army General Staff, Heusinger had repeatedly been taken to Nuremberg to participate as a witness in both the main trial and some of the subsequent proceedings that involved the trials of a number of senior generals. Because the tribunal had made a firm decision to exclude from any indictment the staff officers assigned to duties in the Army General Staff, officers such as Heusinger and Hans Speidel were of interest to the tribunal as witnesses only. Although Heusinger did not dwell on the subject of the war crimes trials in those early conversations, I eventually understood that his role as a witness had been a very difficult experience for him. There is no doubt that events at Nuremberg continued to be a major factor in Germany's remilitarization.

I met with Heusinger many times in the office, and more often in his home under more leisurely circumstances. What could I bring to the conversations? Not very much. But I did, I am sure, display interest and curiosity, which was quite genuine. In my first visit to Heusinger's quarters I told him only enough about my own background to give him some perception of "where I was coming from." I made no pretext of being well versed on either recent or early German history. We were well into our second conversation before I decided to reveal what I thought he ought to know about Americans if he and his friends were seriously thinking about a long-term association with the United States. I told him that I had come to Pullach with the language of Yalta and Potsdam clearly fixed in my mind, but my perceptions of American interests and our country's role in Germany and Western Europe had been modified considerably by my own postwar experiences. My assignment in Nikolaus had been my first personal contact with so many German officers. Since my arrival at the end of November 1948 I had spent many hours in conversation with several dozen members of Gehlen's staff and had met members of their families. I was reassured by my first brief associations with the large number of former officers of the Army General Staff, but I had some reservations about their suitability for clandestine operations (which I myself was discovering was a quite different profession). I assumed that Gehlen had passed on to him my implied criticism on this point. In addition, I had arrived in Nikolaus wholly unable to comprehend how senior German officers as a group had stayed with Hitler to the dramatic and bitter end. I hoped to leave my assignment at Nikolaus with a better understanding of this mystery and Germany's complex history. Heusinger and his associates should accept that it was too soon after the end of the war and the end of the Nazi era for an American to make collective judgments on Germany's past that could be translated into confidence about the future. The world at large had a lot of thinking and reflection ahead of it on the entire history of a war of unbelievable violence and brutality. It would take a lot of time, great patience, and much forbearance in the Western community of nations to draw a shared understanding of the World War II experience. The admonition of the tribunal at Nuremberg that guilt of a crime is ultimately a matter of the individual had real meaning to me. The tribunal had emphasized that the concept of organizational or group guilt was a new legal concept and one that should be approached with caution. I was uncomfortable with the application of collective judgments at Nuremberg, but I found the legal commentary and opinions accompanying the verdict somewhat persuasive. I told Heusinger that after three years of exposure to the German and Austrian people I had resolved to view every German or Austrian as an individual to be taken at face value until proved otherwise. Heusinger smiled and remarked that many Germans and Austrians had quite a lot in their backgrounds that they would never candidly reveal. I noted that such was the reason we routinely requested background checks from the vast official records —the Berlin Documents Center files—that had fallen so remarkably intact into the hands of the U.S. Army in 1945. In my opinion the average American officer probably saw the German military in much the same way as I did—impressed by its military performance but still perplexed by its relationship with national socialism. The amassing of documents and witnesses at Nuremberg had contributed to our understanding that the relationship between the German military and the Nazi Party had not been as simplistic as perceived in Washington when U.S. policies were being formulated in 1944 and early 1945. I told Heusinger that I had come away from the verdict session at Nuremberg on 1 October 1946 somewhat confused about the judgments on the German military. Not until we (the staff of the occupation army) had the opportunity to study the accompanying commentary of the tribunal did we recognize that the decision regarding the "General Staff and High Command" had nothing to do with avoiding the declaration of criminality as an organization. We also had noted differences between the opinions of the tribunal and those of the U.S. Military Government as reflected in the denazification law adopted in the U.S. Zone earlier in 1946, and months before the verdict of the tribunal. With discussion of the tribunal I touched a very raw nerve in this outwardly composed former general. I dropped the subject by observing that American officers would probably tell him— and more often than he wished to hear—that what had happened in the German Army could not happen in the United States.

Moving to a subject with which I was more familiar, I told Heusinger that I could foresee a future in which he would have numerous close associations with American military leaders. Regardless of the educational level of American officers he would likely meet, he should assume that they all were thoroughly familiar with the origin of the United States in the American Revolution, with the Declaration of Independence, the Constitution, and the Bill of Rights. They would know something of the history of the Civil War, since training at Leavenworth focused on that war in some detail. Most could probably quote from Lincoln's Gettysburg Address. As a last thought I told him that I had started every school day in a small Midwest American farm community, 98 percent first- and second-generation European immigrants, by standing up, facing an American flag at the front of the classroom, and reciting the Pledge of Allegiance. In my assessment of the two great wars that had started in Europe in the first half of the twentieth century, I attached special importance to the phrase "one nation indivisible," which I saw as the advantage we Americans had over the Europeans in handling questions of peace and war. While West Point instills in its graduates a simple but strong code of values—"Duty, Honor, Country"—American military officers were not as preoccupied as German officers in the tangled web of questions concerning tradition, loyalty oaths, honor, obedience, and the relationship of the military to the state and to society. As I ended my remarks I sensed that Heusinger probably considered my performance as either naive or even pompous. Nevertheless, I felt I had made a modest contribution and had the impression he was listening thoughtfully.

Throughout 1949 Heusinger participated in an active and expanding dialogue with senior U.S. military officers and a number of CIA officers, including analysts who covered a wide range of specialized areas of interest to his evaluations staff. This was Heusinger's first extensive exposure to Americans beyond the historians at Allendorff and Neustadt. It is difficult to judge how much this contact influenced his thinking. The decline in the number of U.S. forces deployed in Europe was continuing. Whatever their reasons, by the end of 1949 the three German generals had concluded that a major role by the United States was the key to any viable defense of Europe. The creation of NATO seemed to be the most encouraging sign on the horizon.

Discovering from Heusinger how little we seemed to know about remilitarization, I had proposed to Washington that it would be prudent to establish an intelligence-collection requirement, backed by an analytical effort in Germany, on German remilitarization as Heusinger broadly defined it. Washington promptly gave a negative reply. I was told to turn over any information on this subject to the American generals in Heidelberg and to High Commissioner John J. McCloy in Bonn. I thought it an odd response and concluded that a duty officer had written it on a Sunday afternoon when the Washington Redskins were playing at home. In a discussion about this series of events some forty-eight years later, Tom Polgar, head of the CIA's Frankfurt base at that time, confirmed that he had received no requests for intelligence on the subject and that the German station had made no effort to collate or analyze fragmentary information on the activities of German generals.

By the end of 1949 I had concluded that Heusinger's presence in Pullach was fully as significant as Gehlen's. Until the Korean War, however, re-arming Germany was not on anyone's agenda. Heusinger's role and potential importance in Pullach was not understood or acknowledged by many individuals who read my reports on conversations with this remarkable man. If Germany were to emerge as a democratic ally of the United States it would be useful to know as much as possible about both its future Army leaders and its intelligence service. If things did not go well with the U.S. effort it would be wise to know what we were leaving behind. The CIA would have to judge whether both of these efforts were within the framework of its policy on the Gehlen Organization. The Heusinger effort had added a new dimension, but it was little more than a small think tank in 1949. Nevertheless, I gave it a high place on my own priority list.

Networking among former generals and admirals in the federal republic was becoming more active. Perhaps the existence of the new German government in Bonn against the backdrop of the onset of the cold war and the emergence of NATO provoked interest, dialogue, and movement among the disenfranchised German military leadership. Clearly a consensus was developing on how the new Federal Republic would eventually play a role in the defense of the West. The networking was in part a process of selection about who should play an active role in remilitarization and who should not. Generally these contacts remained spasmodic, informally and discreetly organized, and limited to small groups.

HERMANN BAUN—THE NONSURVIVOR

The CIA staff was disposed to believe the best about anyone's Abwehr credentials, and to assume that those claiming to be experienced professionals who served in the Abwehr under Admiral Canaris were legitimate. The Abwehr had an aura of political acceptability that came as a result of our knowledge that the service had been a center of resistance to Adolf Hitler and the Nazi Party. The British secret service had known a great deal about Canaris and his organization, but until he appeared at Wiesbaden in 1945 almost no one had ever heard of Reinhard Gehlen. Against this background the CIA was prepared to look favorably on the large number of Abwehr officers whom we had identified. Only gradually did it become apparent that inherent security problems existed in the wartime cooperation of the Abwehr with elements of the RSHA. A number of former Abwehr officers became security problems of one kind or another. Looking back, the record of the Gehlen Organization indicates that the outside elements interested in penetrating the Gehlen Organization had considerably more success with Abwehr and former RSHA members than with officers of the General Staff. Gehlen had always argued that a General

Staff officer was a lower security risk than others with more complicated backgrounds in intelligence.

The Gehlen Organization was still strongly influenced by Baun men when I arrived in Pullach; they clearly remained a faction, an asset, and a problem. With the disdain and snobbery that is often found in intelligence officers with operational backgrounds, the Baun men regarded most of the General Staff officers who ventured into agent operations as amateurs. It was not until several years after the move to Pullach that some of the slightly younger officers with General Staff backgrounds were making progress in running productive operations. They also discovered security problems left by too rich a mixture of former Abwehr officers, who had residual connections with the SD, and the Gestapo, which were formed in wartime circumstances. Operations officers in the CIA were distinctly partial to ex-Abwehr men. Chief of Operations Walter Schenk and Siegfried Graber, a much younger veteran of Abwehr operations, were quite popular with the CIA staff. A front line combat soldier who had been highly decorated, Graber was Baun's deputy during the last year of the war and served as his key operations man. Schenk, an old Abwehr hand with Middle East and South Asia experience, nominally supervised both agent operations collecting military information and all counterintelligence matters. On the counterintelligence side there were several senior officers whose precise responsibilities were not entirely clear. Nominally, Dr. Kurt Kohler, an Austrian who had served in the Abwehr on the eastern front, was regarded as chief of counterintelligence, but a former Abwehr colonel named Radke also had considerable authority. The operations staff appeared to us somewhat loosely organized and obviously had far less control of its work than did the evaluations staff. Gehlen was not giving detailed attention to either staff, and demonstrated more interest in what was developing in Bonn than in the details of operations. Hans von Lossow, an Abwehr officer who had turned up on Baun's staff in the Jagdhaus, did not join the operations staff in Pullach but became Gehlen's personal emissary to sensitive political connections in Bonn.

Baun's fate led him in a different direction. Gehlen sidelined Baun by giving him the new task of planning strategic intelligence operations. I met with Baun several times and heard his descriptions of a number of fairly innovative ideas for operations around the periphery of the Soviet Union. But he had obviously been put on the shelf. I think Baun was more at home with Russians than with Germans, certainly those of the General Staff kind. He spoke no English and was not comfortable with Americans, but he did make an effort to open the door for the CIA to join him in his imaginative vision of Soviet operations. If I had met Hermann Baun before coming to Pullach my colleagues and I might have offered him what he wanted—support for his unorthodox ideas on penetrating the Soviet Union. The CIA had a large stable of ethnic Russian case officers whose lifestyles and strong anti-Bolshevik convictions resembled Hermann Baun's.

After Baun's removal from the operations staff, Siegfried Graber carried on. Graber became respected as a competent officer but demonstrated little respect for most of the General Staff officers attempting to prove useful in an operating intelligence environment. Running West German agents into East Germany and maintaining loyalties and connections to both sides of the bitter Gehlen-Baun conflict was mission impossible for even the experienced and respected Graber. Baun never regained status in the Gehlen Organization and, while still working as a strategic planner in the early 1950s, developed cancer and died. This ill treatment of Baun was not carried out without some cost to Gehlen and many officers (Baun men) only reluctantly adjusted to the dramatically changed circumstances. These men pragmatically accepted their future in Pullach, but many remained faithful Baun defenders despite his known shortcomings.

Looking back, I think we unduly harassed the operating elements of the Gehlen Organization that were collecting intelligence in the Soviet Zone. Siegfried Graber was making an honest effort to adjust his operations within the constraints of our quite miserly support. In our first year we followed the Army practice and each month committed only $125,000 of American taxpayer money into the Gehlen Organization, easily worth it for the reporting we got on the Soviet armed forces alone. We were also acquiring equity in a long-term asset: an intelligence service of a major NATO ally.

Col. James H. Critchfield, a.k.a., Kent J. Marshall, during the years at Pullach, 1949–1956.

Colonel Critchfield and Maj. Parkhurst Hough at the end of the war, just outside of Ulm, Germany, in 1945.

Reinhard Gehlen in 1944 as head of Fremde Heere Ost.

Hermann Baun (*right*) with his deputy, Siegfried Graber, at Bad Elster, Germany, on 1 April 1945, at the time of the secret meeting between Baun and Gehlen. *Herr Graber*

The Pullach compound, acquired in 1949 by the U.S. Army for the Gehlen Organization, built in the mid-1930s by Nazi Party leader Martin Bormann to accommodate senior Party officials assigned to Bavaria. Rudolph Hess also lived there. The compound is to this day the headquarters of the German Federal Intelligence Service, the BND. *BND*

CIA Director Allen Dulles, 1957.

CIA Director Richard Helms and James Critchfield in Helms's office, 1968.

Gen. Adolf Heusinger, 1956.

General Gehlen displaying his
Order of the Sovereign and Military
Order of Malta in 1948.

Lt. Gen. Gerhard Wessel in 1973.

Reinhard Gehlen and Heinz Herre touring the United States in 1951.

Reinhard Gehlen and James Critchfield in New York City's Central Park in 1951.

New York night club during Reinhard Gehlen's U.S. visit in 1951: (*left to right*) Heinz Herre, Mrs. Critchfield, John Boker, James Critchfield, Mrs. Boker, Reinhard Gehlen. Sign in background says, "Here one can embrace his partner."

Reinhard Gehlen in 1973 after his retirement.

James Critchfield, Konrad Kuehlein, and Mrs. Astrid Kuehlein in 1986 at the celebration marking the fortieth anniversary of the beginning of U.S.–German intelligence cooperation. *BND*

Gerhard Wessel and James Critchfield in 1998 at a reception in Pullach, Germany, honoring CIA-BND cooperation. *BND*

Visit to Reinhard Gehlen's home in Berg, Germany, in 1977. James Critchfield, Gehlen, Mrs. Critchfield, Mrs. Herta Gehlen.

Fiftieth anniversary celebration of the BND-CIA relationship held in July 1999 at CIA Headquarters, Washington, D.C. Former BND presidents pictured here are Eberhard Blum and Dr. Hans-Georg Wieck, along with current BND president Dr. August Hanning and DCI George Tenet. Fifth from left is Christoph Gehlen, son of Reinhard Gehlen. *CIA*

BND president Dr. August Hanning (*right*) and James Critchfield at a ceremony held at the German Embassy in Washington, D.C., in February 2001, in which Critchfield was awarded the Officer's Cross of the Order of Merit of the Federal Republic of Germany.

10

Adenauer's Search for
a National Security Policy

WHILE MY relationship with Reinhard Gehlen was cordial and proper during the months after my arrival in Pullach, he frequently registered his concern about CIA requests for information about his organization's finances and operations. After the installation of the Adenauer government in Bonn on 15 September 1949, Gehlen expected political developments to clear the way for achieving some legal status for his organization and solve some of his problems, a point the CIA had yet to address. He wanted us to give him freedom to initiate an active political effort in Bonn that he hoped would lead to establishing contact with the Adenauer government, a request more complicated than it might appear. On 1 July, John J. McCloy replaced Lucius Clay as U.S. military governor; with the inauguration of the German Federal Republic McCloy became the U.S. high commissioner. The CIA station had not yet worked a full briefing into McCloy's demanding schedule on its acceptance of responsibility for the Gehlen Organization. Therefore, neither the CIA nor the high commissioner had said a word to Adenauer about the U.S. support of the Gehlen Organization.

Major world events were also beginning to overtake our thinking about the Gehlen Organization. In April 1949 President Truman took the lead in founding NATO. The Soviet Union as a military power was rapidly changing in character. The successful Soviet testing of an atomic bomb in June 1949 signaled the emergence of the Soviet Union as a world-class nuclear power and the end of the U.S. monopoly on the technology. Containing the Soviet threat in Western Europe by itself was beyond the defense capability of any independent European military alliance. The communists were victorious over the nationalists in China, and Moscow and Peking had signed a Treaty of Friendship.

Konrad Adenauer became the first postwar chancellor of the German Federal Republic. The pace of these events forced us to understand that we would not have a leisurely one or two years to study the Gehlen Organization. Clearly the issue of Germany's role in the Western alliance had to be resolved sooner rather than later, probably in months not years. The broader picture—upgraded Soviet forces facing Western Europe—eventually worked in Gehlen's favor.

Adolf Heusinger and his comrades Hans Speidel and Hermann Foertsch had already reached the conclusion that the defense of Western Europe was feasible only in the wider geographical and political context of an Atlantic community being led by the United States with a participating re-armed Germany. It took the American president and the German chancellor most of another year to reach the same conclusion. For agreement among the Western Allies it took a full five years.

Late in 1949 Heusinger showed me a paper that he described as the "Heuss-Adenauer policy" that had come to him via Speidel from Eberhard Wildermuth, a Free Democratic Party political figure from Wuerttemberg who served as the housing minister in Adenauer's first cabinet. Wildermuth explained that Adenauer, who had little interest in military affairs, looked to him for advice on military matters. The text of the report, which had not been made public, read: "It was their [President Heuss and Chancellor Adenauer's] conviction that the first move to open the question of remilitarization of Germany as a member of the Western European Union must come from the United States and the Western European Union. Any unilateral action by the German government, by any organized group of former German officers, or by any well-known former German commander to precipitate the issue of German remilitarization would have a damaging effect."

Heusinger had concluded, probably correctly, that Heuss and Adenauer formulated the policy after an outburst of press attention following an interview Adenauer gave to John Leacacos of the *Cleveland Plain Dealer* in November. The article focused international attention on the question of German troops and their part in a European army. The Allied High Commission passed a law, Decree Number 7, on 19 December 1949, banning involvement "directly or indirectly [in any] activities that promoted the revival of militarism." Despite the interview Adenauer had not and did not want to address the issue of rearming Germany. At the top of his agenda was the end of the Occupation. Beyond that, his real priority was to lead the German Federal Republic (which was industrially centered on the Ruhr and the Rhineland) into membership in a united states of Western Europe.

Press interest on German generals, however, did not abate. On 13 January 1950 the Paris edition of the *New York Herald Tribune* ran a story by reporter Don Cook, alleging that former general Hasso von Manteuffel, one of Hitler's top commanders, was playing a prominent role in a shadow organization called the Bruderschaft (Brotherhood). As it turned out Cook had been poorly informed on the Bruder-schaft, which in fact had been penetrated and controlled by the East German communists as an "active measure" to attract public and international interest and opposition to German remilitarization—a high priority of the Soviet KGB. The *Herald Tribune* story, like Adenauer's interview with the *Cleveland Plain Dealer*, produced a surge of interest in the former German generals and strengthened the convictions of Chancellor Adenauer and President Heuss that any initiative on remilitarization would be counterproductive to their goals.

In Pullach I got the impression that the von Manteuffel incident had touched a sensitive nerve in Adolf Heusinger's group and demonstrated to them how little public and political support there was in Germany for the idea of a new German Army. Heusinger and Speidel were considering the idea of one or both of them talking with von Manteuffel, an idea apparently abandoned after I suggested there was more to the von Manteuffel story than reported by the *Herald Tribune*. A few months later an investigative journalist of the *Sueddeutsche Zeitung* in Munich reported that the Bruderschaft had been organized by two former Nazi officers and from the outset had been penetrated and probably controlled by the communists in the East. Eventually Franke-Grietsch, one of the group's founding members, took refuge in communist East Germany. The Bruderschaft affair probably served a useful purpose in demonstrating the wisdom of the Heuss-Adenauer policy.

By this time Gehlen was politically active in Bonn. He did not consider the Heuss-Adenauer policy applicable to him or his plan to build a civilian intelligence service. Just six weeks after the CIA took responsibility for Pullach, Gehlen was impatiently exploring ways to get a political foothold in Bonn. The CIA informed him that his actions were premature and asked him to observe a moratorium on all political activity. Gehlen did not listen. Hans von Lossow, a former Abwehr captain who had been with Hermann Baun's organization, was working as Gehlen's eyes and ears in Bonn. Von Lossow was politically savvy and Gehlen came to rely on him in the coming months to help him in Bonn.

By the end of 1949 and the first days of 1950, and despite our admonitions, the combination of unresolved financial problems and Gehlen's continuing activities in Bonn produced added problems between the two sides of the courtyard in Nikolaus. Gehlen told his immediate staff that he was seriously considering closing down the entire operation. Gehlen never made this threat directly in any conversation with me, but from time to time he resorted to the device. He assumed—correctly—that I would be quickly informed of his statements to his staff.

Because his organization had no legal status, Gehlen was still entirely dependent on the authority of the United States as an occupying power. However, the CIA had not yet gone beyond its 1948 policy decision for dealing with the Gehlen Organization and was doing nothing to alleviate Gehlen's chronic financial crisis. My requests for increased funding fell on deaf ears in Washington. Gehlen's office in Pullach echoed with angry comments about the Americans.

There was something to be said for Gehlen's arguments concerning the importance of establishing a Bonn connection. Gehlen had developed a national intelligence service that had no government to which it could turn and no legal status beyond what it had derived from the United States as an occupying power. The establishment of the German Federal Republic in September 1949 gave the West Germans a symbol of hope. But as of early 1950 Gehlen could only make small promises to his associates about sharing his ambitions and hopes for the future. He could point out the improved conditions at Pullach since the dark days of early 1945 and the two years at Oberursel. Their operations in East Germany, many of which relied on communication lines running through Berlin, had been affected by the ordeal of the Berlin Blockade. After resolution of the blockade in June 1949 a new spirit prevailed in beleaguered West Berlin, and an even higher level of optimism came with the creation of the German Federal Republic. Gehlen also could point out to his colleagues the fact that they were now in the hands of America's senior intelligence authority, the CIA, which should have been an advantage. Unfortunately thus far he himself was not convinced. Meanwhile, my staff in Pullach was pressing for more insight, more operational information, and a better accounting of funds—all without giving any sign that it was interested in creating a long-term relationship. The CIA, in taking over from the Army, had not been informed of any agreements Gehlen might have reached with General Sibert in 1945 and 1946. The Germans, who knew the United States from earlier days before the war (and who were back in touch with contacts in the United States), were reporting a powerful resurgence of isolationism and a call for the United States to withdraw from Europe.

Some of Gehlen's associates were obviously concerned that he would break with the Americans. In early January 1950 Heusinger and Speidel, in a meeting with

Foertsch at his home in Nymphenburg, sent Gehlen a cryptic message warning him not to be too hasty in abandoning American support in exchange for support from the Bonn government. They opined that the United States was the best hope for the future of Europe. Heusinger had cast his lot with Gehlen and any break in the relations that Heusinger was developing with the Americans or the loss of any advantages he enjoyed as a senior member of the Gehlen Organization was not what Heusinger and his friends wanted.

Gehlen believed that things were now moving forward in Bonn and he wanted to be a part of it, but this was largely an illusion. Chancellor Adenauer was not hopeful that the occupying powers were moving toward an early end to the Occupation, and nothing was lower on his list than creating a national intelligence service or any form of a new German armed force. Reinhard Gehlen and, for that matter, most of the other generals did not personally know the chancellor. Adenauer had come from the Rhineland and was a man of simple parochial interests. As a politician in the Weimar period he had developed an aversion to army generals, particularly those of Prussian background. Not only was he unacquainted with Gehlen, he had no idea of Gehlen's background or postwar history, or the character of the organization in Pullach.

At some cost to management and operations Gehlen became preoccupied with how to go about establishing a tie to Adenauer and how to obtain more support from the CIA until his connection to Bonn was established. The CIA was not cooperating in either effort. Though John McCloy had been living in Germany for six months, he had not been briefed by the CIA on the Gehlen Organization. In early January, in a change of mind concerning Gehlen's staying away from Bonn, Gordon Stewart, the CIA station chief in Germany, proposed a course of action that would test the willingness of the chancellor to meet with Gehlen. CIA headquarters supported the move. The formula was simple: the CIA would inform High Commissioner McCloy of the existence and history of the Gehlen Organization; McCloy would then use an opportunity to provide the chancellor with the same information, ending with a recommendation that Chancellor Adenauer invite Gehlen to meet with him. Gehlen's senior associates unanimously supported the idea. Heusinger, a key person and currently troubled by Gehlen's state of mind, was pleased about the plan. Gehlen assented to the proposal, although it was apparent that he would have preferred to contact Adenauer on his own or at least to make his own case with McCloy directly and personally. The plan was simple enough, provided everyone cooperated and acted in good faith. It would also offer the occasion to bring McCloy up to date on the remilitarization interests of Heusinger and his associates. How and whether to use this information with Adenauer would obviously be a matter for the high commissioner to decide.

We saw this as a way to put to the test Gehlen's assumptions about the readiness of the chancellor to address the existence of the Gehlen Organization and the known aspirations of its leader. We would recommend that the high commissioner not go beyond giving Adenauer a factual account of the enterprise, including Gehlen's demonstrable current interest in meeting with the new government in Bonn. It appeared uncomplicated and it offered a way to reduce some of the tensions developing in Pullach that detracted from our efforts to focus on intelligence matters. It also addressed some of the concerns of Gehlen's closest and oldest associates that he was putting the relationship with the Americans at risk.

McCloy agreed with the scenario and sent Ben Shute, a trusted counselor, to Pullach for a full briefing, including meetings with Gehlen and his staff. Shute, a New York lawyer who had been persuaded by McCloy to join him in Bonn, was regarded in Bonn as one of McCloy's closest and most influential advisors. As the member of McCloy's staff concerned with intelligence and security matters he was highly regarded by the CIA officers who knew him. Shute and Gordon Stewart visited Pullach on 23 and 24 January. Shute met many members of the German and American staffs and was given numerous briefings, including one by Heusinger, Wessel, and the top analysts from the evaluation staff on the Soviet armed forces. Shute was obviously impressed. Gehlen personally gave him a description of the history, character, and objectives of his organization. I separately provided a summary of what the CIA staff was doing and my appraisal of the two-track character of the Gehlen Organization. At the dinner that night he mingled with Gehlen, Heusinger, and other senior members of the German staff. During a conversation with Gehlen following dinner he offered a cryptic summary of McCloy's attitude: "The boss thinks things are going okay." I learned several years later the statement was too cryptic for Gehlen to understand; his record of the event revealed that neither he nor his aides were sure who "the boss" was.

Following Shute's report of his Pullach visit, I went to Bonn to meet with McCloy and answer some of his questions; McCloy was satisfied and would proceed with the plan. On 16 February I returned to Munich on the evening train. On the morning of 17 February, in Gehlen's absence, I gave Heinz Herre a summary of my meeting with McCloy and asked to meet with Gehlen to give him a fuller version of my conversations in Bonn. At that point our plan went awry.

Gehlen's man, Hans von Lossow, had an active connection with State Secretary Ritter von Lex of the new Interior Ministry in Bonn. In a discreet meeting held in his office on 19 January, von Lex had offered to make Gehlen the government's candidate to head the new internal security service, which was to be called the Bundesamt fuer Verfassungsschutz (Federal Office for Protection of the Constitution, or BfV). Von Lex had learned from von Lossow of the security group that he and Baun had organized in early 1946 in Karlsruhe at the request of USFET G-2 (while Gehlen was at Fort Hunt; Gehlen only learned of it after he returned). Gehlen was intrigued with this operation while the CIA viewed it with skepticism. Faced with rapidly developing penetrations from the east, von Lex saw Gehlen's security group as an existing asset that could fill an obvious need of the Interior Ministry in organizing the BfV.

The BfV position was attractive to Gehlen as a way to become officially established in the Federal Republic. He saw it—probably unrealistically—as a position through which he could expect to influence the creation of a foreign intelligence service. Gehlen's candidacy—leaked to the press while he was still secretly considering it—caught him riding two horses in the same race. After the press report the CIA told Gehlen that it would support his candidacy if it became official, but added that were he to become head of the BfV and it did not work out, there would be no returning to his position in Pullach. The whole affair ended abruptly when a British intelligence officer made an informal visit to the ministry's office to inform von Lex that the British would veto the selection of Gehlen. The British wanted to put forward their own candidate, Dr. Otto John, who later in 1950 became the first president of the BfV—not an unqualified success, since in July 1954 Otto John went over to the Soviets in East Berlin.

Because he had taken neither his colleagues nor the CIA into his confidence about the matter, Gehlen's image in Pullach suffered on both sides. McCloy withdrew from the plan to brief Adenauer and never picked it up again. Gehlen was back on his own. Adolf Heusinger was convinced that Gehlen had done additional damage to his already strained relations with the Americans. I was surprised that Gehlen had taken the risk of simultaneously pursuing both the BfV and the McCloy-Adenauer options, all within such a small circle of influential people in Bonn. It was predictable that his actions would be leaked and damage his reputation. It had been a poor performance.

Once he had impulsively accepted the von Lex proposal, Gehlen had explored the possibility of using the BfV position to test the feasibility of somehow bringing part of the internal security mission into an official intelligence service. I attributed this naïvete to his lack of experience in police or internal security matters. In his book, *The Service,* an older and wiser Gehlen described his own conviction—with 20-20 hindsight—that internal security had to be kept separate from foreign intelligence. In my early discussions with Gehlen he always supported the idea of combining security and intelligence, noting the very unusual circumstances that existed in a divided Germany where the line between East and West and between domestic and foreign operations was less clear. Gehlen was correct in citing the divided character of Germany as a complicating element in the design of an internal security service in West Germany. He was aware of Adenauer's politically pragmatic position that the threat of the Volkspolizei from East Germany came from within Germany's 1937 borders and thus was an internal security matter. Regardless of Adenauer's true hopes and aspirations about a future in a united states of Western Europe, however, politically the chancellor had to remain publicly committed to a reunified Germany.

The end to Gehlen's candidacy for the BfV position did not stop his active effort to preserve a counterespionage responsibility within the Gehlen Organization. The BfV episode passed and Gehlen acted as though it had never happened. The unofficial threat by the British to officially veto Gehlen as a candidate gave everyone a way out of the mess. Gehlen showed no resentment toward the British for their role. In the immediate aftermath of the affair Gehlen's anger was still focused on the Americans, largely because we were making life in the Gehlen Organization so difficult.

Gehlen's impatient political maneuvering in Bonn and the Americans' unwillingness to support him produced stresses across the courtyard that separated his office from mine, but our regular contacts remained cordial. Nevertheless, his repeated performances for the benefit of his staff did little for his image among our group or, for that matter, among his own associates. I found it a challenge to be detached and objective in observing and analyzing Gehlen's performances. My deputies Peer De Silva, Tom Lucid, and Henry Pleasants were indispensable in their assumed role as a board of clinical psychologists watching Gehlen's behavior. We didn't always agree on how we should deal with him. Lucid was the most detached and never advocated any action beyond continuing to observe "the patient" while proceeding full bore with the work at hand. But De Silva and Pleasants couldn't contain themselves, and one day they marched into my office, shoulder to shoulder, to recommend that I forthwith fire Gehlen based on his recent performance, including the BfV affair. I believed there was one difference between us: for better or worse, I was responsible for our CIA operation. My answer was no. I regarded Gehlen's problems as having far more to do with style and personality than with substance. The political repercussions in the new government in Bonn were difficult to predict, and Heusinger's efforts were growing in significance. And Gehlen enjoyed considerable support and solidarity within his own organization. Peer and Henry likely expected no other response, but they had made their point.

Gehlen had two major complaints about the CIA: we were pressing too hard on financial accountability, and, in the demand for operational details, we had insisted on separating all activities—including intelligence operations outside of East Germany—into single, identifiable activities that could be examined, analyzed, judged, and funded on a project-by-project basis. Lump-sum budgeting was not realistic and Gehlen's subordinates, particularly those in outlying bases that were running agent operations, were giving him a difficult time on both issues. The project system was devised mainly in Pullach but was supported by the German station and the CIA in Washington. The CIA had left the Pullach staff very much on its own in devising ways of learning more about the Gehlen Organization.

Life with the CIA would have been much easier for Gehlen had mutual trust been an element of the relationship from the start. Though Gehlen was by nature more secretive and less cooperative in providing information than many of his senior staff, he and they never permitted exchanges with us to become confrontational. When facing questions he preferred to obfuscate and procrastinate by assigning them to one of his more senior aides "to study the matter," especially in regards to the counterintelligence operation centralized in Alfred Bentzinger's GV L and in the so-called strategic intelligence operations against the U.S.S.R. and its communist satellite countries (where, in the current circumstances, he actually had little or no potential for genuine espionage operations). But the United States and the Allies were not doing appreciably better in the way of intelligence production, considering their advantage of retaining diplomatic and commercial representatives in the Soviet Bloc.

Gehlen was under growing criticism from many of his senior staff for failing to assign authority to handle pressing management issues. Day-to-day operations and the production of intelligence created management problems that competed with his other priorities of developing a relationship with a new government, coping with his critics and opponents in the intelligence circus in Bonn, selectively developing liaison relations with a dozen NATO services, broadening his support base in the political parties that controlled the Bundestag, and, finally, getting along with a generally unhelpful CIA. Only a strong deputy with fully delegated authority to manage the intelligence job could have significantly reduced Gehlen's problems, but Gehlen never seemed willing or able to delegate that kind of authority.

On 1 April, Gehlen assembled his senior staff and made his strongest attack on the Americans when he announced that he once more was considering dissolution of the organization; he stopped just short of a decision to do so. He emphasized the lack of financial support, attacked the hated project system and the CIA's emphasis on accountability of funds, and announced that it would be necessary to curtail any new or expanded initiatives. Though Heusinger typically remained quite aloof from Gehlen's problems with the Americans and he sat silently through the meeting listening to Gehlen's entire litany of complaints, shortly after it Heusinger and Gehlen had one of their rare one-on-one private meetings. Many of Gehlen's senior associates had been shaken by the intensity of Gehlen's assault on us. Herre privately urged Gehlen not to throw away a large opportunity in the face of transient problems. Among themselves a number of Gehlen's senior staff discussed the situation and agreed on a concerted effort to stop the decline in relations with the Americans, the *befreundete seite* (the friendly side).

As was usually the case, Gehlen worked off his tensions on his staff, confident that I would quickly get the word. I cooperated by easing our pressures on several fronts. I was sorry that Gehlen had felt compelled to go this far. Not once during those troubled months did he suggest to me directly that he was considering closing down his operation, though I thought he was justified in some of his criticisms of agency performance. Actually our frequent meetings were always civil. I recognized that he was genuinely under intense financial pressures resulting from the organization's uncontrolled expansion in the Baun period of 1946 and 1947, followed by a significant expansion of Gehlen's headquarters staff in 1948 and 1949. In the face of its own serious early growing problems, the CIA was not very interested in the history of Gehlen's financial difficulties. I strongly believed that the U.S. Army had been irresponsible in encouraging the Gehlen Organization to finance itself through institutionalized black marketing operations.

A few comments about Heinz Herre are appropriate here, because he played a unique role that went far in cementing U.S.–German intelligence relations. Herre had an extensive background as a professional intelligence officer and he was well informed about the Soviet Union and spoke Russian. He was involved in the entire process of producing finished intelligence and had all but memorized Sherman Kent's *Strategic Intelligence*. For a time Herre headed the evaluation staff in Pullach after the departure of Heusinger in 1951 and Wessel in 1952. He also maintained an active interest in operations. During all of those early years of the Gehlen Organization he remained a central influence. In the end he accepted the opportunity to become the BND representative in Washington, where he worked for six years. Although I maintained a personal connection with Heinz Herre after his return to Germany, I was not in a position to observe his last years in the BND after his assignment in Washington. It seemed that his relations with Gehlen were less close than they had been in the war years while they were both in Fremde Heere Ost or during my time in Pullach. Herre, like several other members of Gehlen's inner circle, probably ended his career with some sense of dissatisfaction. My own view is that Herre, more than any other single person, made crucial contributions in developing and maintaining the American connection in the decade after the end of the war. To my knowledge he gave Gehlen a great deal of good advice, a good percentage of which was not accepted. No member of the Gehlen Organization did more in the years that I was in Pullach to bring the Germans and Americans together in an effort to achieve a better understanding of two related but different cultures.

My personal life took a significant turn in June 1950 when I married a girl from Ohio who was in Germany with the CIA as a code clerk and communicator. Louise had served in OSS late in the war, leading to assignments in Prague and Berlin in the immediate postwar period. After a week's honeymoon in Venice we returned to Pullach on 25 June, the same day North Korea attacked South Korea. A few days later the Germans held a reception in our honor at the White House in Nikolaus, with Heusinger playing host. He presented us with a silver tea service on behalf of the organization. Gehlen did not attend and at the time I did not know why. Later I learned that he was in Bonn arranging for his first meeting with Dr. Hans Globke, a senior official in the chancellor's office (the Bundeskanzleramt, or BK). He had his priorities right.

Although the U.S. ambassador in Seoul had warned Washington of the growing military imbalance between North and South Korea, and several CIA predictions had been made regarding North Korean aggression across the 38th Parallel, much of the world and certainly the new German Federal Republic were taken by surprise by the North Korean attack (a full-scale conventional war offensive launched by North Korea on the secret order and support of the Soviet Union). In Pullach we went on high alert, looking for indications of possible Soviet initiatives in central Europe.

Soviet documents released from archives in Moscow in 1997 make it clear that Stalin had taken the initiative in deciding and organizing the attack as a result of his own concern about the rising power of Mao's Chinese communism in Asia. Simply stated, Stalin's conduct of a brief limited offensive was meant to acquire Soviet control of the strategic ports of Pusan and Inchon in order to protect his own interests in Asia. Many in the United States and Europe were concerned that the attack in Korea might be followed by a similar conventional war offensive by the Soviet Union in Western Europe. Stalin perhaps did not understand that his action in Korea would have a tremendous impact on geopolitical thinking in Washington and Europe and in three months would precipitate a decision in Washington to militarize NATO in order to strengthen the U.S. presence in Europe and rearm Germany. When President Truman moved rapidly to a decision to rearm Germany, the United States quickly discovered that France and Britain were opposed to the move and that Adenauer had given little thought to the defense problems of Germany and Western Europe.

In Washington the CIA estimated that having risked a surprise full-scale attack by conventional communist military forces in Korea probably meant that the Soviets might exploit their comparable military advantage to launch an attack into Western Europe. The military concurred in its estimate that Soviet forces could probably drive through the meager military forces of the Western nations stationed in Europe to reach the English Channel and, drawing on their reserve divisions in the Soviet Union, occupy all of Western Europe, except the Iberian Peninsula and Norway.

11

Korea and Adenauer's
National Security Policy

THE NORTH Korean attack marked the beginning of an improved level of understanding between the CIA and the Gehlen Organization. It set in motion the consolidation of the strengths of the noncommunist world that in the end defeated international communism, led to the collapse of the Soviet empire, and ushered in the reunification of Germany. In this context 1950 was a significant year of decisions. The outbreak of war in Korea immediately enhanced the value of the Gehlen Organization's experienced watch on Soviet forces in East Germany. The tempo of activity in Pullach increased. Our staffs went on full alert and all sources were instructed to watch for any changes in the disposition and readiness of Soviet forces. Our highest priority, which governed the daily efforts of both the German and American staffs, was discerning Soviet intentions.

At the same time I found Gehlen himself a somewhat isolated and lonely figure. That summer he appeared restless and uncertain about his immediate priorities. Despite his comparatively more assertive personality, and considering his equity as the founder and major shareholder in the Gehlen Organization, we accepted at face value that he was not an equal partner in the remilitarization effort, and began to look for indications of German thinking concerning its defense and the defense of Europe. Henry Pleasants, working closely with von Mellenthin's Special Connections staff, had firsthand knowledge of some of the orderly networking that was taking place among former German generals and admirals. Henry's access made him

131

the most knowledgeable member of our Pullach staff about which German generals had survived and were likely to play a role in Germany's rearmament.

Henry believed that Gehlen was potentially a "latter-day von Seeckt," a reference to the German general who led the German General Staff in circumventing the terms of the Versailles Treaty. Gehlen, Henry thought, might well find a revived German Army an irresistible attraction for his political aims. I did not share this opinion, but I could well imagine Gehlen might attempt to play a militant political role were Germany to slide toward neutralism or a prolonged period of genuine political and economic instability. I believed that the most likely development for Germany in the 1950s, in contrast to the 1920s, would be the one foreseen by Heusinger and Speidel—the integration of Germany as a developing democracy into an Atlantic alliance.

Adolf Heusinger, Hans Speidel, and Hermann Foertsch continued their cooperation in planning German remilitarization. In reality the British were opposed to anything more than a new armed and mobile police force. The British and the French were unprepared to see Germany rearmed, and the United States was unwilling to commit itself to the defense of Western Europe without the participation of some conventional German land forces. The situation posed a quandary for the UK since it could not put at risk its ties to the United States; Britain had to find some way to remain an influence in Europe. Between January and May 1950 the British Labour Party moved toward a policy that supported the development of a lightly armed, mobile, uniformed German police and the arming and training of German labor battalions similar to those seen in the British Zone. It opposed the formation and arming of conventional German land forces. France opposed German rearmament in any way.

Konrad Adenauer was prepared to go along with the British policy. Nevertheless, achieving a rapprochement with France remained an essential objective of German policy. Germany was forced to make some compromises in meeting the inevitable French initiative to secure its place as the leader of a Western European defense effort. But in its cooperation with the French the Germans could not accede to any arrangement in which German military manpower would serve directly under French officers, except as a member of a unified Western European defense force.

Adolf Heusinger's discovery that the United States brought a unique and indispensable character to any European alliance was perhaps the Germans' driving conviction toward the creation of a European defense force. Through a process of intellectual analysis the European nations, including Germany, had proved that on their own they could not keep the peace in Europe. Heusinger and his associates only had to look at the history of wars among European nations to be firmly convinced that there was no possibility of developing a mutual viable defense of Western Europe consisting of these nations alone. Technology had changed the character of war. The basic concept of an Atlantic defense community had developed in World War II under the leadership of the United States, which after two centuries had emerged as the only democratic world power. They saw no future for Germany except as a member of an Atlantic alliance led by the United States. Unfortunately neither Adenauer (nor Gehlen, for that matter) had come as far in his own thinking.

This line of thinking emerged among a wide variety of Germans residing in Pullach, most of whom were interested and aware of the new strategic thinking developing in their country. I spent a great deal of time with members of the German organization, both men and women, skiing in the Alps and during the summer I and a small group of Germans and Americans frequently enjoyed mountain climbing together. Our Alpine excursions were conducive to just this kind of discussion. Attempting to build upon our dialogue, and taking a long-range view of the relationship developing in Pullach, we initiated some small-group orientation visits to the United States. A member of the CIA staff in Pullach escorted each group of not more than six nor less than four selected members of the organization to satisfy a great curiosity about America, since few had ever visited the United States.

To advocate and advance Britain's policy the British high commissioner successfully proposed that Graf Schwerin, a former German tank general, be installed as an advisor to Adenauer. During several visits to Britain prior to taking up his task, Schwerin met with a large cross section of influential British leaders and several from the Labour regime. Gen. Sir Kenneth Strong, Eisenhower's wartime intelligence connection, told Schwerin that the British were disturbed "by that whole complex of the Gehlen Organization in Pullach," including the group of generals surrounding Heusinger and Speidel. The Labour Party took the position that Admiral Hillenkoetter had taken with the U.S. Army intelligence unit in 1947: supporting the Gehlen Organization was risking the revival of the Army General Staff. General Strong and others urged Schwerin to do everything he possibly could to oppose both the remilitarization and intelligence efforts of the Gehlen Organization.

Schwerin spent his time and energy establishing an office in Schaumburg Palace by assembling a staff and expanding contacts in official circles, including from among members of the British, American, and French high commissions and their intelligence organizations. Working closely with ministerial director Herbert Blankenhorn, Schwerin continued to advocate the British ideas on forming a federal police force and arming labor units and other auxiliary elements that had been organized by the occupying powers. On 17 July, Schwerin and Blankenhorn participated in a comprehensive discussion of emergency civil defense planning and internal security matters with Gen. George Hays, a deputy to High Commissioner McCloy. Schwerin also explored the possibility of forming a group of German experts, headed by former general von Vietinghoff, to work with a comparable Allied group. Although General Hays reacted positively to the idea when Schwerin first presented it, at a subsequent meeting on 9 August he rescinded (at Washington's direction) his support of the British position. Hays emphasized that the issue was primarily political, and it was probably premature for any combined working group to be considered. Discreetly Schwerin held additional meetings with several members of the high commissioner's staff, including at least one more meeting with General Hays, and other meetings with several Americans he knew to be CIA officers. Schwerin wanted to broaden his area of discussion with the Americans. He presented a list of thirteen points describing Germany's total vulnerability in the event of a Soviet attack. McCloy found the list useful when reporting to Washington.

Schwerin met with Adenauer's other advisor, Eberhard Wildermuth, on 25 July to discuss his contacts with General Hays's office and request a meeting of former generals (chaired by von Vietinghoff) to advise the chancellor about military and security concerns. Wildermuth was astonished to hear of two separate and distinct remilitarization efforts—his own, in conjunction with Heusinger, Speidel, and Foertsch, and Schwerin's. Wildermuth may have rationalized that Schwerin's task concerned only internal security, that is, police affairs and civil defense, while he was concerned with external security and the Soviet threat. Nevertheless, the fact remained that Schwerin and von Vietinghoff were addressing remilitarization as well.

Schwerin assumed control of an existing intelligence group led by former Abwehr officer Friedrich Wilhelm Heinz. Achim Oster, son of the famous Hans Oster of the Abwehr who had been executed as a member of the resistance, became the Schwerin organization's staff intelligence officer. Schwerin found a supportive element among former OSS officers in the CIA station. Gehlen, of course, became aware of the situation. He knew that the CIA was in contact with Schwerin and his hastily assembled organization and suspected that the CIA was at least theoretically supporting him. The situation quickly developed into a competitive and hostile opposition movement in Bonn to Gehlen's intelligence aspirations and the role of Heusinger and Speidel in remilitarization.

The British had caused Gehlen a great deal of anguish, but in some ways Gehlen had been his own worst enemy. He had a certain appetite for perishable political intelligence and the gossip continually circulating in Bonn. He fixated on what he saw as conspiracies by CIA officers in Bonn against him and his plan. Latent opposition to Gehlen had a brief revival when some CIA officers in Bonn urged U.S. support of the British opposition to Gehlen. Taking note of the situation, CIA headquarters directed the station to back off.

Adenauer was suddenly confronted with a critical policy issue: determining his responsibility for the defense of Germany and satisfying himself on the nature and seriousness of the threat to the new-found peace in Western Europe. The West, particularly the United States, appeared to be convinced that the attack by North Korea had to be taken as a sufficient reason to consider the possibility of a Soviet attack against an equally undefended Western Europe. The Americans had engaged in unilateral demobilization, leaving little more than a symbolic military presence in Germany. The British and the French had sent their armed forces to all parts of their rebellious colonial empires and cut their forces at home and in Germany.

For the first time Adenauer was faced with the possibility that the Soviet Union had become an actual threat to West Germany, regardless of the republic's status as an occupied and demilitarized nation. Adenauer's political colleagues understood the situation and pressed him for some expression of policy. Adenauer hesitated. On 13 July he left for a month's vacation in Switzerland. His duplicitous position was evident in the fact that he left two advisors behind in Bonn who had been advocating entirely different approaches to defending the republic, each convinced that he was to assemble a group of military experts to advise the chancellor on a national security policy.

Prior to his departure Adenauer gave a third man, Dr. Hans Globke, the idea that as his principal advisor on government organization, Globke should be thinking about a national security system and possibly even some kind of armed force that would at least defend Germany against any violation of its borders by the growing Volkspolizei (Peoples Police) in East Germany. Globke, a senior official in the chancellor's office, was responsible for financial affairs, government organization, and personnel policies who thought that Adenauer's absence for a month would give him the time he needed to study the whole subject of a national security system about which he knew very little.

As a start Globke made plans to meet in Bonn with Gehlen and Heusinger on 17 July, his first meeting with Heusinger. He had met Gehlen earlier on 29 June to get an intelligence briefing on the Korean crisis. Almost as an aside during the June meeting Globke asked Gehlen if he could help in dealing with the growing subversion from East Germany, a question that would have a profound effect in the future; nothing interested Gehlen more than the possible subversion of Germany by its neighbor to the east. At the 17 July meeting Globke asked Heusinger and Gehlen for their off-the-record opinions of a list of former generals being considered as candidates for heading the border police. Heusinger gratuitously offered the opinion that developing a police force as an alternative to a conventional force was a poor idea. It can be argued that this meeting marked the beginning of Globke's influence within the BK on national security affairs. He surely recognized that Heusinger—with whom I had been engaged in long discussions on this subject—was a unique German asset on which to expand his own role within the BK.

Shortly after this meeting Globke saw a report from Washington, an important study on the defense of Europe reportedly authored by Heusinger that was circulating in the Pentagon. Since my arrival in Pullach, Heusinger had conducted at least two studies, one examining a theoretical Soviet attack to take all of Western Europe and the other proposing how the Western nations might defend Europe. The two reports were not intelligence documents, nor were they classified; they simply were products of the analyses that Heusinger and Speidel had put together prior to the time Heusinger joined the Gehlen Organization. Speidel had sent these reports to Truman Smith, a retired military attaché in Germany, who circulated them to carefully selected officials. The reports definitely got around. I suspected Globke was curious about possibly creating a separate Heusinger connection with the Pentagon, but in truth he was looking for a plausible excuse to visit Pullach and see Gehlen and Heusinger in their milieu.

Globke's very discreet visit to Pullach on 21 July gave him a superficial but firsthand impression of the size and complexity of the organization about which he knew almost nothing. He had not missed the significance of the Stars and Stripes flying from a flagpole at the center of the Pullach compound alongside the red-black-gold colors of the German Federal Republic. He carried back to Bonn additional reports on the Korean War and the evolving reactions to it by the Americans, the British, the French, and the Soviets.

Adenauer's advisors in their newly appointed roles spent a dizzying few weeks drawing on numerous contacts for ideas on how to proceed from the status quo of "no policy on defense" to creating a solid policy proposal on the matter. In anticipation of the chancellor's return on 14 August, Schwerin requested from a CIA contact an American intelligence estimate of the European defense situation after events in Korea, something he could use with the chancellor. General Hays intervened and informed the CIA that Schwerin was not recognized as a bona fide official and that it was U.S. policy not to provide intelligence until the issue of German participation in the defense of Europe had been settled. The phrasing of General Hays's decision suggests that by mid-August news of the debate in Washington about the evolving U.S. policy aimed at strengthening NATO and arming Germany had filtered back to Bonn and the U.S. high commission. Generally, Schwerin had failed to gain acceptance as an official of the Bonn government.

Schwerin, apparently not aware of the Heuss-Adenauer policy, was quite open and indiscreet in developing a plan to convene a meeting of former generals. He scheduled it for 29 August at the Walberberg Abbey near Bonn. Schwerin was either not aware of Hays's policy or simply did not take it seriously. In the meantime Eberhard Wildermuth, still of the view that Schwerin's efforts related only to internal security and his to external security, met with Heusinger, Foertsch, and Speidel on 31 July to ask them to put their thoughts on the remilitarization question into a memorandum to be presented to Adenauer upon his return to Bonn. They immediately went to work and returned a week later with their report, titled "Gedanken ueber die Frage der aeusseren sicherheit der Deutschen Bundesrepublik" (A Thinkpiece concerning the Security of the Federal Republic of Germany) dated 7 August 1950. The memorandum was in fact a response to a request from the chancellor conveyed through Minister Wildermuth. It allowed the three generals to act with the authority of the chancellor and thus avoid any suggestion that they were acting inconsistently with either the Heuss-Adenauer policy or Military Government Law 16.

On 11 August the CIA in Washington informed us about a report they had from Truman Smith concerning the activities of a number of former German generals. The report noted that the following former generals were being considered for important "General Staff" positions: Heusinger, Speidel, von Schweppenberg, von Vietinghoff, von Senger und Etterlin, Roettinger, Staedke, and Koestring. Smith also reported that Speidel was in Paris participating in the Schumann Plan on coal and steel negotiations. The list of names roughly corresponded with the group of former generals who had attended the conference at Walberberg on 29 August. Smith's report revealed exactly the type of information that the Heuss-Adenauer policy was designed to avoid. The timing was unfortunate for the three generals, coming just days after they had completed their report. Heusinger visibly winced when I quoted the reports from Washington. He noted that the information was untrue on two counts: Adenauer was not planning to create a General Staff, and Speidel was not participating in negotiations in Paris. Truman Smith had not revealed his source or sources in Germany, though he clearly had several dating back to his prewar assignment in Berlin. The cabled 11 August report from the CIA in Washington also went to Bonn. It was certainly passed to McCloy's office and may have made its way to the BK in the form of an inquiry. This report may have contributed to Adenauer's determination to tighten his control over remilitarization matters. Nevertheless, there was no doubt in my mind that by this time there was a Germany evolving out of the ashes of World War II that was seeking a place in the Western community of nations.

The first man to brief Adenauer upon his return from Switzerland was Eberhard Wildermuth, who had with him the seventeen-page memorandum prepared by Heusinger, Speidel, and Foertsch. At Adenauer's request Wildermuth presented the report to the full cabinet the following day, without revealing the identities of the report's authors. The cabinet reacted positively. Only one dissenter, Minister of Interior Gustav Heinemann, disagreed with the substance of the report and tendered his resignation, which Adenauer accepted. By all historical accounts Adenauer was profoundly impressed by the 7 August memorandum—which he dubbed the "Sommer Denkschrift" or "Summer Thinkpiece"—and instructed Wildermuth to direct the three generals to further address the issue of a German role in a Western defense alliance. The report began with a description of the situation of the Federal Republic:

> The German Federal Republic has not as yet achieved the status of peace. It is not sovereign. It has not yet been integrated into the European Community or the Atlantic defense pact. It is, however, the one most immediately exposed to the threat posed by the east to the European-Atlantic nations. The people of the federal republic have adopted the ideals of freedom of the Western powers. Still, these ideals are not yet so firmly rooted that the populace would be ready to sacrifice possessions and blood on their behalf. So long as the people do not themselves enjoy complete freedom, they will not necessarily be ready to die for freedom. And in spite of the election defeat of the communist party, the populace remains susceptible to communistic-Bolshevistic propaganda. That does not mean that there is support for this ideology, but rather that there is fear and anxiety among the people. The thought, "What shall I do if the Russians come?" preoccupies individuals to a much greater extent than is expressed openly in public opinion.

The report presented in concise military terms and specific details the strength of Soviet ground, air, and naval forces in central Europe and in the Soviet Union. It credited the thirty front-line Soviet divisions in East Germany with a capability of launching an attack within forty-eight hours after a decision to do so. (The authenticity of this section clearly rested on the knowledge of Adolf Heusinger as head of the evaluations staff, which at the time was the foremost group of experts in Europe on Soviet armed forces.) The security of the federal republic could be had only by a Western military alliance of Europe and the Atlantic community in strength sufficient to support a forward strategic defense. A forward defense strategy, to contain at or near the front line any Soviet attack along the Elbe, would require acceptance by the West of a sovereign and rearmed federal republic within the Western alliance. Germany, the authors said, could provide up to fifteen divisions of modern, conventionally armed German forces fully integrated into the military command of the Western alliance. That the German people would be in the forefront of a battle area if the Soviets were to launch an attack out of East Germany was a primary consideration. A political and military protective defense of Germany during the German buildup of forces would be required to deter the Soviet Union from an early, preemptive attack. During this period the deterrent influence of a U.S. strategic air force and atomic weapons was particularly important. (It was assumed the American monopoly on such weapons would last at least two more years.) The agreement would be founded on a commitment to the principle of equality in the treatment of German forces within a Western alliance, including a commutation of sentences in the cases of German soldiers convicted of war crimes for their actions in battle taken on the orders of higher authority (provided such actions were not in violation of German laws prior to World War II).

The "Sommer Denkschrift" recommended the creation of an official federal office staffed by civil servants and initially camouflaged to obfuscate and conceal its purpose as defense planning. This office would provide a firmly and officially funded *arbeitstab*, or work staff, to exercise the functions as the sole and central authority for the entire process of Germany's rearming within the framework of a Western alliance. Initially the *arbeitstab* was seen as a task force to conceptualize and begin the organizational planning of a new German armed force; eventually it would participate in the drafting of related legislation and performing civil defense matters. In the end, the authors acknowledged, they were proposing the creation of a "defense ministry" without actually using the term. The staff would coordinate closely with the Western powers in order to be kept fully informed of the planning and development of a common and integrated Western defense. In this coordination the authors emphasized the significance of the United States as the most capable contributing partner. The group held a basic conviction that, left to their own devices, Europeans would be wholly incapable of organizing themselves to meet the Soviet threat. On this point their influence on Adenauer became most evident in the second half of 1950. Adenauer's basic inclination was to find a future in a predominantly Catholic "little Western Europe" without German reunification. Adenauer's own doubts on the viability of such a solution in the polarizing world of the cold war may have contributed to the alacrity with which he began to rely on an Atlantic community led by the United States.

Adenauer adopted the thrust of the "Sommer Denkschrift" as the basis for further development of a new defense policy. As the authors prepared a comprehensive proposal for the federal republic's defense planning, he would continue to adhere to the Heuss-Adenauer policy of leaving any public or official remilitarization initiative to the Western alliance. Intending to disengage somewhat from the British initiative of May 1950 with as little damage as possible, he imposed a strict secrecy classification on the work. Adenauer was not capable of going beyond these initial decisions in the first days after his return to Bonn; the next steps would depend largely on Hans Globke, a trusted advisor.

In the meantime Adenauer met with Blankenhorn for a report on Graf Schwerin's activities. Blankenhorn had maintained an ongoing official dialogue with the Allied High Commission and had met with its representatives on the creation of a proposed police force and emergency planning. Schwerin had made progress in organizing a group of officers around the central figure of former general von Vietinghoff, and proposed to convene a conference later that month to obtain their collective views on the security problems of the Federal Republic. Blankenhorn was able to provide intelligence on the East German Volkspolizei and Soviet forces in East Germany that had been produced by Schwerin's own intelligence organization run by Friederich Wilhelm Heinz. Schwerin had also expanded his own contacts with some of the American and British intelligence officers in Bonn. Blankenhorn found Adenauer somewhat preoccupied. Nothing he had reported seemed to be of particular interest to the chancellor. What Blankenhorn did not know was that his report did not fit into the scenario described in the "Sommer Denkschrift," which Adenauer had embraced as the direction for the future.

On 17 August, Adenauer presented to the high commissioners a long list of desired goals, ranging from a broad request to end the Occupation and give Germany sovereignty to admission to the Western community of nations. More specifically he requested permission to form the lightly armed police force advocated by the British. He went on record as being prepared to provide a German contingent to participate in the defense of Europe. The Allied High Commission made no response, and requested that Adenauer collate his ideas into a memorandum that would be put on the agenda at the September meeting in New York. The three high commissioners were obviously stalling for time in order to see what could be done in New York to bring the highly divided positions of the Big Three together on the German issue, amidst the heightened concern about the defense of Europe in light of the attack in Korea. American High Commissioner McCloy assured Adenauer his positions would be addressed in New York. Adenauer realized that he was being put off. He left the meeting even more determined to undertake defense policy planning independently, using the "Sommer Denkschrift" as a point of departure. Most political observers in Bonn were unaware of what was transpiring between the chancellery and the German organization in Pullach. In the spring and summer of 1950 exaggerated importance was being given to the British initiative and the activities of Graf Schwerin, who had suddenly emerged as a figure of considerable interest. Almost nothing was being reported on Adenauer's shift in policy and advisors. In the disarray after June 1950 relations between Adenauer and McCloy were at least superficially strained as the Allied High Commission, with McCloy in the chair, failed to take Adenauer into his confidence on the problems among the three occupying powers.

The memorandum McCloy requested, to be prepared by Blankenhorn and his staff, turned out to be two separate reports. The first draft, completed on 21 August, was followed by second and third drafts (in English) on 24 August; the cabinet met to discuss the drafts on 25 August. The first memorandum dealt with internal and external threats, describing in considerable detail the size and character of the Soviet military and the East German Volkspolizei. Adenauer chose to describe the Volkspolizei of East Germany as an internal threat, the Soviets as external. The report noted that the Allied High Commission had not responded to the government's proposal to form a lightly armed and mobile federal police force. The second memorandum addressed the issues of relations with the occupying powers, sovereignty, the occupation statutes, and Germany's acceptance into the Western alliance. Adenauer sent the memoranda to McCloy on 29 August, who in return assured him they would be placed on the agenda in New York. The urgency of these issues seemed fully justified to Adenauer and his cabinet due to changing circumstances: the creation of NATO, the establishment of the federal republic, and the impact of the Korean War.

In the meantime Graf Schwerin continued to make plans to convene his meeting at Walberberg Abbey on 29 August. Clearly the chancellor was working at cross-purposes in permitting both initiatives to continue. Adenauer's concern that news of the meeting might leak and be unsettling to the foreign ministers meeting in New York finally led him to order that the Walberberg meeting be canceled.

At this point the role of Wildermuth in defense matters declined and Dr. Globke, who was then directly in touch with the three generals, took over. Wildermuth's contributions during 1950 are clear. On his initiative the "Sommer Denkschrift" was written; he presented the report to Adenauer in a way that got his full attention; he briefed the full cabinet; and he carried Adenauer's instructions back to Speidel and through him to Heusinger and Foertsch. But Wildermuth was not destined to become the first minister of defense of the Federal Republic. Adenauer apparently believed in the old rule that a new policy takes a new man. The chancellor gave Globke responsibility to oversee the trio of Heusinger, Speidel, and Foertsch in secretly developing a plan for German remilitarization without consulting the Allied High Commission, including the Americans. Globke realized such secrecy might be difficult to achieve, since two of the three generals were members of the Gehlen Organization run by the Americans. He simply passed on to Heusinger the chancellor's orders on secrecy and let Heusinger figure out how to keep his activities hidden.

Globke faced one other minor problem. It was absolutely illegal under Military Government Law 16 for a group of German generals to meet to discuss rearming. Schwerin and Blankenhorn had gotten some kind of waiver from General Hays in planning their conference (which Adenauer ultimately canceled). The waiver granted by McCloy's deputy was presumed to be still valid and applicable to the conference that Globke was now organizing with the help of Heusinger, Speidel, and Foertsch. The decision to include Schwerin in the new effort was primarily a way to gracefully disengage from Schwerin. Schwerin had become a problem for Adenauer, but he wanted to disengage from the British-Schwerin situation with some grace.

By the end of September Adenauer had become increasingly vexed by the inability or unwillingness of the divided Allied High Commission to continue the exchange they had begun. McCloy privately admitted to Adenauer that the meetings in New York had produced nothing favorable for him. Adenauer saw the political environment steadily deteriorating throughout all of Germany. The severe reverses of the UN forces in North Korea (mostly U.S. forces) had brought a new wave of despair and fear to the West German public.

After the outbreak of war in Korea, Gehlen was drawn into a relationship with the chancellery and provided intelligence on the ensuing crisis. The CIA officially approved Gehlen's request to do so, a policy that remained in effect after 1950. Gehlen had his initial meeting with Adenauer on 20 September. Although Gehlen was a Protestant and Adenauer was a devout Catholic, Adenauer could not have missed Gehlen's seemingly good relationship with the Catholic Bavarians of the

Christian Social Union. Adenauer could see that Gehlen had gotten his start as a young General Staff officer mainly under the Bavarian monarchist Franz Halder, whose opposition to Hitler had marked Halder's career. By December 1950 Adenauer assured Gehlen that the Federal Republic would take over the Gehlen Organization "in the appropriate circumstances," and make it into a German centralized intelligence service directly responsible to the chancellor. Things were definitely looking up. Just twenty-four hours after Gehlen's meeting with Adenauer, Gehlen and Heusinger met with Dr. Kurt Schumacher, head of the opposition Social Democratic Party (SPD). I thought it a truly remarkable "coincidence" that these important events had been separated by exactly twenty-four hours. In hindsight I am certain that someone in Adenauer's office, probably Dr. Globke, had learned of the Schumacher appointment and had arranged the Adenauer-Gehlen meeting the day before. Both Gehlen and Heusinger had been wholly committed to supporting a nonpartisan political base for both the intelligence and remilitarization objectives and it is why they cultivated a connection with the Social Democrats, seeking support for their aims.

On 25 September Gehlen told me that High Commissioner McCloy was planning to invite him to dinner. While at the Tripartite and NATO council meetings in New York earlier that month, McCloy had talked with his old friend, banker Eric Warburg, and casually mentioned he would like to meet Gehlen. McCloy was a clever fellow. He wanted to meet Gehlen in a situation disassociated with either the CIA or the chancellor. Warburg contacted Gert Whitman, an American of German origin working on McCloy's political staff, who, not surprisingly, was an established contact of Gehlen's man, Hans von Lossow. Gehlen was obviously pleased that this meeting was planned without our help, though prior to the meeting we had fully updated McCloy on all aspects of our relations with Gehlen.

The dinner went off well. In addition to the two German guests—Gehlen and Heusinger—it included Gen. George Hays, Ben Shute, Gert Whitman, and several other members of McCloy's staff. McCloy guided the conversation into a general discussion of Korea and how the issue of Western European defense was becoming complicated by that crisis. McCloy avoided any reference to the failed effort to put Gehlen in touch with Adenauer earlier in the year, and everything else related to intelligence. Gehlen, not eager to discuss the BfV fiasco and assuming correctly that I would have already reported to McCloy on Gehlen's Adenauer connection, did not mention his meeting with Adenauer. It was the most Byzantine of affairs. The McCloy dinner was an important occasion for both Gehlen and Heusinger; as a gesture and the way in which it was done the scenario was typical of McCloy. Likely the first to hear a report on the dinner was Dr. Globke and the second was Chancellor Adenauer. Adenauer no doubt appreciated the timely action by the U.S. high commissioner, a subtle way of conveying American agreement with the steps Adenauer had taken with both Heusinger and Gehlen.

A year that had started badly and gotten steadily worse had suddenly, in its second half, turned remarkably better for Reinhard Gehlen. The Korean conflict had dramatically increased the chances that the Gehlen Organization would survive and become part of the government in Bonn. Gehlen concluded that the senior officers in the CIA in Washington, all of whom were making decisions on CIA intelligence interests in Germany, appeared to have tacitly accepted and supported Gehlen's plan and objectives.

Military planning was also moving ahead. By September specific planning for a secret meeting at the secluded Himmerod Abbey just a few miles from the upper Mosel valley near Trier was under way under Dr. Globke's direction. Globke expected the three generals to be in charge of developing a plan for the German armed forces that could be used in defense negotiations. Hans Speidel had some reservations about Graf Schwerin's role. Speidel had broken off relations with Schwerin late in 1949 after Schwerin had failed to persuade Speidel (with his important French connections) to join him in his efforts for an incremental approach to remilitarization, that is, establishing police and auxiliary forces now and conventional forces later. The process of identifying individuals to be included in the Himmerod conference was somewhat complicated by the fact that Schwerin, von Vietinghoff, and the generals who had been invited to the aborted meeting at Walberberg, were all waiting in the wings, expecting to be called to a rescheduled meeting. Globke found it to be a sensitive matter that would take careful handling. Adenauer wanted to spare Schwerin and von Vietinghoff embarrassment but did not want to weaken the position of the three generals.

The preparations for the Himmerod meeting and developments in Washington were moving forward on separate but parallel tracks. The effort of the three generals in Germany were, taken together, the counterpart of the actions of the Joint Chiefs that had produced the "Single Package" proposal to reverse the decline in the U.S. military presence in Europe and to rearm Germany—in essence the National Security Council policy proposal that went to President Truman for his approval on 8 September. Truman's approval of the policy was not known to the public for some time, but it was presented to the British and French at the foreign ministers meeting in New York in the week that followed. Both the French and the British harshly rejected Truman's Single Package proposal, but knew they had not seen the end of it. In deference to the French the Americans put it aside.

With planning for Himmerod moving forward, Globke had obviously felt uneasy that he had not yet met the third general. On 14 September General Foertsch accompanied Heusinger to a planning session at the chancellor's office. While Adenauer had made the original decision to reach out and expand the connection with the three authors of the "Sommer Denkschrift," Globke was responsible for either validating the decision the chancellor had made or advising the chancellor if he had any reason to question it. Adenauer had a great deal at stake. His secret unilateral defense policy planning had been quite effective. At the time I never saw any of the German defense policy milestone documents. Heusinger returned to Pullach on the overnight train from Bonn, arriving in Munich early on 15 September. My conversation with him later that day was, looking back, the most important of that entire period. Heusinger did not tell me that he had met with Globke the day before to discuss the list of former officers that were being invited to the planned conference. All he said was that "things were looking up" for the convening of a group of military experts. Our conversation of 15 September was as close as he ever got to revealing the firm plans being developed for the meeting at Himmerod. Heusinger also told me he had dinner with Schwerin and Blankenhorn on the evening of 13 September. He had found Schwerin still confident in his position and, as he wryly observed, "in the saddle." He did not, however, find Schwerin well informed on what had been going on in the month since Adenauer's return from vacation.

On the evening of 5 October, before the group assembled at the Himmerod Abbey, Adenauer invited Speidel to meet with him at Schaumburg Palace. Adenauer made it unmistakably clear to Speidel that the "Sommer Denkschrift" was to provide the basic document for the work taking place in Himmerod. He added that Blankenhorn and Graf Schwerin had been made fully aware of this strategy. Though Schwerin was ostensibly the organizer of the conference, Adenauer was engaging in a delicate disengagement, since Globke and Heusinger actually had made the arrangements. The chancellor had personally selected the Himmerod Abbey, a secluded place not frequented by the press, diplomats, or intelligence officers in Bonn, and imposed strict security on all aspects of the October conference, including obtaining a promise of silence from the local Cistercian Order.

Of the conference's fifteen participants, five were former Army generals: Heusinger, Speidel, Foertsch, Fridolin von Senger und Etterlin, and Hans Roettiger. Roettiger and Senger und Etterlin had both been on Schwerin's original list and their inclusion at Himmerod was, presumably, a matter discussed and agreed to by Globke and Heusinger. Army colonel Graf von Kielmansegg acted as the executive secretary of the conference, and his friend and member of the Gehlen Organization, Col. Eberhard Graf von Nostitz, was, I think, a nomination of Heusinger and Speidel. At the last minute the former colonel Bogislaw von Bonin, whom Heusinger had proposed as one of the fifteen, was unable to leave his new position with Daimler Benz in Stuttgart; a former Army major, Graf Wolf Baudissin, was his substitute. Several former Navy officers were also in attendance: Vice Adm. Friedrich Ruge and Adm. Walter Gladisch; and former Navy captain Schulze-Hinrichs (whose presence was attributed to his current knowledge of the postwar expanding maritime power of the Soviet Union); Schulze-Hinrichs, who headed the Navy group in Heusinger's evaluations staff in Pullach, came with the support of the group of German admirals who had been working with Heusinger. The group included two former Air Force generals, Robert Knauss and Rudolf Meister, a former Luftwaffe major, Horst Krueger (who at thirty-four was the youngest of the experts), and former Army general von Vietinghoff who participated as pro forma chairman.

The introduction of Kielmansegg as the self-confident executive secretary, the use of von Vietinghoff as chairman, allowing Schwerin to make the opening remarks but then departing, and the presence of Blankenhorn as a political backgrounder who otherwise stayed in the background, all reflected the skillful hands of Adenauer and Globke. The conference committee was divided into four working groups, three of them chaired by Heusinger, Speidel, and Foertsch, and the fourth by the former Air Force major General von Senger. It was apparent to the planners at Himmerod that the weapons of air and missile warfare were in a revolutionary era of rapid technological change to which the Germans had contributed in the last years of the war. The new German Air Force would be confronted with the most dramatic changes in the five years since the end of the war. To some extent the tempo of change in ships and maritime weapons was likewise dramatic; the German maritime mission would initially be focused on the North Sea and the Soviet Navy, which also was experiencing a period of great change. For German Army officers the professional scene and the weapons and military principles of ground warfare had changed far less dramatically.

The Himmerod conference produced a plan for creating a ground force of twelve modern, heavily armed German divisions organized at the corps level, with appropriate air and naval forces determined by the presumed missions, all under NATO command in a geographical setting that stretched from the Elbe west to the English Channel. The memorandum clearly identified the military ideas on strategy that the Germans would bring to NATO if invited to join. The concept of a forward defense that would challenge a Soviet offensive at the Elbe rejected any idea of falling back to a defensive line on the Rhine. The Germans were committed to relying on a strong conventional force and strategy that would not rely primarily on the U.S. atomic weapons advantage. With this strategy strongly tilted toward an Atlantic rather than a European defense force, the Germans envisaged a heavy reliance on U.S. and British forces for assistance in training, particularly the new air and naval forces.

After the conference Kielmansegg, nominally a member of Schwerin's office, was charged with preparing the final report. The fifteen military experts signed their names to this report that, in the face of some difficulty, had been agreed upon in four days. As a group these experts were never called upon to meet again. The Himmerod plan was not simply the result of four days of intense debate, it reflected many months of networking and planning among military experts with whom Heusinger, Speidel, and Foertsch had been communicating. The basic intelligence data used to create the document had obviously come from the evaluations staff in Pullach. The ongoing efforts had produced the widest possible consensus on the central and most perplexing issues involved in forming a new German armed force. Like the presentation of the "Sommer Denkschrift," the conference at Himmerod was a landmark event in the history of how the national security system of Germany developed in the postwar era—a German "shadow" Joint Chiefs of Staff had held its first meeting in postwar Germany.

No leaks on the Himmerod meeting made it to the press or the public. Three days before the gathering Heusinger had dinner with McCloy at his home and later gave me an account of the dinner. There was no reference to the planned meeting at Himmerod, although General Hays and several other members of McCloy's staff were present. During the previous summer Hays sent several requests for German comments on fairly routine planning questions to Blankenhorn in the chancellor's office. Adenauer intervened in each case and forbade any response, proof that the Heuss-Adenauer policy was still in place and being followed.

While the creation of the "Sommer Denkschrift" was the turning point in Adenauer's thinking, the memorandum prepared at Himmerod—which noted a five-year period of planning and negotiation of a Western defense alliance—provided the blueprint for the German forces that did in fact become the Bundeswehr. On 29 October Adenauer announced the creation of a kind of minister's post described as "Der Beauftragte des Bundeskanzlers fuer die mit der Vermehrung der allierten Truppen zusammenhaengenden Fragen." Theodor Blank, a Catholic labor leader and a CDU member of the Bundestag, had been appointed. Because of the sheer length of Blank's title, the name of the office, in truth a camouflaged Defense Ministry, was quickly reduced to "Dienstelle Blank" or simply "Amt Blank"—Blank's Office. Officially Blank was to look after matters relating to the expansion of the Allied forces in Germany. By the end of 1950 Heusinger, Speidel, and two former General Staff officers, Kielmansegg and Baudissin—all participants at Himmerod— became the hard-core cadre of Amt Blank.

Adenauer faced a sensitive and politically delicate problem of disengaging from his pre-Korea policy coordination of defense matters with the British, mainly through Herbert Blankenhorn and Graf Schwerin. Adenauer simply set aside the relationship. He dismissed Schwerin. British policy on Germany's role in the defense of Europe had moved into an area of ambiguity, where it remained until late 1953 when Churchill led the rescue of the NATO defense policy.

On the evening of 27 October Fred Wesemann of the *Frankfurter Abendzeitung* broke the story that Schwerin had been fired from his position as Adenauer's advisor because of an "indiscretion with the press." Other reports circulated that Adenauer had dismissed Schwerin simply because Schwerin had overstepped his assigned task. Dr. Globke gave selected members of the press an off-the-record explanation that Schwerin had engaged in drafting military legislation that had come to the chancellor's attention. My own view of the Schwerin affair, that it had been an operation casually run by both the British and Adenauer, meant that Schwerin had come and gone in this brief period and left virtually no mark on the history of 1950, the year of decisions.

Kielmansegg delivered the official report of the Himmerod conference to Adenauer on 2 November. Schwerin attached his comments, signed on 28 October, even though he had "resigned" the day before. On major issues Schwerin expressed support, sometimes strong, for the expressed conclusions and recommendations. He took exception to the exclusion of armed labor units and auxiliary forces from the remilitarization effort, and correctly identified as far too ambitious the two-year plan for creating the first armed and trained German forces. He emphasized that such haste would create mistakes which would later require costly correction. On the whole his commentary was professional, brief, well written, and balanced.

When it was all over and the finished report was delivered to the chancellor in four numbered copies, Globke became the custodian of copy number one; Blankenhorn the second; and the other two were held in the secretariat headed by Kielmansegg. All four numbered copies were held in the BK files and remained there until the Allied High Commission the took the initiative to invite the Germans to join them at talks on how Europe could be defended. In the meantime Kielmansegg and two others from Schwerin's staff, Achim Oster and Axel von dem Bussche, had been assigned to the new offices of Amt Blank.

Coinciding with the events surrounding the Himmerod Memorandum, a French initiative was put forward by Prime Minister Rene Pleven. In a speech to the French parliament on 29 October, Pleven presented a concept for an essentially European defense of Western Europe anchored in developing the political and economic institutions of Western Europe. Pleven's plan may have fitted nicely into the concept of a Western Europe built around a rapprochement between France and the German Federal Republic, but it did not fit the concept of a Western defense alliance built around a U.S.-led NATO military alliance. The Pleven Plan was clearly discriminatory against Germany and incompatible with the concept of the Himmerod Memorandum, the contents of which remained secret in Bonn.

On 2 November, the date that Adenauer approved the Himmerod Memorandum and met with a group of his key advisors on matters of national security, the German Federal Republic was on a collision course with French policy. Ambivalence on the issue tugged on the political heartstrings of Adenauer, Speidel, and Gehlen, all of whom had well-established ties to the French. Speidel was actively in contact with both French military and civilian officials and knew where the French stood. Although he had long since become a convinced Atlanticist, Speidel felt that achieving a rapprochement with the French was a difficult task that nevertheless had to be pursued. Gehlen was in close and continuing contact with French intelligence officials as well, and he too felt a rapprochement with France was all-important.

During the early afternoon of 2 November, Adenauer asked Heusinger and Speidel to serve as his military advisors. Heusinger told the chancellor that the two of them were prepared to serve as unpaid advisors without titles or any official status but only with the provision that they did not appear to be replacements for Graf Schwerin. Because Adenauer had still not been invited to sit down with the Western alliance to discuss a German defense role, the appointments of Heusinger and Speidel would be delayed until Christmas Day. On 23 December the Allied high commissioners met with Adenauer and on behalf of the NATO council formally invited the German Federal Republic to officially join in defense talks.

Later, on 2 November, the chancellor met with Globke, Blank, Blankenhorn, Heusinger, Speidel, and Gehlen to thank them for the accomplishment of the Himmerod Memorandum and to convey his ideas on the role they, particularly Amt Blank and the two generals, would play. Adenauer had chosen his team and for the present he would act as his own foreign minister. Dr. Hans Globke was emerging as the key figure in Adenauer's version of the National Security Council in Washington.

Probably as a gesture of recognition for his contribution, Reinhard Gehlen was invited to the meeting, but remilitarization and intelligence had been separated in the eyes of the chancellor and would remain so. From his first contacts with Gehlen and Heusinger, Globke saw the necessity of separating Adenauer's relations with the two men. The CIA explicitly supported this separation. Gehlen did not see himself as a participant in Heusinger's remilitarization initiatives, though Heusinger demonstrated a remarkable ability to draw on the entire resources of the Gehlen Organization without jeopardizing the separate character of his own role. The most intangible but probably most important asset that Nikolaus offered Heusinger was the implicit American connection. Though Heusinger was obviously ambivalent about his association with American and German intelligence, he also realized that Adenauer was quietly reassured to know that Heusinger and Gehlen lived and worked in a compound over which the Stars and Stripes—as well as the new flag of the Federal Republic—flew.

The Himmerod Memorandum was written in language that ultimately could be presented, unchanged, to the German parliament, her people, and the press. Though its immediate purpose was to create a plan that could be given to the three occupying powers once they had reached a political decision to invite Germany to the negotiating table, it also became the basic planning document for Amt Blank. The essentials of the report were ultimately accepted by NATO and followed by the military and political leaders of the Federal Republic for the next two or three decades.

12

The Politics of Acceptance

THE PETERSBERG Hotel, an old resort at the top of a mountain overlooking the Rhine, served as the headquarters of the Allied High Commission. On 9 January 1951, under the aegis of NATO, the American, British, and French deputy high commissioners invited a German delegation, headed by Theodor Blank and supported by military advisors Adolf Heusinger, Hans Speidel, and Graf Kielmansegg, to join them for talks at the Petersberg. The talks got off to an awkward start, since Blank and his team had come with ironclad orders from Chancellor Adenauer that the principle of equality was a prerequisite to progress. However, previously established protocol at the Petersberg reminded all German visitors that they were second-class citizens of an occupied nation. Minor arrangements, such as parking facilities away from the building and other inconveniences, were part of the calculated discriminatory plan. Blank insisted on equal treatment at the meeting, not only in parking vehicles but in seating arrangements and procedural issues. Equality issues, a central theme in the negotiations, eventually were resolved.

The representatives of the three occupying powers came to the Petersberg negotiations with unresolved differences of opinion on Germany's role. The French were thinking that not more than 100,000 German soldiers would be required, and those forces would be delivered to the proposed European army in small military units of less than a division strong. The U.S. Joint Chiefs of Staff had something closer to 500,000 in mind. The British were cautiously supportive of the French. To further complicate the issue, parallel talks were scheduled to begin in Paris in February to address the Pleven Plan. Though the Germans would be participating in those talks, the Americans, the Canadians, and the British each planned to send only an observer to Paris.

During the next five months twelve meetings were held at the Petersberg. The German delegation was fully prepared and presented the plan that had been developed at the Himmerod Abbey the previous October. Their proposal included Germany's entry into NATO, with fully accorded equality, and submission of a conventional force of 250,000 troops integrated into NATO forces under the NATO supreme commander. German troops would be assigned to twelve highly mobile and heavily armored divisions organized up to a corps level, a supporting air force of four hundred military aircraft, and a naval force that would participate in coastal defense including the threat of Soviet or East German naval forces in the Baltic. The Occupation would end. Germany would appoint a minister of defense, and a German inspector general (a general officer in the defense forces) would serve in the Defense Ministry as the senior officer in the new federal armed forces. The inspector general would report directly to the minister of defense, who in turn would be accountable to the Bundestag. Strategically the Germans envisaged a major buildup of Allied troops to establish a forward defense strategy capable of meeting any Soviet attack at the Elbe or in the Fulda Gap.

I have always assumed that Adenauer was fairly well informed on the character of the debate in Washington in the months after Korea, though he likely was unaware of the specific NSC policy paper signed by President Truman on 8 September 1950. The paper proposed the rearming of Germany only within a broader policy of a U.S. role in a NATO defense alliance, and called for a halt of the withdrawal of American forces from Europe. The national security and defense policies put before Adenauer between August and October were essentially the same. But a week later when the U.S. delegation took to New York the policy that had been adopted in Washington on 6 September, the French, supported by the British, flatly opposed the rearming of Germany. The United States had simply put aside its policy to be reopened at a NATO council meeting set for December in Brussels. Against this backdrop the Petersberg negotiations began with no agreement on how Europe was to be defended and what the German role should be. The Petersberg negotiations ended on 4 June 1951, producing a simple factual report of the meetings and the plan presented by the Germans with virtually no semblance of an agreement by the three. The report went into the record and on the shelf.

A far more sensitive and more relevant issue that could not be put on the agenda at the Petersberg meetings was General Eisenhower's view of the Germans at the end of the war. Eisenhower had accepted at face value the underlying formula stated in JCS 1067 that German militarists, industrialists, and senior civil servants shared equal guilt for the criminal deeds of the Nazi Party. Eisenhower had refused to meet with German officers at the surrender and had asserted that, because of their support of Hitler and the Nazi Party, German soldiers had sacrificed all claims to honor on the battlefields of World War II.

Adolf Heusinger had discussed these views with us in Pullach and was so perturbed that we agreed to send Henry Pleasants to Bonn to review the problem with senior members of John McCloy's staff. Henry met with Ben Shute and Gert Whitman and put the problem in their hands; they promised to discuss it with McCloy and get back to us. Eisenhower's scheduled arrival in Europe as head of the newly established Supreme Headquarters–Allied Powers Europe (SHAPE), led us to suggest that Eisenhower meet with Heusinger and Speidel. Though it was clearly not our decision to make, at a minimum we recommended to Shute that Eisenhower be briefed carefully on the concerns and backgrounds of Adenauer's two military advisors. It was equally important for Eisenhower to understand the role that they had played in shaping Adenauer's current policies on defense and foreign relations, and their strong convictions on the integration of German forces into NATO under the leadership of an American commander.

Eisenhower agreed to meet the German generals. He was staying with McCloy at his residence near Bad Homberg on 23 January when McCloy hosted a dinner at which Heusinger and Speidel were among the guests. When the Germans arrived together General Eisenhower was standing at the opposite end of the room, engaged in a conversation. Interrupting his conversation, he walked toward them, displaying the famous Eisenhower grin and exclaiming in a clear voice that momentarily stopped all other conversation in the room: "Ah, the generals!" Eisenhower warmly shook hands with each and escorted them into the room. After dinner McCloy arranged for Eisenhower, Blank, Whitman, Heusinger, and Speidel to withdraw to an adjoining study. Eisenhower went directly to the point of his statements at the end of the war. He described the circumstances in which they were made and emphasized that they represented his own convictions at the time. He had been wrong in 1945. In the intervening years, he told them, he had learned a great deal more and had adjusted his views. Most German officers and soldiers had conducted themselves in battle with courage and honor. The two German generals genuinely expressed their appreciation for General Eisenhower's statement and later reconstructed a version that was subsequently circulated among Germans and never challenged by anyone. On the following day Eisenhower issued a declaration on the honor of the German soldier in World War II that was released to the press. In essence it followed the statements of the previous evening. The exchange, a landmark event in the relations of the armed forces of the United States and the German Federal Republic, had cleared the air and set the tone for the future. On his next visit to Pullach Adolf Heusinger related the events of his evening at McCloy's home. Whether we deserved it or not, Heusinger attributed some credit to us and expressed his profound appreciation for our assistance.

To President Truman, who was under attack for his European defense policy, General Eisenhower brought only good news. In an informal meeting of the Senate and the House at the Library of Congress, Eisenhower reported that, "Western Europe is so important to our future, our future is so definitely tied up with them, that we cannot afford to do less than our best in making sure that it does not go down the drain." Eisenhower's prestige and reputation with Congress was evident. His presence in Europe ensured the support of many members of Congress who might have opposed the Truman policy of expanding America's involvement there.

Both Truman and Eisenhower were committed to NATO, but were prepared to give the French all the time they needed to test the concept of a European army that they would firmly control. The French saw no need for a German defense ministry or a general staff, and they certainly did not foresee German generals occupying high staff or command positions in a European army. Truman was aware that the Joint Chiefs and Secretary of Defense Gen. George Marshall were skeptical; they knew the French had entered the talks with no intention of giving the Germans any equality in forming a European defense. As the participants talked an impasse developed over the central reality that the German and French delegations were deeply divided about an integrated European army. The talks ended in a stalemate in June. The Germans tabled the same report they had presented at Petersberg.

John J. McCloy's swing toward support of the French initiative on Europe's defense resulted partly out of his concerns over a resurgence of Nazi influence in the Lower Saxony election in May 1951. A right-wing pro-Nazi party, the SRP, led by the notorious Otto Ernst Remer, had gained 11 percent of the vote. The SRP supported neutralism as the proper political course for reunifying Germany. McCloy's attitude also may have been influenced by his irritation with what he saw as the irrational position held by German industrialists, former officers, church leaders, and both Adenauer and Dr. Kurt Schumacher on the issue of clemency for convicted prisoners being held in the Landsberg facility. The question of reparations to the victims of Nazi Germany was actively being addressed, and McCloy was fully engaged in putting pressure on the Germans to move quickly and decisively in granting reparations to Jewish individuals directly, through international Jewish agencies or through the Israeli government.

McCloy was perhaps the strongest advocate of the idea of the Pleven Plan. He had not been entirely comfortable with the outcome of the Petersberg negotiations earlier, believing that the Germans had come almost too well prepared. Changes in American relations with the Germans had rapidly moved quite a distance since his personal participation in the evolving JCS 1067 as assistant secretary of war in Washington. During the early months of 1951 he had been mildly irritated with the positions the Germans had been taking on a number of issues. He was uncomfortable with Adenauer's persistent pleas to revise the occupation statutes, if not call an end to the Occupation altogether. He doubted the wisdom of creating a new German Army, and continued to give public assurances that Germany would have no national Army or General Staff. At the same time he was fully aware of the rehabilitation of a number of German General Staff members who worked in Pullach, all with his full support.

McCloy relentlessly pressured Adenauer to continue the talks in Paris. The United States was clearly committed to the principle of a European army and saw the Petersberg talks as having contributed to ideas that could be merged into an agreed-upon solution in Paris. McCloy argued that the European army had three essential and positive characteristics: it would overcome French objections to a self-contained German Army; it was consistent with long-term U.S. aims to establish a united Europe; and it provided a cooperative economic solution to the cost of defending Europe. Adenauer, sensing that American policy was now shifting away from the clarity achieved in the summer of 1950, cautiously reiterated his opinion that German forces under a NATO commander represented the best and most expeditious way to meet the Soviet threat in Europe.

Adenauer's own thinking was closer to those of the Pentagon than to McCloy's. He sent Blank and his two defense advisors, Heusinger and Speidel, to Paris for another try. On 10 July Blank presented the same German position, which had been tabled at the Petersberg talks months earlier. The French called the proposal "Le Bombe Blank." Eisenhower replied in a cable to Secretary of Defense Marshall that he was willing to participate in the Paris talks and try to bring the Germans around. He immediately engaged in the talks and proposed abandoning the term "European army" and replacing it with "European defense force." The principle of equality for all participating forces, established at this point, led to an aura of optimism. It was also agreed that SHAPE would develop a common armaments system and a common supply system—both NATO systems. The concept of a European defense force and a European defense community had gained acceptance.

McCloy and American Ambassador to France David Bruce had orchestrated the development. In a cable to Washington they urged the earliest possible conclusion of a treaty covering a European defense force. However, though it was agreed to in principle, the French continued to argue against accommodation to the German insistence on equality, and French anxieties concerning their own security remained a fundamental disagreement.

In late 1951 there seemed to be little more the chancellor could do related to the security of the Federal Republic. All the relevant decisions had been made in 1950. and subsequent related actions had been taken in 1951. The stalemate over defense matters was not one in which he had any obvious choice. He would continue to go along with the European defense planning in Paris and build relations across Europe, including relations with the French. Above all he planned to continue to work closely with the Americans, who seemed to offer the greatest hope for continued peace and stability in Europe.

LEGALIZATION BEFORE SOVEREIGNTY

Reinhard Gehlen remained an impatient man. He always thought his objective of achieving legal status in Bonn was within reach. The Adenauer government did in fact have real problems related to its unchanged status as an occupied nation. Many of the military government laws and regulations that derived directly from JCS 1067 were still on the books. The legality of the Gehlen Organization's activities was derived solely from the authority of the United States as an occupying power. The entire move toward remilitarization and organization of a national defense system could be considered an illegal action, although no one would attempt to make such a case.

After accepting Adenauer's proposal that Heusinger and Speidel become official employees of Amt Blank, Heusinger formally advised Gehlen that he was ending his status as the head of the evaluations staff and an employee of the organization. Heusinger turned over his responsibilities to Gerhard Wessel, though I have no recollection of any official or social event marking the occasion—true to form for the Gehlen Organization. Quite often a member of the organization would appear at my office simply to say goodbye.

On 31 March 1951 Gehlen gave Konrad Adenauer his first comprehensive briefing about the structure of a new German intelligence service. We had provided Gehlen a copy of the 1947 National Security Act that had created the CIA and contained a great deal of language that was useful in educating Adenauer and others in Bonn. The briefing presented Gehlen's known ideas regarding a central civilian service having broad responsibility for the collection and evaluation of foreign intelligence; it did not include any internal security responsibilities, leaving those to the BfV. From all reports the briefing went well. Also in March 1951 Gehlen presented to us a proposal that his organization become a legal part of the German Federal Republic but with the CIA continuing its financial support. This second proposal was turned down. (The idea reappeared attired in a different costume later in 1951.) Gehlen amplified the March briefing with a second presentation to Adenauer in May.

One of Gehlen's primary concerns was the presence of the intelligence effort in Amt Blank headed by a former Abwehr officer Friedrich Wilhelm Heinz. Heinz had become active in intelligence operations immediately after the war and had developed his own small group with a variety of well-established clients, contacts, supporters, and operations. He had established contacts with the Soviets and with Allen Dulles's short-lived OSS group in postwar Berlin. When Graf Schwerin decided he needed an intelligence organization he had brought in Heinz and Heinz's group. The British welcomed the fact that Heinz was positioning himself as an opponent and competitor to the Gehlen Organization. After Schwerin left, Dr. Globke acted to see that the intelligence operation headed by Heinz did not get swept aside. After an unsuccessful effort to pass them off to the Gehlen Organization, early in the year Globke elected to transfer Heinz to Amt Blank. A CIA officer in touch with Blank noted Blank's support of Heinz because the Gehlen Organization was "too big, too expensive, and too American." Yet when Gehlen refused to deal with Heinz Amt Blank eventually let Heinz go.

Gehlen and I agreed in principle that his intelligence production should go through American channels to the intelligence unit of SHAPE, with recognition of the information's origin and, in particular, assurance of its delivery to General Eisenhower's staff. Though Gehlen wanted to be able to tell Adenauer that his organization was contributing to the evolving NATO command, 1951 was too early to address any questions regarding future communication channels with the NATO commander. A great deal would depend on the agreed role of Germany in a Western defense alliance.

In June 1951 Gordon Stewart, the Bonn CIA station chief, met with Dr. Globke, who, in the time-tested German tradition, was enjoying a restorative cure at Bad Gastein in Austria. Noting Adenauer's assurances to Gehlen in December 1950,

Stewart told Globke that the CIA would "hold in trust" the Gehlen Organization until such time as the "federal republic in the appropriate circumstances would take it over." Globke replied that he would undertake concrete measures to prepare for the legalization of the organization. When I informed Gehlen of the agreement he attached particular importance to the "hold in trust" provision. Over time the "hold in trust agreement" acquired some of the mystique of his "gentlemen's agreement" with General Sibert in 1946—nothing in writing but a matter of record in Pullach, Bonn, and Washington.

In August Dr. Globke made his first official visit to Pullach and received a full briefing by Gehlen and his staff. I was away from Nikolaus at the time, having departed on my first home leave since my arrival in Germany in the late summer of 1948. As was customary in those days, my family and I returned to the United States on one of the large transatlantic oceanliners, the *Ile de France*, a vacation in itself. Before departing Germany I invited Gehlen to join me in the United States for a tour and a visit to CIA headquarters. He agreed and, accompanied by Heinz Herre, arrived in New York on 21 September.

It was Gehlen's first visit to Washington after being in Fort Hunt as a POW in 1945 and 1946. We spent about three days in Washington, where he met the DCI, Gen. Walter Bedell Smith, briefly for an exchange of pleasant and appropriate remarks. Gehlen's own record of the meeting states that the DCI thanked him for his contribution to a common defense and wished him well. Gehlen and Herre received general briefings by Bob Amory's Intelligence Directorate covering the communist countries, the war in Korea, and the situation in French Indo-China. Allen Dulles, who was in the agency at the time but not present at the meeting with General Smith, did not become DCI until 1 January 1953. Dulles hosted a small private dinner at the Metropolitan Club for Gehlen and Herre and about ten other CIA officers. Among those present were several that Gehlen had met before, including Richard Helms, Bob Amory (who had visited Pullach in 1950), and Sherman Kent (who had met with Gehlen and Herre at Fort Hunt in early 1946). Kent, the CIA's wizard on national intelligence estimates, made an impression that later shaped Gehlen and Herre's own thinking on the German estimates process.

Frank Wisner, the CIA's deputy director for plans—the clandestine arm of the CIA—was not at this dinner, though over the years considerable speculation has persisted that Wisner and Gehlen were in contact regarding operations in Eastern Europe. As a matter of fact Gehlen only met Wisner once, in a small conference room at CIA headquarters where Gehlen was receiving briefings. Wisner joined us for perhaps ten minutes and welcomed Gehlen to Washington, assured him that he was in good hands, and wished him success in his efforts. No operational discussions took place. To my knowledge Wisner never had any other contact with Gehlen. Wisner never came to the Pullach compound during my years there nor have I ever heard a reliable account of a Wisner-Gehlen meeting in any circumstance.

Gehlen's visit to Washington was remarkably uneventful. Most of the outstanding policy issues related to the Gehlen Organization had been settled in 1950. Our relationship with Gehlen was now a positive and well-established one. Gehlen was in a holding pattern, waiting for his future to be resolved by the German government. We became tourists. We had a reunion with Eric Waldman there and one with John Boker in New York, both of whom were warmly greeted by Gehlen and Herre. While in Chicago my closest college friend, Michael Hurdlebrink, a highly decorated Third Division officer in Italy during World War II and later a chief executive of a major paint company in Chicago, took Gehlen, Herre, and me to a 1930s-vintage speakeasy where, much to the surprise of all of us, we were greeted by a famous member of the mafia. This mafioso, a young man during World War I who had been a highly decorated sergeant in the Third Division at the Battle of the Marne assured us it had been the high point of his life. For years he was a strong supporter and most generous contributor to the Third Division's veterans organization in Chicago. The nightclub was a gambling house, dimly lit with a clientele of well-heeled visitors from out of town. The staff included a number of beautiful hostesses, whom Gehlen viewed somewhat nervously—not Gehlen's typical milieu, but he was clearly amused by the whole experience.

Gehlen and Herre proved to be enthusiastic and wholly congenial traveling companions. Herre was always on the move, exploring every accessible niche of the United States and American life. Gehlen and I had hours of discussion on long train trips through the industrialized East Coast, the Great Plains, and the scenic mountains of the West. Outside of Denver we spent a Sunday afternoon with Rudolph Glinsky and his wife, who in 1946 had met and married in the Blue House at Oberursel before they emigrated via Venezuela to the United States. The Glinskys were in the process of building their own house in the mountains; friends and neighbors were helping them. The endeavor impressed Gehlen enormously. We looked out on the Rockies from the top of Pike's Peak and walked among the great redwoods outside of San Francisco. Gehlen was an insatiable photographer and Herre, like the trained General Staff officer that he was, equipped himself with maps and sought out the highest observation point for surveying each tourist objective. One of my younger brothers, who had just completed his doctorate at the University of California in Berkeley, gave us a student's eye view of that great American university. We ended our visit in New York by attending the last game of the World Series at Yankee Stadium. For Heinz Herre, a true baseball buff, it was a dream come true.

Gehlen and Herre returned to their real world in Pullach. The problems Gehlen had left behind hadn't disappeared, but perhaps the trip did help him gain a wider perspective on the United States, which he had seen only as a POW at Fort Hunt. I stayed behind for a few weeks at headquarters and returned to Pullach just before Christmas. The immediate future seemed to be in the hands of Konrad Adenauer and the European Defense Community (EDC) negotiators in Paris.

Adenauer had taken almost every possible action available to him to develop a well-rounded national security system. He had pressed the Western Allies on the need for more allied forces in Europe to deter a Soviet attack during the period of building a new German force. His representatives had participated in the Petersberg negotiations, and Germany's proposal for rearming itself within the framework of NATO was on record. He was taking part in the continuing efforts in Paris to develop a European defense force and was prepared to join in a treaty if that was what the Paris talks produced. Adenauer did not believe the Pleven Plan would provide a timely and workable defense of Western Europe, but he understood that for the present the United States had officially opted for the French solution. The return of Winston Churchill to power in 1951 brought a major shift in British policy on the Adenauer government and its efforts to rearm within the NATO alliance. As Eisenhower shifted toward supporting the Pleven Plan between 1952 and 1954, Churchill moved away from it and into a position of full support for Adenauer.

The internal security service, the BfV, was in its infant stages and the formation of a federal border police was being vigorously pursued. The Bundestag passed legislation in February authorizing a ten thousand–man federal border police that later was expanded to twenty thousand. Adenauer had accepted the view of his military advisors and the experts at Himmerod: while a lightly armed police force was no substitute for a conventional military force, it should be developed without delay as a deterrent to any adventures that the East German Volkspolizei across the border may take. In an emergency the border police could assist in the maintenance of internal security and stability.

Adenauer had established direct contact with Gehlen. Dr. Globke, responsible for intelligence matters, had reached agreement with the CIA that it would "hold in trust" the Gehlen Organization until the Federal Republic could take it over. Few other initiatives related to the security of the Federal Republic were open for the chancellor to take. Above all, Adenauer would continue to work closely with the Americans, who seemed to offer the greatest hope for continuing peace and stability in Europe.

From 1951, the time of the "hold in trust" agreement, until the collapse of the European Defense Community treaty in August 1954, a closer and more equal professionally oriented relationship developed in Pullach. We concentrated our efforts on the "intelligence war" with the Soviet and other communist services centered in a divided Germany and Berlin. In blocking Germany's entrance into a NATO defense alliance the Kremlin's principal strategy was to offer a reunified, politically neutral Germany at the center of Europe.

13

The Intelligence War in Germany

DIVIDED GERMANY during the Occupation was an intelligence jungle. Both the Allies and the Soviets multiplied their intelligence forces through the widespread use of thousands of former German intelligence officers on both sides of what Churchill described as the "Iron Curtain." The two sides waged the largest, most concentrated and intense intelligence warfare in history on German soil. Although the Soviet Union of 1945 recognized itself as an economically devastated nation that had lost twenty million of its people in the war, Soviet leaders were confident that the combination of numerous strengthened communist parties and the sheer threatening presence of the Red Army in Europe would permit them—without the actual use of armed force—to bring Western Europe, including Germany, into the Soviet sphere of influence.

Stalin's sanction of the war in Korea produced a dramatic shift in policy in Washington. The highest levels there suddenly mandated an intelligence war against the Soviet Union and its satellites. The Truman administration threw itself into an almost frenzied debate of cold war policies—both military and intelligence. A CIA-produced National Intelligence Estimate concluded that a Soviet attack in Europe could not be ruled out. Up to that point, our main intelligence interest in Germany had been to rehash and research German activities throughout World War II. A major shift developed toward utilizing German wartime and postwar intelligence that targeted Soviet intentions and capabilities. Germany became the front line of the intelligence war that started in 1950 and did not end until the Berlin Wall came down in 1989.

GEHLEN JOINS THE COUNTERINTELLIGENCE GAME

Counterintelligence is the most sophisticated, intellectually demanding, and professionally complex of all intelligence tasks. The CI organization's mission is to identify security problems and propose preventive actions. These steps usually involve sensitive and complicated individuals with psychologically complex personalities, the types that seem to abound in the field of counterintelligence.

Gehlen's entry into counterintelligence was the result of actions taken by the U.S. Army in 1946. Responding to a USFET G-2 request for the German organization in Oberursel to develop a capability to monitor the activities of the Soviet missions in the U.S. Zone, Hermann Baun organized Dienststelle 114 (later designated GV L) which was located in Karlsruhe and headed by Alfred Bentzinger, an individual with no experience in counterintelligence. At the time Gehlen was in the United States as a POW. Even though the U.S. Army counterintelligence corps had developed numerous police and security connections and had extensive coverage of East German and communist party activities in West Germany, oddly the Germans were selected for the task. During Dr. Globke's first contact with Reinhard Gehlen in 1950 he asked, almost as an afterthought, if Gehlen could help with the growing problem of hostile intelligence and subversion coming out of East Germany. Gehlen violated his own policy and allowed former SD members, a small group in Stuttgart working under supervision of Bentzinger, to be hired and brought into GV L. Bentzinger openly recruited SD officers to work in the area of Karlsruhe and Stuttgart on the information and operations concerning communist penetration of West Germany. (I contend that coverage of communist infiltration into West Germany had been GV L's principal effort from its inception.) Gehlen was a profound believer in the danger communism posed to Western society. The word quickly got around, and the recruitment of one former SD officer soon led to the recruitment of his friend, which led to another, and so on—a veritable chain reaction. Bentzinger's actions, though obviously taken with Gehlen's knowledge and approval, were almost certainly not followed in any detail. Gehlen presumably saw this action as an acceptable political risk, considering the importance of his contact with Dr. Globke. Gehlen did discuss the issue of employing former SD officers with Heinz Herre, who later told me that he recommended that Gehlen drop the idea for fear it would inevitably turn into a political liability in the anticipated legalization of the organization. The decision to employ former SD officers was perhaps Gehlen's most costly mistake, and opened the door for the KGB to insert two agents—Heinz Felfe and Hans Clemens—into his sensitive CI organization. The decision probably cost the lives of numerous agents in communist countries, and caused lasting damage to Gehlen's reputation and that of his organization. It was a decision that for a brief period he concealed from both the CIA and much of his own senior staff. If Gehlen had not made the error there would almost certainly have been no Felfe case nor other KGB penetrations.

The existence of an organization in Karlsruhe that primarily conducted internal security operations was from the beginning a controversial matter between the CIA and Gehlen. The information it produced was difficult to pass to the CIA without provoking debate. The product was, however, probably well received by a select clientele in Bonn, including the interior ministry and the chancellery. The organization's record of preventing penetration by hostile intelligence services was not at all impressive, but one must consider the handicap caused by a divided nation, two countries with a single history, language, and culture. The intensity of espionage across the East-West dividing line throughout the intelligence war from the early 1950s to at least the early 1960s was unique in the history of espionage. A CIA study at the time revealed that of all the espionage cases involving a communist service and actually brought to trial, 95 percent of those that occurred over a three-year period after 1955 were found in West Germany.

My understanding of the situation in GV L has come only from information acquired in the 1980s and early 1990s. The CIA's first awareness of the consequences of employing SD officers came with our identification of Felfe as a suspected KGB agent in 1957. Surprisingly, it was not until reviewing information acquired in the 1980s and early 1990s that I developed a real understanding of the situation in GV L.

THE KGB IN KARLSHORST

KGB operations throughout Europe were gaining momentum as the cold war proceeded. KGB penetrations of British intelligence by Kim Philby, Donald MacLean, and Guy Burgess are well known. Not so well known were KGB penetrations of the French intelligence service, which provided the Soviets with its most detailed coverage of West Germany's political and defense matters. But it was the KGB group in Karlshorst, East Germany, that most successfully penetrated the Gehlen Organization, particularly through Hans Clemens and Heinz Felfe, both of whom landed jobs with Alfred Bentzinger's GV L.

Hans Clemens was an older SD officer from prewar Dresden. He had abandoned his start as a classical pianist and achieved an infamous reputation in wartime northern Italy, meting out retribution after the Italians had bowed out of the Rome-Berlin alliance. After the normal pattern of arrest, interrogation, and internment at the end of the war, Clemens had been employed by British intelligence in the Rhineland and the Ruhr areas. After leaving the British in the spring of 1950, Clemens was contacted by his estranged wife, still living in Dresden (then East Germany), who was having an affair with a KGB colonel named "Max." Under the guidance of her KGB lover Clemens's wife persuaded Clemens to visit Dresden. Clemens met Max, and was recruited and returned to West Germany with the task of identifying some of his former SD colleagues who might be willing to serve as prospective agents for the KGB. Clemens sought out Willi Krichbaum, a former colonel in the Geheime Feldpolizei (Secret Field Police), who had joined GV L and was a resident staff member in Bad Reichenhall on the Austrian border. To Clemens's surprise, Krichbaum offered him employment with the same task he had received from Max but with a different twist; Willi Krichbaum offered Clemens an operational mission of spotting and assessing former SD officers in West Germany to join Krichbaum's organization. Clemens accepted the offer and began scouting for former SD members; no candidate seemed more promising to meet the requirements of both Max and Krichbaum than a young SD colleague from his prewar days in Dresden, Heinz Felfe.

Prior to the war Heinz Felfe was a bright young man with a promising future as an SS police and intelligence official. Born and raised in Dresden, one of Germany's most beautiful cities, he finished his schooling, including his early police training, at the age of twenty-three and married a Dresden girl of his own age, Margarete Ingeborg. In his first year out of school Felfe was employed in Dresden by the Sicherheitspolizei (the security police), and began his career as a criminal "commissioner."

In August 1943 Felfe received a desirable assignment well isolated from Germany's wars: under the cover of being a teacher he was sent to Switzerland as an intelligence officer in Walter Schellenberg's RSHA Amt VI. There, he later claimed, he had contact with an aide of Allen Dulles and obtained reports of the meetings of Roosevelt, Churchill, and Stalin at Teheran and Yalta. It is possible that some version of those reports was intentionally leaked, since they contained nothing but very bad news for Hitler's Germany. It is likely that this experience helped prepare the young Felfe when he resumed his career as an intelligence officer in postwar Germany. His tour in Switzerland also left his record untouched by any suggestion of the kind of war crimes associated with the likes of Klaus Barbie.

Late in the war, holding the rank of obersturmfuehrer in the SS, Felfe was briefly stationed in Holland. Arrested by the Canadians and sent to a POW camp in the British Zone, he was eventually discharged from internment on 6 November 1946, then settled in Honnef in the British Zone and joined by his wife and son, who had been living in Dresden.

Early in 1947 Felfe was employed by the British intelligence office in the Rhineland, which used him in operations directed against the German communist party. Felfe was pleased to find that Hans Clemens, a senior SD leader from Dresden, was also working for the same British officers. In early 1950 Felfe left the British and went to work for the German ministry concerned with refugee affairs. He worked as an interrogator in refugee camps, looking for information on the Soviet forces, the Volkspolizei, and the East German state security service. Felfe was successful enough in his work for the ministry that he developed personal connections with several officials involved in political matters, most of whom were prepared to attest to his job performance. The odyssey of Heinz Felfe was about to take an interesting turn.

Hans Clemens persuaded Felfe, still an employee of the Ministry of All-German Affairs in Bonn, to accompany him on a visit to see Max in Karlshorst. During the visit the two were entertained lavishly, and Felfe agreed to go to work for Max and the KGB. Felfe was instructed to apply for employment in the Gehlen Organization.

How did the KGB recruit Felfe so easily? My view is that this generation of Germans, so thoroughly indoctrinated by the Nazi Party, the SS, the SD, and the Gestapo, were psychologically less capable of resisting recruitment. The destruction of national socialism had left them inherently more vulnerable. Hundreds of other former members of the SD and the Gestapo were more susceptible to serving foreign intelligence once the Third Reich had been defeated.

A recruited Felfe returned to his job in the ministry in Bonn while Clemens (with guidance from Max) considered how Felfe might be maneuvered into the Gehlen Organization. In October 1951 Felfe left the Ministry of All-German Affairs to join Bentzinger's GV L. Gehlen wrote in his book *Der Dienst* that Felfe was recommended for employment by the Minister of All-German Affairs and that Felfe's work with the British was known to Gehlen and had been viewed as a positive factor. The KGB now had at least two agents, Felfe and Clemens, working from within Alfred Bentzinger's counterintelligence outfit. The web had been woven.

In 1952 and 1953 Heinz Felfe was a KGB agent in place and reporting. Hans Clemens in nearby Stuttgart was part of Felfe's support structure. Felfe served within the GV L facility in Karlsruhe for almost two years but reportedly did not get along well with Bentzinger and several other senior members there. Felfe was described as pushy, ambitious, and inclined to pry into the work of everyone else. His superior, former Abwehr lieutenant colonel Oskar Reile, the top German counterintelligence officer in Paris during the war, found him bright and surprisingly well informed on a number of subjects of professional interest. Whenever possible Felfe sought to expand his association with Reile and his connections to the Gehlen headquarters in Pullach. During this period he regularly communicated with his KGB handler, having at that point been turned over by Max. Periodically he risked a visit to Berlin or elsewhere to have direct contact with his KGB case officer, whose aim above all else was to get Felfe into the central CI staff in Pullach and perhaps to actually have some contact with the mythical Reinhard Gehlen. He succeeded in late 1953 when Dr. Kohler, the head of the Pullach CI staff, took a personal initiative to request that Felfe be assigned there. Bentzinger and his entire organization were by then under attack within the Gehlen Organization as a result of the spy trials in East Germany. GV L had not distinguished itself in performing its counterintelligence mission. With Felfe's transfer from GV L to Pullach the KGB thus had better access to more sensitive information. By the end of 1953 Felfe was regularly observed to be inquisitive and prying into matters beyond his official duties. I learned many years later that the KGB avoided the risk of conducting direct meetings with Felfe for some months after his move to Pullach, relying solely on communications through Clemens.

At about this time Clemens quietly contacted British intelligence, reported a connection with the KGB in Karlshorst, and offered to develop a British double-agent operation out of it. The British declined to join the game and only many years later did a senior British intelligence officer in Germany tell an experienced CIA counterintelligence officer about this offer. The British, who had established a formal liaison with Gehlen in March 1953, never passed this information on to Gehlen or his CI staff. MI-6 was probably unaware in 1953 that either Clemens or Felfe had joined the Gehlen Organization.

CIC PENETRATION OF THE GERMAN
NATIONAL SECURITY SYSTEM

At some level an early decision was made for the U.S. Army counterintelligence group to penetrate the German national security system (an operation that probably originated and evolved in the 970th CIC). Although the date of approval and sponsorship is not well documented, by 1952 at the latest it was an active operation being run by Region III's 66th CIC, the successor to the 970th. No one in the CIA was made aware of this activity.

All or most of these CIC penetration operations were run out of Region III in

Offenbach and were supported by a small but competent team assigned to CIC headquarters. CIC officer Thomas Wesley Dale was the central figure in the activity, which was given the code name "Campus." Dale, his office, and his critically important files were all located in Offenbach, but the principal supporting structure for Operation Campus was located at CIC headquarters near Stuttgart—a three-hour trip via the autobahn.

Three CIC team principals—Dale, William Parkinson, and Daniel Benjamin— have been consistently identified as the hard core and "elite team" that conducted Campus and other comparable operations. All were civilian employees of the CIC. Parkinson and Benjamin regarded Dale as a brilliant intelligence officer and the recognized leading expert in CIC on international communism. The CIC's operations against the Gehlen Organization rested on almost a decade of unusual access and familiarity, particularly to Bentzinger's GV L. The Gehlen Organization at the time did not perceive the CIC as a potentially hostile service. But the official confidential relationship between the two was often confused.

Between 1950 and late 1955 when Campus was terminated, Region III produced a large number of reports on the Gehlen Organization, on the Friedrich Wilhelm Heinz operation in Amt Blank, and on other targets in the same category. In 1983 many of these reports were released under the Freedom of Information Act to Mary Ellen Reese, the American author of *General Reinhard Gehlen, The CIA Connection.* I have reviewed more than a hundred of these reports. In another search during the late 1980s I found none of these same reports in CIA or Pentagon records. Possibly none of the sensitive CIC reports from Germany ever reached the Pentagon or CIA. I have concluded that Region III had at least three sources reporting on the Gehlen Organization—at least two and possibly all three were in Bentzinger's GV L. All three were being contacted separately and on different dates.

One of those sources was Ludwig Albert, a former senior police official who worked for the GV L in Karlsruhe as a regional security representative in the Frankfurt area. A second likely CIC source was Bentzinger himself. The circumstances of Bentzinger's relationship with the CIC in the summer of 1946, also described in documents received under FOIA in 1983, suggest that he was a sensitive connection at that early date. Bentzinger had probably developed access to the central files in Pullach in the early 1950s. I once heard that when Gehlen asked to see the file on Bentzinger, it had simply disappeared.

Heinz Felfe was the subject of many CIC reports on the Gehlen Organization, although information on other SD members in his circle was often included in these reports. By the summer of 1954 Felfe clearly had emerged as the central figure in CIC reporting. CIC files also contained extensive data on the entire Bentzinger organization, including the staff in Karlsruhe, and the principal figures such as Bentzinger himself, Oskar Reile, Ludwig Albert, and Willi Krichbaum. Region III was aware of the entire ring of former SD officers led by Felfe in Karlsruhe.

Two CIC reports produced by Dale stood out as critical intelligence. Both were issued in 1954. One dated 24 June 1954 reported that the CIC's continuing investigation into information furnished by the communists concerning the Gehlen Organization had revealed that at least 70 percent of the information could have come only from the former SD group within the Gehlen Organization in which Felfe belonged. The second, dated 13 July 1954, reported that the investigation within the Gehlen Organization to locate and identify the source of the "treacherous act" of supplying information to the communists the previous year had concentrated suspicion on Heinz Felfe and his SD cohort in Stuttgart, Karl Schuetz.

The 13 July report is the only evidence I have found of Gehlen's interest at that time in Felfe as a possible communist agent. Only after I became aware of the CIC reports did I learn that Gehlen did investigate Felfe as early as 1954, but his investigation did not produce any supporting evidence. Gehlen's suspicions of Felfe and Schuetz may have simply been feedback from the Dale CIC team to Ludwig Albert and Alfred Bentzinger. The situation in the mid-1950s created the potential for information to move in any part of a closed circle touching Gehlen, Dale's CIC team, or the major CIC agents in Gehlen's CI organization, that is, Albert and Bentzinger. Also in this same circle were the KGB control in Berlin and the KGB agents Felfe and Clemens in the Gehlen Organization. It was a circle within circles. At the time no mention of suspecting Felfe was made to me or to any of my staff. (Most of the critical information here remained concealed in American, Soviet, and German files until thirty or more years later.)

During those days Gehlen used a variety of trusted individuals to investigate vexing security problems. I know, for example, that at one point he instructed his special assistant, Walter Lobedanz, to make an independent examination of Bentzinger's background. At the same time Conrad Kuehlein, by then serving in the important post of chief of operations, was given some responsibility related to security.

After the onset of the propaganda attacks in early 1953, Armin Eck of the CI staff was put in charge of a small group to work with Ed Petty of my staff on the specific subject of operational security cases. Eck, a former General Staff Corps major, had come into the Gehlen Organization after its move to Pullach. Eck was entirely free of any GV L background. The special relationship between Petty and Eck was reaffirmed and made more explicit starting in 1957 when Gehlen received

Ed Petty's analysis of Gehlen's mole problem. Finally, there was the uniquely close position held by Wolfgang Langkau, who appeared in Pullach in about 1950 and was identified as a comrade from Gehlen's first regimental assignment. Langkau became a senior special staff officer handling sensitive matters of special interest to Gehlen. Thus an established pattern existed within the organization of placing great reliance on selected individuals to look into security and other sensitive matters regardless of formal position. I would have expected that any suspicion of Felfe in 1954 would have been handled in this way.

In recent years I have learned something additional about Gehlen's relations with Felfe. After 1956, when all Gehlen Organization employees went through a screening process for civil service status, Felfe had come into focus because of his SD background. Gehlen had removed the Felfe case from the list under review by a Bonn screening team and later negotiated separately to have Felfe made an exception. Gehlen was so impressed by Felfe's knowledge and value that he was blind-sided on the security questions surrounding Felfe. These were simply unwise and unnecessary risks.

Gehlen, in the English version of his book *The Service,* noted that he and Globke had recognized, when they faced up to their initial suspicions of Felfe, that a major spy scandal would be very damaging to the organization. They wished to pursue it quietly if at all possible. But it soon became entirely clear to Globke and Gehlen that Felfe's arrest and trial and publicity about the case were unavoidable. At that point the question of what Gehlen had known about Felfe and when he had known it would become of interest to the court and of even greater interest to the media and to the political opposition. Until the end Gehlen maintained that he had not known of Felfe's Nazi Party or SD background. What Gehlen did not know in 1961 when Felfe was arrested was the existence of the 13 July 1954 CIC report in the archives at Fort Holabird concerning his own investigation of Felfe and Schuetz.

We never knew at the time about Operation Campus. The operation was never coordinated with the CIA in Germany or Washington, and was never discussed or approved by the intelligence community. A significant number of counterintelligence officers with either CIC or OSS experience served on my CIA staff in Pullach. But these officers had almost no contact with the 66th CIC in Germany. Neither the CIA nor the Army G-2 in Heidelberg appeared to recognize or address the schism that existed between the CIA and the CIC. Information on Campus first became public in 1990, long after Gehlen's book appeared and years after Gehlen's death, when Mary Ellen Reese described the operation in her biography of Gehlen. While the specific reports from Campus were tightly held within the CIC, the need to penetrate the Gehlen Organization did, I believe, contribute to the 1954 decision of the Army G-2 staff in Washington to initiate an effort to persuade Adenauer and his senior advisors to drop Gehlen and to shift Bonn's policy to building a German intelligence service within a revived defense establishment.

THE PROPAGANDA WAR OF 1953 AND 1954

By late 1952 the KGB had made a decision to conduct an extended propaganda attack calculated to damage the reputation and credibility of the Gehlen Organization and, if possible, to destroy it before it could be legally established as the national intelligence service of Adenauer's West Germany. The KGB planned and orchestrated a campaign to create an image of the Gehlen Organization as a loosely run, badly penetrated, and very large spying operation in East Germany and a sinister presence in West Germany. The campaign would demonstrate to the East German public the ability of the East German police and security agencies to detect and arrest Gehlen agents. The KGB planned to use spy trials as propaganda platforms to demoralize Gehlen's agents in East Germany and his employees in West Germany.

On 13 February 1953 Alfred Bentzinger's operating base in Karlsruhe reported that Wolfgang Hoeher, head of the GV L's two-man office in West Berlin, had been drugged and kidnapped while having dinner at a restaurant near the border that separated West Berlin from the Soviet sector. Gehlen's CI officer Armin Eck and my CI specialist Ed Petty investigated the incident and concluded that Hoeher had been an agent of the East German Ministry for State Security (MfS) for some time and had undoubtedly identified a number of Gehlen agents to the MfS. He likely had reported at great length on the Gehlen Organization, particularly its counterintelligence operations. Hoeher's withdrawal, staged as a kidnapping, almost certainly related to Soviet and East German plans to launch a propaganda war against Gehlen. Hoeher was needed as a "captured" member of Gehlen's Organization to play out the role the KGB had planned for him—an informed agent in the enemy's own CI organization who, under interrogation, would tell quite a story. Although we assumed the KGB was in charge of East German intelligence operations of any consequence, it was apparent that the Soviets wished to give the attack on the Gehlen Organization a German character by attributing the propaganda operation to the MfS. By October 1953 the outpouring of propaganda on the Gehlen Organization made it entirely clear to us that its purpose was to discredit this large German intelligence effort that was being supported by the CIA.

During this same period a Gehlen staff member in Berlin named Hans Joachim

Geyer heard that he was under investigation by the West Berlin police. Geyer in fact had been an MfS penetration agent for some time. Assuming the investigation related to his intelligence work, Geyer fled to East Berlin. As it turned out, police interest in him had nothing to do with intelligence operations. Geyer's flight to East Berlin was followed by an immediate increase of arrests of Gehlen agents in East Germany. The MfS decided to turn the loss of Geyer into a more significant asset in the propaganda war. On 29 October Geyer appeared at a press conference as a "defector from the Gehlen Organization," who in his initial appearance seemed to have impressive information, considerably more than anyone would have expected.

On 13 November 1953 a "Gehlen agent" named Werner Haase was arrested while laying a communication cable across a canal that formed part of the East-West boundary in Berlin; an MfS agent in the Gehlen Organization in West Germany had apparently compromised the operation. A few weeks later a major press conference was held in East Berlin at which the MfS again displayed Geyer and Wolfgang Hoeher—this time joined by Werner Haase.

On 21 December 1953 Werner Haase was arraigned at a show trial that continued into early 1954. At the peak of this trial the communist regime of Walter Ulbricht sent a much-publicized letter to the Soviet authorities, requesting that they take action to protect East Germany from the hostile activities of the Gehlen Organization. Haase, on the basis of his own "confession" which had revealed him as an important and knowledgeable agent of Gehlen, was convicted and sentenced to life imprisonment.

A certain Colonel Bormann, introduced as an official of the East German counterespionage service, had finally exposed Wolfgang Hoeher, who was still presented as a "captured agent." Hoeher's surfacing was accompanied by the release of a report based on Hoeher's "months of interrogation." The MfS attributed an impressive amount of information to Hoeher, which was explained by his experience as a member of Gehlen's counterintelligence organization. Wolfgang Hoeher and Hans Joachim Geyer were presented as extremely valuable sources of information on the Gehlen Organization, including personnel, operations, and communications. To the public it appeared that the MfS had simply learned a great deal from the arrests, reports, confessions, and interrogations of Gehlen agents that were in the hands of the MfS. At the conclusion of this particular media blitz MfS chief Ernst Wollweber seriously offered a reward of one million marks for the assassination of Reinhard Gehlen.

In November 1953 Gehlen took the long overdue action of shaking up Bentzinger's field organization and announced its "reorganization." What the reorganization entailed was not entirely clear to us, though we had heard in some quarters there was support for its total liquidation. The propaganda operation in East Germany, including arrests of alleged agents, media press conferences, and staged show trials, was expanding and causing consternation in the entire Gehlen Organization. Some discussion took place in Pullach as to the degree of responsibility that could be charged to the GV L for the security flaws that were being exposed. Gehlen and his staff were forced to help the rank-and-file employees understand what was factual and what was not. Enlightening Bonn on the same issues was obviously of critical importance. The continuing "exposé" in East Germany of these allegations aroused apprehension within the organization that the course of events might not merely delay but actually endanger Adenauer's promise to create an intelligence service in the appropriate circumstances.

In December 1953 Gehlen began to give more personal attention to the growing security problems. Cooperation tightened between my CI staff and some individuals in a harried Gehlen CI staff headed by Kurt Kohler. Although we were not informed of the details of the GV L reorganization, we noted that an officer who went by the cover name of Friesen was brought into Gehlen headquarters from GV L. Not until some time later did we learn that Friesen's true name was Heinz Felfe.

The attack on the Gehlen Organization in 1953 was the first major communist propaganda effort to expose the Western intelligence network. Over a period of eighteen months the Soviets, through a variety of scenarios, pulled agents out of Gehlen's field organization in East and West Germany, including divided Berlin, to put them on display in media events or as defendants or witnesses (sometimes both) in show trials. The KGB and the East Germans obviously calculated that the cost of expending some of their own agents in order to round up and bring to trial known or suspected Gehlen agents, was worth the exposure of counterintelligence assets in West Germany. The pattern of "arrests of Gehlen agents" in East Germany continued on into 1954. The East Germans, with obvious Soviet support and guidance, brought their propaganda campaign to a peak in early 1954.

By late 1953, it was apparent to us that the Soviet propaganda effort, although demoralizing within the Gehlen Organization, was not achieving its intended purpose of disrupting the process of legalizing the Gehlen Organization and blocking the creation of an official German intelligence service. The West Germans had become partially inured to the rhetoric and propaganda of the cold war. The 17 June 1953 uprising in East Germany by a large part of the German population was obviously an unanticipated embarrassment for the communist regime and the Soviets; conversely, it helped Gehlen. Many interested political leaders in West Germany accepted Gehlen's interpretation of events, that the scope and character of the Soviet attack against him was a reliable indicator of the importance the Soviets attached to his intelligence contributions. Whatever his personal concerns, Adenauer remained firm and unwavering in his commitment to the Gehlen Organization. In July 1954 Adenauer's cabinet voted unanimously for the inclusion of the Gehlen Organization (without actually referring to a timetable). Gehlen's rapport within the government appeared able to withstand the Soviet propaganda attack; indeed, his popularity seemed to be growing. Many years later a retired general of the KGB, who had been active in German operations in the 1950s, told me that the Ulbricht regime had "overplayed its hand" in the propaganda effort and had, in fact, provoked increased support for Gehlen in Bonn.

REPERCUSSIONS OF THE INTELLIGENCE WAR

Gehlen was caught in the crossfire of a silent and invisible counterintelligence war been waged within his own CI organization between the KGB and the American CIC. In February 1954 a KGB defector from Vienna named Peter Deriabin had told the CIA that the KGB had two agents in the Gehlen Organization known as "Peter and Paul," but he could offer no additional details. The CIA had not yet identified Felfe as a security suspect and the Army's CIC was not sharing any of its information on the Gehlen Organization with the CIA, including the conclusion that Felfe was probably the principal communist agent in Pullach. If Dale, Parkinson, and Benjamin had sat down with my CI officers at any time during the summer of 1954 and openly and cooperatively analyzed the entire situation in Gehlen's counterintelligence organization, the history of both U.S. and German intelligence efforts in those years would have been significantly changed. Felfe would have been exposed and the entire CI organization in Karlsruhe probably would have been eliminated. At a minimum all of the former SD officers, including Felfe and Clemens, would have been dismissed and prosecuted.

I think Gehlen could have survived a crisis of this magnitude. A USFET intelligence project had created the Karlsruhe operation of Alfred Bentzinger and had not permitted the CIC to become involved. The CIC had been permitted to pursue an adversarial policy from the day the CIA took over the Gehlen Organization. Gehlen's record in the matter was not defensible, but in my opinion a lion's share of the responsibility for the whole CI fiasco in Germany must be given to the Americans. The CIA's share of the blame is mainly a matter of neglect. The CIA never addressed the issue of the overall counterintelligence protection of the Gehlen Organization. James Angleton was the principal counterintelligence staff officer in CIA, but not until 1954 did the agency formally establish the CI staff with Angleton as its chief. Angleton never displayed any interest in or responsibility for counterintelligence in Pullach. I found the CIA leadership weak and passive in dealing with the U.S. military on security matters. Thus, while Gehlen's record on counterintelligence was deplorable, it was largely at a cost to his own organization and reputation. It was a major intelligence failure. Gehlen's secrecy and lack of candor in dealing with the CIA on security matters had created the situation. Nevertheless, while Gehlen can fairly be charged for his own failures, a major part of the blame must also go to the deplorable lack of coordination and cooperation within the U.S. intelligence community.

Anyone familiar with a reasonably accurate version of wartime and occupation history knows that the United States left major gaps in its denazification and war crimes policies. In the U.S. Zone very large numbers of former SD officials were acquitted or never brought to trial by German denazification courts. As denazification ran out in 1949, Gehlen was probably aware of the pragmatic positions taken by the widely popular German courts. A quiet process of rehabilitation of many "denazified" members of the SD took place in the 1950s, many of whom were, like Felfe, well-trained professional police. The trend received little attention and publicity and was to some degree accepted by the Western nations in the chaotic environment of the cold war. Most former SD officers were able to gain employment in positions in law enforcement or security in the states or municipal governments, somewhat out of the public view. These people were not considered war criminals. The SD influence within the Gehlen Organization had been limited by the large number of younger generation Army General Staff officers who from the beginning occupied most key positions. After 1952, when Gehlen engaged in detailed planning with the chancellery for legalization, we in the CIA left it up to Gehlen and the chancellery to examine the political background of its employees. In addition, the practice of using "consultants" on the fringe of the organization was established at Oberursel and had continued at Pullach. In the end the transfer of Gehlen's employees into the civil service or the Bundeswehr was a matter left to the chancellery and the defense ministry under the active oversight of the Bundestag, which left the SD issue, if there was one, to the federal republic.

Except for Clemens and Felfe, other former SD officers brought into GV L proved to be inconsequential and appeared to have come and gone from the rolls of the late Gehlen Organization and the early BND without doing any discernible damage. But Felfe, supported by Clemens, served the KGB for a full decade, inflicting immense damage to the evolving BND, to the security of its government, and to the personal reputation of Reinhard Gehlen.

14

Germany's Acceptance in the West

ONE OF President Eisenhower's first post-inauguration acts was to send Secretary of State John Foster Dulles to Europe on 20 January 1953 to put pressure on the Europeans to complete the ratification of the European Defense Community (EDC) Treaty. France was having difficulty getting a parliamentary majority willing to give the Germans any degree of equality in a defense force. Then Joseph Stalin's death in March caused a wave of expectation and hope among the noncommunist world that the face of communism would become kindlier without the reviled leader. Politicians in Western Europe briefly demonstrated hope that Stalin's death would revive cooperation among the four Allies of World War II in settling the German question.

By the summer of 1953 the French concept embodied in the EDC Treaty got bogged down in the Paris negotiations and a prolonged ratification process. The French were agonizingly ambivalent and obviously dragging out the negotiations that Washington still expected to lead to French ratification. Adenauer had become reconciled to going all the way with the French. That old war-horse Winston Churchill reappeared on the scene and observed that his friend Dwight Eisenhower was determined to go to the end with the French. Churchill, who described the whole idea of the EDC as a "sludgy amalgam," went about devising a rescue operation following the EDC's inevitable collapse. In July Churchill and Anthony Eden visited Washington to discuss alternatives. Eisenhower replied that the United States was staying with the EDC. Churchill believed Pierre Mendes-France would never be able to bring to life the whole idea of a united Europe within the context of a European Defense Community, and was charting an alternative course. Simultaneously the CIA took the initiative to connect the British secret service, MI-6, with the Gehlen Organization in a direct and continuing liaison relationship. All of Gehlen's problems with the British—real or imagined—disappeared overnight. Concurrently, British support of Gehlen was positive and consistent. The dramatic shift of the British to Adenauer's firm adherence to the NATO solution was taking place behind the scenes as well.

On 19 August 1954 at a meeting preliminary to a formal conference among Brussels Pact countries, Mendes-France announced his intent to propose sweeping amendments and delays in implementing the EDC treaty. The Brussels Pact nations rejected his proposal and on 30 August the French parliament, by a vote of 319 to 264, rejected ratification. Eisenhower was likely somewhat surprised, knowing that France and Italy were both in serious political trouble. He, Foster Dulles, and the State Department had thrown enormous support to the treaty and were confident it would be ratified. Eisenhower referred to the Mendes-France performance at Brussels as "an act of mayhem."

Within West Germany the collapse of the EDC produced criticism of Adenauer for having lost at least three years in pursuing Pleven's European defense initiative. The charge was not justified. Adenauer, at McCloy's insistence, had merely gone along with U.S. support of the French plan for the defense of Europe after the United States had failed to support the NATO solution in January 1951 at Petersberg.

After the collapse of the EDC Churchill immediately stepped in. On 28 September 1954 the British hosted a Nine-Power Conference in London—which included representatives from the Brussels Pact group as well as the United States, Canada, Italy, and the Federal Republic of Germany. The British proposed expanding the Brussels Pact, adding Italy and Germany, to form the Western European Union (WEU). The Big Three would negotiate to grant sovereignty to Germany, end the Occupation, and take Germany into NATO. The solution would permit a WEU sufficiently connected to NATO to preserve much of what had been agreed to in the lengthy EDC negotiations. Linking the WEU with NATO was a significant step toward the creation of a united Europe and the defense of the Atlantic community. The negotiations took place in Paris and two German delegates, Hans Speidel and Gerhard Wessel, actively assisted in identifying the elements of the EDC treaty that would be taken over by the WEU and carried into its new relationship with NATO. Both Amt Blank and the Foreign Office carried their treaty negotiation experience into the agreements and treaties signed in Paris, referring to them as the *lenkung*, or linking negotiations between the London Nine Power Conference and the talks in Paris. Ironically, it was the French by failing to ratify the EDC Treaty and by joining in the Paris negotiations that finally ensured the formation of a genuine German armed force with full-sized and heavily armored divisions commanded by German generals. Not much of the French and British policies of 1949 and early 1950 had survived.

After five days of meetings representatives to the conference signed more than twenty-four treaties, protocols, communiqués, and special agreements, all described as the "Paris Treaties." The numerous treaties created an expanded WEU and brought West Germany into NATO. They ended the Occupation and produced an agreement on the Saar. They brought all WEU troops under NATO command, and Germany accepted the imposed limitations on chemical, biological, and nuclear weapons. Berlin would keep its four-power status.

The British salvaged a great deal from the failed EDC by their initiative in the London Conference, but in breaking with the British position on non-involvement in the European defense effort, they contributed to the positive atmosphere in Paris by undertaking a commitment to maintain a long-term British military presence of four divisions with tactical air support on the continent for as long as the Western European Union remained in favor of the British presence. The French, still contesting genuine equality for the Germans, fought the process of linking the failed EDC to the NATO solution, but they were unable to slow down the rush of events that had led to the signing of the Paris Treaties. In the end, after fighting every inch of the way, the French accepted the results.

THE GEHLEN ORGANIZATION AWAITS LEGALIZATION

Meanwhile, in Pullach the CIA's contingency planning for the transfer of the Gehlen Organization to the Bonn government had been completed and was only awaiting the word from Adenauer. A certain kind of stability had been achieved in the size and character of the Gehlen Organization. The CIA staff had leveled off at fewer than twenty-five. The operation of the compound, its administrative services, and its security and protection had been transferred to Horst Wendland's staff using a system of "opposite numbers" (Germans and Americans) working together.

By this time most of the married German staff members had taken advantage of a CIA program that provided interest-free housing loans to resettle outside of the compound. At our encouragement Gehlen found a modest Bavarian-style wooden house in the village of Berg on Lake Starnberg, for which he borrowed DM48,000 or about twelve thousand dollars. He allocated a significant part of his monthly salary to repayment. Most of these loans, including Gehlen's, were repaid prior to the founding of the BND. After he retired Gehlen built a small prefab dwelling just behind his home, and turned over the home to his son Christoph and family. He and Herta lived in the prefab until his death.

Gehlen had fervently hoped for the establishment and legalization of a federal intelligence service on 1 April 1953 and again on 1 April 1954. Both dates passed with no decision from Bonn. In both Adenauer's and certainly McCloy's minds, such a service was linked to the broader issues of German sovereignty and the role of German armed forces in the defense of Western Europe. Obtaining permission from the Allied High Commission to create the BfV had been both a hassle and not a great success. In July 1954 the BfV's chief, Dr. Otto John, had defected to East Berlin and eventually to Moscow. Adenauer clearly saw the advantage in simply waiting to establish a federal intelligence service without the involvement of the three high commissioners, and Gehlen most likely accepted this unstated plan too.

The show trials in East Berlin had drawn heavily on sensitive data on the Gehlen Organization that could not be attributed to the KGB and SSD sources identified in the trials. Adenauer likely knew the concerns regarding a mole in Pullach. A solid consensus that the KGB had one or more agents in Pullach arose among the analysts in Pullach and quite separately in Tom Dale's CIC team.

On the surface it appeared late in 1954 that Gehlen's sidetracked train was likely to be given the signal to proceed and arrive at its end station in Bonn without further problems or delays. The optimistic picture was of course not the whole story. In reality Gehlen was sitting on two ticking time bombs—the undetected CIC and KGB penetrations, and a determined but surreptitious effort to discredit him by the intelligence unit of the U.S. Army.

Within the CIA it was generally assumed that a German intelligence service would simply fall into place. Horst von Mellenthin was selected to travel to Washington to lay the foundation for formal liaison relations that undoubtedly would be established after the creation of the German intelligence service. Von Mellenthin's prewar position as head of the military attaché system in the Army General Staff proved to be useful background to the Germans' first venture into the diplomatic community in the Washington. Gehlen intended his representative to be the central figure of the federal republic's liaison with the U.S. intelligence community, and initially in contact with CIA, with the Department of Defense intelligence and security agencies, and with the Federal Bureau of Investigation.

It had not occurred to Gehlen that the U.S. Army, which had sponsored him so decisively in 1945, would turn against him once his legal status in Bonn loomed. But a conspiracy to destroy his organization was afoot. During the first week in November 1954 the Army G-2 invited retired colonel Truman Smith to the Pentagon to discuss pressing problems regarding the rush of events in Germany. A week later, on 14 November, Smith sent a long letter to Hans Speidel, informing Speidel of his meeting in the Pentagon. The Pentagon was interested in who would be named the top officers in the new German Army and other matters related to German intelligence.

Smith was looking for confirmation information he had heard from reliable German sources that Gen. Ludwig Cruewell of the Afrika Corps would be named the top commander of German armed forces; Heusinger was to be a kind of chief of staff and Speidel would be concerned with NATO and foreign military relations. On the subject of intelligence Smith wrote to Speidel:

There is a matter which currently causes Washington concern, namely, the relationship between the numerous intelligence organizations which currently coexist in Germany. One can only characterize the present situation as chaotic. Unless one deals with it, this situation can bring unpleasant consequences. The Otto John case indicates the dangers we can be confronted with. In my view, this can occur again. Whether the Gehlen organization has also been penetrated, I cannot judge. I have the impression that this is completely possible. . . . I am nevertheless convinced that once Germany's sovereignty is restored in the larger context, neither Chancellor Adenauer nor a successor will allow these countless intelligence organizations—like the Gehlen Organization, for example, to continue to exist. On the other hand, NATO forces will require a strong military intelligence agency on German soil. In my opinion, the problem could be solved by placing the intelligence services within the military. In this way, they can be most effectively coordinated. If the German Army conducts intelligence, along with the American, British, and French armies, the intelligence activities can be coordinated and important information can be shared. This cannot take place if a dozen civilian intelligence networks are independently controlled and directed by a half-dozen regional authorities outside military control. We do not want to forget that foremost, the intelligence function belongs with the Defense Ministry. If not, then it has no significant value. . . . I believe that the relationship between our G-2 and the comparable organization is of utmost importance. It will primarily depend on the personal relationship between the respective leaders of the two organizations whether this relationship is warm or cool, and based on cooperation or rivalry. In my view, both leaders should be honorable and noble-minded soldiers from the old school, who are convinced of the inherent justice of the West's position. They should also recognize that cooperation in the area of intelligence between our countries is only slightly less important than comradeship on the battlefield. I can imagine that Washington would want to assign someone with the qualities and expertise of someone like Col. Richardson, whom you know from the negotiations in Paris, to G-2 in Germany. It occurs to me that it may not be easy for Bonn to find the right man for that post. Even though the post requires a military man with diplomatic abilities, and there are a number of officers with this combined background in the German Army. Nevertheless, I am very interested in this choice; as are my friends. For this reason, I lay this matter before you for your urgent consideration. In the event you can disclose the name of this individual to me through protected channels, I will handle it in confidence. This would make the choice for the position of G-2 in Europe, as well as of military attaché in Bonn, much easier. We wish to assign honorable and capable military men to these posts, and not men who are merely intelligence specialists.

In closing Smith requested Speidel burn the letter after reading it.

Speidel obviously did not burn the letter. He discussed it with Heusinger, who in turn informed Gehlen. Speidel answered Smith's letter in two installments, an initial reply letter dated 30 November and a second from Paris on 14 December. Both Heusinger and Gehlen were informed of the entire exchange. In his response Speidel rejected the Smith's proposals point by point. These are excerpts of the 14 December letter relating specifically to Gehlen:

In recent years, the Gehlen Organization has achieved preeminent status among these organizations as a result of the integrity of its leadership and its achievement. The Gehlen Organization has been operating for several years with the approval and support of the United States. With the emergence of the Federal Republic, the Federal government has directed the organization's activities without changing the close relationship to American authorities. As a result of this cooperation there developed a connection between the Gehlen Organization and the Amt Blank office. The Gehlen Organization's achievements in the areas of military, political-military, and defense policy came to my attention, along with that of other organizations this way. Hence my assessment: For some years, the Gehlen organization has provided a near complete picture of the Soviet-occupied zone, as well as extensive documents pertaining to Soviet satellite states, and of the Soviet Union itself—which provides essential information for future military leaders. . . . Your proposal to create a military intelligence service is in my view already achieved through the cooperation of the Gehlen organization and Amt Blank. . . . Regarding Gehlen himself: I have known Gehlen since prior to the war as a particularly capable and noble-charactered General Staff officer of the best type. He is no one-sided intelligence functionary; rather he emerged from the leadership ranks of the General Staff (until 1942 he was General Staff Officer in the operations division under Heusinger and did not become involved with intelligence matters until the middle of 1942 when he assumed command of the Foreign Army East). The same applies for Gehlen's military inner circle, who in the age range of 40-45, are far from being one-sided intelligence types, but are general staff officers with the requisite "all round" training. Among others, General Heusinger for over two and a half years led the Evaluation Staff under Gehlen.... Your suggestion, to fill the ranks of the military intelligence service or G-2 with "honorable and capable soldiers, not merely intelligence specialists" has already been achieved.... You are concerned that the Gehlen Organization could be penetrated by the East. I believe that every organization of this kind which finds itself in a perpetual "state of war" faces the possibility of infiltration. It solely depends on institutionalizing security measures which can identify any and all attempts to infiltrate it early on and to paralyze them. It appears to me that these precautions have been taken by the Gehlen Organization.... It is not surprising that the Gehlen Organization has some critics in the United States along with numerous genuine friends and supporters—the organization credits its existence to the courage of certain American officers—it also has critics in Germany. It has become apparent over time that various internal or external powers want to discredit the organization—either out of envy, ambition, or in terms of Eastern infiltration. In the view of most governing bodies in the Federal Republic, the Gehlen Organization is the sole organization which could effectively assume the role of an intelligence service in the Federal Republic. The unrelenting effort to discredit the organization from the East appears to me to be the best testament regarding the value of this service for West Germany, as well as for the West.... In order for you to gain a deeper insight into the Gehlen Organization, I would propose that you meet with Gehlen personally during your next trip to Europe. I am convinced that any remaining doubts will be dispelled at that time.

The G-2 initiative so explicit in character and attributed by Truman Smith to the Pentagon had clearly failed. Smith's mission had achieved nothing beyond damaging his reputation in the small circle that learned of his initiative; his letter was an embarrassment to Gehlen but Speidel and Heusinger remained entirely supportive. The episode did not actually damage Gehlen's position, but it was one that Gehlen would not forget. The U.S. Army was out to destroy him.

15

The Year 1955

1955 HAD been a very good year for Konrad Adenauer. Germany was on the road to becoming a genuine democracy. The Marshall Plan had energized the German people and German industry in an economic recovery that was felt throughout Western Europe.

Adenauer's firm commitment to a policy for the defense of Germany and Western Europe within a NATO military alliance had been vindicated. The Paris Treaties had set the stage for an end to the Occupation and Germany's membership in NATO. Theodor Blank and his defense advisors had gone the distance with the French in assessing a concept for the defense of Western Europe. Earlier, under pressure from McCloy and Eisenhower in the summer of 1951, Adenauer had agreed to give the French a chance to persuade the rest of Western Europe that a defense alliance independent of NATO was possible. The French had failed to do so. EDC negotiations that continued until August 1954 had succeeded in narrowing the differences of the negotiators, and brought the French closer to accepting the German insistence on the principle of equality. France remained important in the eyes of Konrad Adenauer. To some extent the French-German rapprochement had been preserved. The French had reluctantly accepted the consequences of the Paris Treaties, but the French connection to NATO remained fragile. The Western European Union was created as a vehicle to preserve much of what had been achieved in the EDC negotiations.

The fifth day of May 1955, the official date of the proclamation of sovereignty of the Federal Republic of Germany, marked the definitive transition of Germany from U.S. enemy to U.S. ally, and ally of all other NATO nations as well. To Adenauer this acceptance was the consummation of his personal commitment to the concept of an Atlantic alliance.

Adenauer turned his attention to the business of transforming the federal republic into a sovereign nation with full responsibilities as a member in a great Western alliance. Until 1955 Adenauer had acted as his own foreign minister and had used his small staff of civil servants and former officers in Amt Blank to make the necessary arrangements related to negotiations in Paris. After 5 May 1955 he created a foreign ministry, headed by Heinrich von Brentano, and a defense ministry, headed by Blank. Herbert Blankenhorn, who in 1950 had been Adenauer's aide handling political relations with both the Allied High Commission and Bonn's limited foreign affairs, was named ambassador to NATO and the WEU. Hans Speidel was appointed senior military advisor and accredited to NATO and the WEU. In this capacity Speidel would supervise the activities of Graf von Kielmansegg, who headed the Bonn military delegation to SHAPE and the Central European Command of NATO. An advisory group on foreign policy and national security affairs had in autumn 1955 already developed around the chancellor; it looked very much like the National Security Council in Washington, D.C.

The government was going through reorganization in virtually every ministry and department as a result of the end of a decade of occupation. West Germany's diplomatic and trade relations were expanding in all directions. Remilitarizing a nation that had been fully demilitarized, however, was proving to be more complicated. The process was not scheduled to begin until 1 January 1956, but rumor had it that plans were under way in the defense ministry to recall large numbers of former officers to active careers. Change was in the air.

Adolf Heusinger was particularly sensitive to the problem of creating a place for the soldier and the army in the new German democratic society. Some former officers who had served with Heusinger in the war were criticizing him for being too sensitive to public opinion. Graf Baudissin, a young and almost unknown officer who at the last minute had become part of the secret meeting at Himmerod in 1950, was a member of Heusinger's team. Baudissin made a unique contribution to the character of the new armed forces and its interface with the German democratic society. He strongly believed that adequate attention should be given to the political problems and psychological factors surrounding the development of the new citizen soldier in German society. That Heusinger, the liberal-minded Speidel, and

Baudissin were involved in the early days of the new German Army was a fortunate historical coincidence. In all things military and in the sensitive interface with the German public and the Bundestag, Heusinger emerged as the forceful moderator. He was the defender of what he and his associates had identified as the indispensable traditional values and principles on which new German forces must be built. His opponents considered him slow in directing the rearming and were pushing for putting more energy into "real military planning." Heusinger's approach won out.

In May 1955 Dr. Globke, supported by Blank, Heusinger, and Speidel, met with Adenauer to discuss a feasible time frame within which to create and train a German force assigned to NATO command. After extensive debate in the Bundestag the chancellor accepted Blank's statement that forty-two to forty-eight months would be needed to produce the first contingents. The Bundestag provided the needed budgetary support and the start date was set for 1 January 1956.

The primary influence in the Amt Blank military planning staff continued to be the small group of younger former officers with training and wartime experience in the Army General Staff. Former air force and navy officers with comparable backgrounds were added to the staff. The group was a carefully selected and highly motivated crew that set the style and provided the professional substance for the work. The staff's productivity was enhanced by its extensive use of consultants among the ranks of experienced former officers and military specialists. To a degree it was a continuation of the system of networks and "Special Connections" that Heusinger had used so effectively in the many months of effort that led to the writing of the "Sommer Denkschrift" as well as the report produced at Himmerod. This group, under the direction of Heusinger and Speidel, set the high standards of performance and provided the continuity that stretched from Himmerod through the early years of the Bundeswehr—the name selected for the new armed forces.

In late 1955 Heusinger was given a new title: Militaerischer Fuehrungsrat (Military Advisor), the first step toward the emerging command and staff structure of the future armed forces. Speidel, although assigned to NATO, was appointed head of Abt IV Armed Forces, Helmuth Laegeler became head of Abt V Army, Werner Panitzki became head of Abt VI Air Force, and Kurt Zenker became head of Abt VII Navy. Heusinger led the entire military planning structure and reported to the defense minister. On the new organizational chart all military staffs remained officially part of the defense ministry but a separate dotted line ran from Heusinger to each senior member of the military staff.

Gerhard Wessel returned to Germany from his three years in Paris to organize military intelligence within the German defense ministry, G-2 Dienst, which included the military counterintelligence group Abwehr Dienst. Wessel's assignment gave Gehlen confidence concerning the key question of cooperation between the civilian service that reported to the chancellor and military intelligence that reported to the defense minister. Of one thing Gehlen was certain: cooperation between his organization and G-2 Dienst would be better than that between the CIA and the U.S. Army G-2 in Germany. Later in 1955 Gehlen attributed the U.S. Army G-2 attacks on his organization to the "deep rivalry" between the CIA and the G-2.

In a modest military ceremony held in Bonn on 12 November 1955, Adolf Heusinger and Hans Speidel were appointed as lieutenant generals—the ranks they held at the end of the war—in the new German Army. One hundred enlisted volunteers went on active duty, only a few of them wearing the new uniform of the still unnamed armed forces. It was a token gesture as a sign of progress. Appropriately, the ceremony was scheduled on the two-hundredth birthday of General Scharnhorst, born on 12 November 1755, who had led a major reform in the Prussian Army at the beginning of the nineteenth century. I have found no account of the rationale for limiting the initial selection of enlistees to such a small number. No doubt Adenauer and Blank were under intense pressure to show some visible sign of progress in forming the new armed forces. The appearance of these two generals in uniform was obviously noted in Germany and at SHAPE.

Heusinger, Speidel, and the small group of former officers working in Amt Blank represented the minimum military cadre that brought the experience and ability to preserve essential military standards in planning and building the new armed forces. The Gehlen Organization had provided Heusinger an ideal functioning support base and a secure and politically protected environment from which to prepare a remilitarization package. In the years leading up to 1955 Gehlen had taken in quite a number of younger General Staff officers who had temporarily joined the Gehlen Organization with the intent to resume their military careers. Heusinger and Speidel knew many experienced officers in the organization were not intelligence staff officers but who nevertheless intended, if the opportunity presented itself, to resume military careers. In fact, Amt Blank had in 1953 prepared a list of 119 former General Staff officers under age fifty-five who had been employed in some capacity by the organization and who were thought to be interested in returning to active military duty.

All of the military officers employed by the Gehlen Organization, including Heusinger, had been provided with a cover story and supporting documents during their years in Pullach. Most had made some use of these cover stories with friends and relatives outside their working world. The official Bundeswehr record, for example, shows that Gen. Adolf Heusinger was a writer during the years 1948 to 1951, and no mention is made about his position in the Gehlen Organization. Many former members of the Gehlen Organization who became top-level officers in the Bundeswehr provided only their cover occupations when submitting their biographic data about those years. Considering the circumstances in Germany and the atmosphere of the cold war, it was an understandable and practical move. More than fifty years after the fact the major role that Heusinger played in the Gehlen Organization and Gehlen's major contributions to the development of the German national security system, including the Bundeswehr, needs to be told accurately and fully. Heusinger saw in the Gehlen Organization a well-formed intelligence service that would fit well into the national defense establishment that Speidel, Foertsch, and he envisioned. Gehlen did not see a role for himself in Germany's remilitarization, but fully supported their concept of a defense establishment.

On 11 May 1955, in response to the newly created NATO, the Soviets hastily assembled in Warsaw the communist nations of the Soviet Bloc; on 14 May they signed a treaty creating the Warsaw Pact. Adenauer and his intelligence and military advisors concluded that the Soviets had promptly formed the alliance as an act of resignation and acceptance that their ambitions in Western Europe had been unrealistic. Our view in Pullach was that the situation in Europe appeared more stable and less threatening than it had appeared in 1950 following the Korean crisis. An element of containment could be detected in Soviet European policy, which added an element of stability, however tenuous. Adenauer was hopeful that the consolidation of NATO and the emergence of the Warsaw Pact would persuade the Americans to reexamine their cold war policies of "rollback" and "liberation" to which he had never subscribed. In fact, just a year later he saw that very U.S. policy tested in Poland and Hungary.

For the Americans and Germans working together in the Pullach compound in mid-1955 nothing had changed. The Gehlen Organization was not officially a part of the new sovereign government. It remained a responsibility of the CIA. While the flag of the Federal Republic was raised on 5 May 1955 at SHAPE, receiving no more than a pro forma protest from the French, in Pullach we had been flying it alongside the Stars and Stripes since 12 September 1949. It had taken six years to fly the flags together at NATO headquarters.

Gehlen remained entirely aloof from the whole NATO development in Bonn. Still, he was uncertain whether the NATO decision would affect his own plans for a German intelligence service. He had not forgotten the letter Truman Smith had sent Hans Speidel the year before in which Smith had proposed that Speidel enter into a conspiracy with the Army G-2 to destroy Gehlen's reputation and create a German service within the German military. Gehlen had been reassured by the promptness and firmness with which Speidel and Heusinger had rejected the Smith proposal. When NATO became the main subject of interest in Bonn, Gehlen found himself at least temporarily neglected and out of the mainstream of activity there. It was a stressful time. He was disturbed by evidence that the CIC was maintaining unauthorized and ostensibly hostile contacts with his own CI organization; he was looking into this. He did not know that in the months immediately ahead other developments would arise—another try by the U.S. Army G-2 to block legalization and an embarrassing arrest and the subsequent suicide of a CIC agent in his own counterintelligence organization.

In May 1955 Col. Truman Smith, on behalf of the Army G-2, was sent to Germany to assess the entire German military situation. Coincidentally Smith was a neighbor of Allen Dulles. When he told Dulles he was planning to visit Germany to survey the progress of Germany's rearmament, Dulles, in an effort to be helpful, offered to put Smith in touch with CIA officers there. Unfortunately for me, Smith said nothing to Dulles about the prevailing hostility within the Army G-2 to the CIA policy on German intelligence. Nor did Dulles know anything about the exchange between Smith and Hans Speidel that had taken place in 1954.

Smith had extensive contacts dating back to officers in the old Wehrmacht, who acknowledged with some bitterness that they were not involved with the new defense ministry and were critical of the "intellectual General Staff generals," an obvious reference to Speidel and Heusinger. It is likely that Smith had found no real opening for advancing the ideas of the U.S. Army G-2. Speidel and Heusinger had elected not to spend a lot of time with him and gave Smith no access to their new ministry, remembering his 1954 effort to disrupt their support of Gehlen.

In response to the personal request of Allen Dulles, I met with Smith socially several times during his visit. He quizzed me at length for information on the performance of the central cadre in the new defense ministry, including Speidel and Heusinger's. I found him an elegant and pleasant officer of the old school who spoke excellent German and had a good grasp, if a somewhat romantic one, of German and European history. Smith never mentioned any connection with the Pentagon or the Army G-2, but spoke warmly of his friendship with Allen and Clover Dulles. I, too, was not aware of the late 1954 exchange of letters between Truman Smith and Hans Speidel. I think had I been I would not have met with Smith at all. Colonel

Smith had clearly imposed on his personal friendship with the Dulles family in obtaining briefings by CIA officers in Germany.

Smith was not pleased with the reception he received in Bonn from Heusinger and Speidel, and apparently made no real effort to achieve a connection with either the chancellor's office or the new defense minister to push his case against the Gehlen Organization. After reading a copy of his letter to Dulles a few weeks later I concluded that he had returned to the United States with a somewhat more realistic understanding of Gehlen's situation and an unnecessarily pessimistic view of the situation in Germany.

One month after Adenauer became head of the government, President Eisenhower invited him to visit Washington. Adenauer felt comfortable in Washington and was reassured by the policies of the president and his secretary of state, John Foster Dulles. Adenauer also met with the director of Central Intelligence, Allan Dulles, who expressed his satisfaction with reports from Germany that Adenauer was proceeding with his plan to take over the Gehlen Organization and form a German intelligence service. Adenauer made clear he was fully conscious of the enormous challenges that he faced and was determined to associate the German Federal Republic with the Atlantic Alliance. He told Eisenhower that he was deeply impressed that Germany had been accepted as a full partner in the Western alliance, and he felt a great responsibility to move ahead with the national security system that he had initiated in 1950.

Adenauer did not discuss with any senior U.S. officials a conversation he had had with Gen. Arthur Trudeau, the top intelligence officer in the U.S. Army. Trudeau, prior to Adenauer's arrival, had made an official request to German ambassador Heinz Krekeler to meet with a member of Adenauer's staff about the Gehlen Organization. When Krekeler told Adenauer of Trudeau's request, the chancellor said that he would himself receive the American general. When Trudeau arrived at the ambassador's residence he was promptly ushered into the garden, then surprised to find himself alone with Adenauer. Trudeau could have changed his game plan at that point and a more prudent general officer would have done so. But he plunged ahead, and, using seven yellow briefing cards pulled from his pocket, ran through seven summarized points (one on each of the cards). The following is my translation of the German translation of the complete original English texts of the cards:

Card 1. Uncontrolled competition and rivalry among aspiring German intelligence efforts was evident and unconstructive; Gehlen was the principal offender.

Card 2. German police and security files contain examples where poor security practices have led to compromises—evidence that the Gehlen Organization is inefficient in devising cover for its operations. In many cases it has, when compromised, used the CIC as a cover. This had caused me to lose confidence in the operational ability of the organization.

Card 3. In late 1953 and early 1954 poor operational cover resulted in the compromise of eighty out of seven hundred Gehlen agents in East Germany. This compromise inspired a major East German propaganda campaign operation by the Soviets and East Germans that has been very damaging to other Western intelligence agencies operating in East Germany. Incidents like this have shaken my confidence in Gehlen's capability.

Card 4. Exposed cases of Soviet and Soviet-controlled communist services operating in West Germany have demonstrated that the German Federal Republic is a major target of Soviet espionage. This fact presents a threat to the security of both the United States and the Federal Republic. It is clear that the Federal Republic has a need for an effective and secure intelligence and counterintelligence mechanism.

Card 5. The defection of Colonel Heinz, former chief of intelligence in Amt Blank, and the defection of Kolb, chief of the Amt Blank intelligence office in Berlin, are indicative of loose security policies permitting unreliable persons to achieve position of trust in Amt Blank.

Card 6. The Gehlen Organization is known to be conducting counterintelligence investigations in West Germany when its mission is supposedly in foreign intelligence. It is unwilling to coordinate its operations in either counterintelligence or foreign espionage with the American Army. This is a cause of my lack of confidence in the Gehlen Organization.

Card 7. A reliable source of U.S. intelligence with good connections in East Germany has reported that the lack of internal operational and personnel security has enabled the communist intelligence services to penetrate the Gehlen Organization in many instances.

Finally, a notation on the German translation of the original cards appeared to be an added remark by Trudeau. He expressed to the chancellor the opinion that the Gehlen Organization was penetrated, and attributed his confidence on this point not to information of such a penetration but to a reliable source in East Germany who reported that Gehlen's operation could be penetrated. Like Truman Smith had done in his letter to Hans Speidel before, Trudeau, in his statement to Adenauer, appeared intent on establishing credibility regarding the claim of Soviet penetration of the Gehlen Organization. Adenauer listened attentively, thanked the general and, mumbling something about the need to remember Trudeau's points, reached out and took the cards out of the hand of the surprised general. The German embassy translated the cards into German for Adenauer and retained a copy in the embassy. Adenauer left for Bonn with the original cards and the German translation in his possession.

Trudeau had not consulted with Allen Dulles or anyone else in the U.S. intelligence community regarding his meeting with Adenauer. Since late 1954 General Trudeau, unknown to Dulles, had been attempting to upset what Dulles believed to be agreed U.S. policy in support of Adenauer's plan to take over the Gehlen Organization. Ironically, the U.S. Army had initially created what had become the Gehlen Organization and had in 1949 passed responsibility for the operation to a reluctant CIA, and had done so under considerable pressure from the Pentagon and the White House. In the intervening six years the Army G-2 in Germany had been generally uncooperative but had not, to the CIA's knowledge, actively proved itself hostile toward the CIA operation. Still, unknown to the CIA, the Army G-2 in Germany had run penetration operations against the Gehlen Organization without revealing them to the CIA. Even worse, by 1954 the CIC had identified Heinz Felfe as a highly suspect KGB penetration of Gehlen's counterintelligence center. While all this was going on the CIA had kept the G-2's resident representative fully integrated with the American and German staffs in Pullach and had hosted numerous visits to Pullach by G-2 officers from Washington and from G-2 staffs in Europe. The CIA had no reason to believe that General Trudeau was hostile to what had developed as an agreed position between Adenauer and the CIA. Trudeau's approach to Adenauer in June 1955 had come as a total surprise.

After his return from the United States, Adenauer had State Secretary Globke look into the Trudeau matter. Globke gave the cards and a description of the meeting to a CIA officer in the U.S. embassy. The officer cabled the text of the cards and a report of his conversation with Globke to the CIA in Washington, to the German Station in Karlsruhe, and to my office in Pullach. I know today what I did not know in the summer of 1955: in his November 1954 letter to Hans Speidel Truman Smith had made many of the same principal points that Trudeau had made to the chancellor in Ambassador Krekeler's garden in June 1955. I believe that Colonel Smith and General Trudeau were ultimately working from the same brief.

After I received the Bonn cable describing the Trudeau episode, I sent my comments to Washington. I thought Trudeau's description of the security situation in Germany was correct. Trudeau had not told Adenauer anything that he and his advisors had not heard before. The Germans believed that the U.S. intelligence community had not distinguished itself in contributing to the temporary counter-intelligence protection of the federal republic to the level that was needed until Germany could create its own national security system. Several of General Trudeau's points were formulated out of the historical context of Army sponsorship of the Gehlen operation between 1945 and 1949; some of his data, such as the defection of Friedrich Wilhelm Heinz, was simply false. Trudeau may have confused Heinz with Otto John, who had defected in 1954.

Reports of the Trudeau meeting with Adenauer turned up almost three months later in the 2 September issue of the *New York Daily News*, and were subsequently picked up by the wire services. It had become an issue among a number of senior officials in the Pentagon, in the intelligence community, and, according to the press, in the White House. The *Daily News* story carried the headline, "Ike Fires G-2 Boss at Bid Allen Dulles." The facts in the press suffered from inaccuracies, but the issue was clear: the DCI, under a National Security Council Intelligence Directive, was responsible for dealing with foreign governments on foreign intelligence matters. Trudeau was clearly testing the authority of the DCI. It was almost certainly Army Chief of Staff Maxwell Taylor and not President Eisenhower who had made the decision to reassign Trudeau. Allen Dulles was uncomfortable with the confrontation but he had no other choice; he had to take issue with Trudeau if the concept of a DCI were to be taken seriously. The episode could have been discreetly handled and would have been quietly relegated to unreported history had it not been for the leaked story.

When Gehlen learned of the Trudeau affair, first from Globke and later from press reports, he noted that he did not know Trudeau and was appalled that the general addressed his concerns to the chancellor directly. Gehlen was obviously both angry and embarrassed and wanted to put the matter aside as quickly as possible. I learned that Gehlen used the occasion to report to Globke that he had known for some time that the U.S. Army G-2 wanted to see a German service, combining both counterintelligence and intelligence, established within the anticipated armed forces and responsible to a defense minister. This was as close as Gehlen ever came to telling Globke about the Truman Smith letter of 1954. Trudeau's action seems to have left little or no impact on Adenauer. In fact, it may have reminded him that the end of the Occupation had created circumstances ripe for addressing the situation of the Gehlen Organization, which he did upon his return from Washington.

In July 1955, just a month after the Trudeau episode and while Colonel Smith was en route home from his visit to Germany, Gehlen came to my office to register a protest concerning CIC operations directed against the Gehlen Organization. In an entirely civil and courteous manner Gehlen stated that he had information concerning the penetration operations of a "Colonel Thomas" into his organization, with efforts concentrated on his CI organization. Several members of my staff knew that Tom Dale had used "Colonel Thomas" as a cover name. Coming on the heels of the Trudeau affair, which Gehlen had not yet mentioned to me, I thought it necessary to take notice of Gehlen's charge. I reported his charge both to the German station and to Washington. I assumed that someone would take it up with the Army G-2. Gordon Stewart had full-time CIA liaison officers within both the G-2 and the 66th CIC. On the contrary, I received no useful response from either the CIA station in Karlsruhe or from Washington. The lack of a response illustrates the situation that existed within the intelligence community at the time. The issue went to the back burner.

Gehlen's reaction was obviously a cumulative response to the three episodes— the Truman Smith operation in 1954 and his visit in May 1955, the Trudeau affair in June 1955, and the CIC penetrations of his organization. It was Gehlen's good fortune that none of these had produced serious problems in his relations with the Adenauer government, or in the evolving liaison relations with the Americans. Beneath the surface, however, the events of 1954 and 1955 had done damage to intelligence relationships in Germany. The KGB understood the changing landscape and developed a series of disinformation operations designed to exacerbate the situation. The destruction of Gehlen and the weakening of his organization had remained KGB objectives.

There was, however, a dichotomy in Gehlen's behavior. He had put his stamp of approval on planned arrangements for future liaison with American intelligence that we had worked out early in 1955 with the certainty that the creation of a German intelligence service was just ahead. He had been entirely positive, and left the details to Wendland, Herre, Kuehlein, Graber, Blum, and others. Gehlen did nothing to disrupt our planning concerning the whole issue of future liaison relations, nor did he dwell at all on the CIC matter. I do not think he shared the suspicions and resentment that grew out of his realization that the U.S. Army had made a genuine effort to destroy him. I believe that Gehlen was embarrassed by the fact that the U.S. Army had attacked his organization just as the prospect of German forces entering NATO was receiving a warm welcome. His discovery of hostile intelligence operations added one more layer to Gehlen's naturally suspicious disposition. It did not help at all when British reporter Sefton Delmer suddenly launched a new series of devastating attacks on Gehlen in July 1955. Since the British were standing firm in their expanding relations with Gehlen, we looked elsewhere for the sponsor of this renewed effort at a time when only the KGB and the U.S. Army G-2 seemed interested in throwing a wrench into the works in Bonn. Gehlen was finding that the role of intelligence chief, whether legal or not, was not and never would be an easy one.

In September 1955 another bombshell exploded. The Security Group, an element of the German federal police within the interior ministry, arrested four Germans, one of whom was Ludwig Albert, the regional representative of Bentzinger's GV L. Albert had been a professional police officer before getting called up for active duty in the Geheime Feldpolizei in 1940. After the attack on the Soviet Union in 1941 Albert had served on the eastern front in several different GFP groups. Albert was in GV L when the CIA took over in July 1949 and became a well-established staff employee representing Bentzinger's CI organization in conducting liaison meetings with German law enforcement and security authorities in Land Hesse and the Frankfurt area. Albert was also an agent of Tom Dale's CIC group.

Albert was arrested by the German Security Group on suspicion of being an agent of a communist service. The first word on the arrest of Albert came to us in Pullach from Kohler's CI staff, which gave a fragmentary verbal report that he was being held in the Bruchsal federal prison. A fuller briefing was later given to several members of my CI staff. The organization sent a security officer to investigate Albert's home and office. Before the investigation could get fully under way Albert committed suicide while in prison. Gehlen's CI staff professed not to know whether the German police had interrogated Albert before his suicide, or any of the circumstances of his arrest and death. Initially we had no reason to link the case of Ludwig Albert with the CIC. We later learned that Albert's office and quarters had yielded a handwritten letter in which he made two startling admissions: he was a well-established agent of the American CIC, and he was also an agent of a communist intelligence service.

Albert's arrest added a far more serious episode to our problems with Gehlen. We were immediately reminded of Gehlen's complaint in July on the operations against his organization by "Colonel Thomas." Gehlen, I am sure, was relieved to see the court clamp tight secrecy down on the investigation; he did not need a major scandal surrounding disloyalty and the suicide of an established employee. The Albert case simply disappeared from sight; in both the U.S. Army and the Bonn interior and justice ministries—a cloak of complete silence descended.

Several days after Albert's suicide Gehlen came to my office and reported that the evidence obtained by his security officer and the Security Group had established that Albert had been an agent of the CIC for some time. Gehlen declined to go into any detail since the case was still under investigation in the federal court. He reminded me of his earlier complaint about "Colonel Thomas." The exposure of the CIC following the suicide of Albert had caused everyone to take cover. When I asked Gehlen a few weeks later about the case, he icily replied that he was sure I knew more about it than he did. Gehlen had concluded that the CIA was a party to CIC penetrations of his organization. Much later I learned from officers in the G-2 not directly involved in CIC operations that a decision was made about this time to close down Operation Campus. Dale returned to the United States shortly after Albert's arrest. We heard nothing further from either the Army G-2 or the CIA about Campus, about Dale, or about the Albert case.

Many years later, long after I had retired, I was surprised to learn that soon after his return to the United States, Dale had left the Army and joined James Angleton's CI staff at CIA headquarters in Langley, Virginia. I asked John Evans and Ed Petty, both former CI specialists in Pullach, about Dale. They told me that at the time each of them had individually approached Dale to discuss the unresolved security problems in Pullach. In each case Dale refused, and stated that he had an agreement with Angleton that he would not be expected to reveal to the CIA any information on his CIC activities. Each of these officers went individually to Angleton and expressed incredulity. Angleton assured them it was true that he had made such an agreement, probably a mistake, but what was done was done and they would have to live with it.

The question arises—and remains unanswered—as to whether Angleton and Dale ever discussed Heinz Felfe and other related security matters. During the five years between the time Dale joined the CIA and the arrest of Felfe in 1961, Angleton was personally and professionally deeply involved in a whole series of CI cases. One CIA agent, Lt. Col. Michael Goleniewski, the Polish deputy chief of counterintelligence, had produced critical information that Maj. Gen. Olef Gribanov, chief of KGB counterintelligence, once bragged at a conference of Soviet Bloc officers that two out of a group of six BND counterintelligence officers visiting the United States in 1956 were controlled KGB agents. Felfe was traveling with that group of six in Washington in September 1956. It is difficult for me to believe that Angleton did not engage Dale in any discussions of the problem of a mole in the headquarters of the Gehlen Organization. I have requested from both the CIA and the Army any evidence of those CIC reports on Operation Campus, reports that apparently were never distributed outside of the CIC. My FOIA requests have provided nothing relevant. I have discussed the matter with the most knowledgeable senior CIA officers, many of whom were later involved in detailed studies on the CI staff after Angleton's retirement, but none have found even a single page of relevant information anywhere in the files.

Many different authors have told the Angleton story, advancing complicated conspiracy theories. Few of Angleton's colleagues share these worst-case analyses. One expressed the view that Angleton's experience with X-2 in London during World War II added to the problems of protecting the sensitive Ultra Operation and the considerable influence that Kim Philby exerted on him, created an accentuated counterintelligence paranoia that became a part of Angleton's professional personality. In later years this paranoia was compounded many times over by the fact that Angleton was Philby's principal contact in Washington. It was also demonstrable in Angleton's deep preoccupation with the Soviet defector Maj. Anatoliy Golytsin, which led Angleton to put labels of suspicion on a number of agency officers involved in Soviet operations. Both Angleton and Tom Dale were fervent anticommunists in the era of rampant "McCarthyism." I never heard Dale expound on this subject, but most who knew him agreed that he was a brilliant student of international communism and carried out his search for communist influence in the emerging Adenauer government with the fervor that is often assigned to the followers of Senator McCarthy.

When Dale joined the CIA he did not work directly for Angleton. Instead he was taken on as a specialist on international communism to work for Lothar Metzl, Angleton's top expert on the Communist Party. Metzl was an older and scholarly expert who approached his position mainly on intellectual terms. For whatever reason, Dale was kept out of any ostensible operational contact with Angleton.

During a telephone conversation in 1997, Tom Dale's widow, a former Agency member herself, described Dale as troubled by his inability to establish a rapport or professional dialogue with Angleton. It was her impression, given without the benefit of the background described above, that Dale had had no contact with Angleton during Dale's long tour in Germany. She believed that Dale never got to know Angleton at all.

In late 1997, while going back over the Dale and Angleton story, I had a long telephone conversation with Bill Johnson, a retired CIA officer I had known intermittently in Germany and Austria in the decade after World War II. After my return to Washington in 1956 Johnson had joined Angleton's staff and had dealt with German operations, including cases relating to unanswered operational questions about suspected KGB penetrations in the Gehlen Organization, by then the BND. I reviewed with him essentially all of the information described above. He recalled the early analysis by Ed Petty in Pullach that put Felfe prominently on the list of suspected penetration agents. Johnson had worked his way through the Goleniewski and Deriabin stories and he knew Dale well. He had much the same impression as Dale's widow. Dale had never established real communications with Angleton and was never one of a group that Angleton assembled to recite his current interests and views on Soviet intelligence. Johnson had no recollection that he had ever seen Angleton and Dale in any operational discussion together. He went even further to say that Angleton had never demonstrated the slightest interest in Germany or to his knowledge had ever visited the German station. The talk with Johnson contributed to my understanding of Angleton but I had drawn another blank and thus am left with questions surrounding Angleton's knowledge and reactions to the CIC penetrations of the Gehlen Organization and Dale's conclusion in 1954 that Heinz Felfe was probably a communist agent. But that is only a part of the larger question of the CIC reporting in the 1950s on its wholly uncoordinated operations against the Gehlen Organization.

While in Berlin in 1997 I met Sergei Kondrashev, a retired lieutenant general of the KGB and a co-author of *Battleground Berlin*. Capping off several days of discussion about the intelligence war, I asked if he was prepared to add to my information on James Angleton. He did not answer for some seconds, then, looking me straight in the eye, said, "I think we should leave the dead to sleep in peace." This was my inclination too.

Much of what I did not know in 1955 became perfectly clear and documented almost fifty years later. In the summer of 1955 I did not know that the CIC had systematically penetrated the Gehlen Organization and produced hundreds of reports, including many on Heinz Felfe in the mid-1950s, that were never seen by the CIA. I did not know that in November 1954 the Army G-2 had secretly initiated an effort to draw Hans Speidel and Adolf Heusinger into a conspiracy to block Bonn's planned takeover of the Gehlen Organization. I had learned, after Ludwig Albert's arrest, that Tom Dale had been secretly and regularly meeting with him. It was not until years later that I learned of Dale's recruitment of other senior CI officers in the Gehlen Organization. We knew from KGB defector Peter Deriabin in early 1954 that the KGB had two established agents in the Gehlen Organization, but we did not know that the CIC had by June 1954 concluded that Heinz Felfe was the principal suspect. We did not know of General Trudeau's uncoordinated meeting with Chancellor Adenauer in June 1955 until the Germans informed us of it after Adenauer's return. My view of the decade after the war has been quite significantly altered by the hard facts of history, many of which have become available over many years. It is obvious that a U.S. intelligence community never was functional in Germany, even though as a concept it was set forth in the National Security Act of July 1947 and the subsequent National Security Council Intelligence Directive 1 (NSCID 1) issued on 12 December 1947. NSCID 1 directed the director of Central Intelligence to coordinate between the Central Intelligence Agency and the intelligence organizations of the Departments of State, Army, Navy, and Air Force, and the Joint Chiefs of Staff. The coordination of intelligence under NSCID 1 was clearly applicable to foreign intelligence. The largest and most complex U.S. foreign intelligence community in the world was based in Germany. In the first two years after the end of the war, circumstances made intelligence coordination, in practical terms, a function of the G-2 of the major commands. At least in theory NSCID 1 imposed a responsibility on both the DCI and the chiefs of intelligence of the departments, including the JCS, to coordinate their activities. In fact, there was never an effort of any kind made in the entire history of the Occupation to coordinate the U.S. intelligence community in Germany. Most of the intelligence problems discussed in this book could have been avoided had NSCID 1 been consciously implemented in Germany.

The last and most lethal bomb ticking away under the Gehlen Organization in 1955 was the presence of KGB agent Heinz Felfe living and working among the sensitive CI staff. Looking back, I am sure that Reinhard Gehlen experienced many anxious moments contemplating the possible cost of a major Soviet spy scandal breaking amidst the problems related to the continuing opposition of the U.S. Army G-2. It is probable that he had not wholly dismissed from his mind the possibility of a mole working in his headquarters staff. It is a problem that every chief of intelligence in the Western world sooner or later has had to live with; the CIA, MI-6, the French, and other Western European services have been through this very same ordeal. For Gehlen there was the added threat to a long-held vision—the creation of a national intelligence service. The stakes were high indeed, and everything depended on Adenauer taking the action to which he had been committed since December 1950.

It was some days after the Albert suicide that I detected for the first time a change in my relations with Gehlen. Always an impersonal man, he now became more so. His manner was more formal, cool, and aloof. Whatever came out of the Security Group's investigation apparently led Gehlen to the conclusion that the CIA and I personally had been at least aware of the CIC operation. He was wrong about me. A distinct chill settled over our offices in the courtyard at the center of Nikolaus. I attributed this partly to Gehlen's preoccupation with the many problems he faced in connection to his long quest for legal status. I also assumed it was at least in part simply a cumulative reaction to the Army G-2's effort to block legalization. But nothing could explain how Gehlen had concluded that the CIA and I had personally been knowledgeable of the CIC penetrations of GV L. Many years later a trusted associate of Gehlen told me that Gehlen's suspicion about me originated with Heinz Felfe.

16

The Founding of the BND

On 20 February 1956 the German government took the long-awaited action to create the Federal Intelligence Service. The entry in the cabinet meeting record for the day was quite succinct: "Es wird ein Nachrichtendienst gegrundet; er sie ist dem Bundeskanzleramt angegliedert." ("An Intelligence Service will be formed; it will be attached to the Office of the Chancellor.") The funding of the Bundesnachrichtendienst (BND) would start 1 April, the beginning of the federal republic's fiscal year. Horst Wendland, charged with the transition, asked the CIA to advance the organization a total of two million deutsche marks between the first of February and the end of March, which would be repaid from the full funding that would be available by 1 April. We agreed to do so.

In anticipation of the creation of the BND my staff had moved out of Pullach to offices in military post headquarters in Munich. Gehlen and his staff easily agreed that the whole business of producing a daily flow of intelligence and in the established English format would continue. By then American forces in Europe were under the command of an American general heading the forces of the NATO military alliance, of which Germany was now a member. Because Germany had been named a sovereign government on 5 May 1955, the formation of the BND was not a matter in which the former high commissioners—now accredited as ambassadors of the United States, Britain, and France—had any role to play. In this sense the creation of the BND was different than circumstances surrounding the formation of the internal security service, the BfV, six years earlier. Although Gehlen had been supported by U.S. occupying forces for an incredible eleven years, his appointment as president of the BND was an entirely German affair.

On the morning of 31 March 1956 an official from the finance ministry in Bonn appeared at Pullach with a package containing two million deutsche marks in currency, the required sum advanced. In Horst Wendland's presence I signed a receipt in alias using the only name I had used in Pullach, Kent J. Marshall. Wendland may have regarded 31 March as no more than an administrative deadline for Bonn to pay the advance. The Gehlen Organization's payroll and budget was now a responsibility of the German government. For years we had made a practice of writing off the value of any equipment or property issued to the organization. Except for the office equipment and file cabinets in the White House, all other property—including that issued to the far-flung facilities of the organization—was to remain.

We left the compound, originally the property of the Nazi Party and as such the property of the United States at the end of the war, very much as the first American troops had found it. We had never painted any of the stucco exteriors, which had aged gracefully into a faded yellow. The White House was a shade of gray. We understood custody would go to the BND on 1 April, and we did not worry about who acquired legal ownership. The Bavarian government seemed to have some claim on such property. It was not my problem.

By 31 March the reception room in the White House was still occupied by a U.S. sergeant and several American soldiers. My secretary and I were the only CIA staff members still in the White House—everyone else had relocated to Munich, though they were in and out of the compound to meet with various members of the German staff and me. Gehlen had indicated nothing about his plans for this long-awaited day, nor did anyone else in Pullach raise the subject. Though the White House was almost empty of personnel it was still fully furnished, including the magnificent oriental carpet that covered most of the floor in the spacious paneled music salon off the central foyer. The Bechstein grand piano was left where we had found it and in well-maintained condition. Even the life-sized bronze bust of Adolf Hitler in the bunker under the White House remained exactly where we had found it—in a heap of rubble in a conference room in the basement.

On that final day I found myself alone in my office as the clock struck five. I rose from my desk and walked out of the office to the window just above the front door. I had a view directly down the center of the walkway leading toward the Colonial House. I observed the backs of two uniformed figures marching in step toward the compound's flagpoles. One man wore the olive drab uniform of an American soldier; the other sported the green and gray uniform of the Bavarian Border Police. In front of the flag pole they stopped, together pulled down the two flags, folded the flags, did an about face, and marched back to the courtyard, halting just in front of the main door of the White House. The American soldier entered and placed the folded U.S. flag on the sergeant's desk. The uniformed guard from the Bavarian Border Police did a left face, marched less than a hundred yards down the road to my right, and deposited the German Federal Republic flag in the guard house used by the Bavarian Border Police.

The Stars and Stripes had flown over this small military compound since American forces first appeared in May 1945. The German flag dated to the creation of the German Federal Republic on 12 September 1949. In fact, the front of the Colonial House probably had been one of the first places in Germany where the American and German flags flew side by side, probably in violation of at least one rule of the Occupation. (After a period of time the Bavarian flag could be seen atop the pole on select Bavarian holidays.) 31 March 1956 was a cold, gray day, and traces of a late snow could still be seen melting along the walls that bordered the courtyard. For perhaps ten minutes as the flags were lowered I saw no person other than the two marching guards. No traffic on the street or in the courtyard below disturbed the scene. It occurred to me that I was probably the only person who had observed the Stars and Stripes and the colors of the German Federal Republic being lowered together for the last time, a daily ritual that had gone on in Nikolaus for years.

I stood for some minutes, conscious that a moment of my own history was passing unobserved and unshared. It suddenly occurred to me that the simple ceremony of lowering the flags had marked the end of a turbulent era in postwar Germany. I knew that in those eight years we together and I personally had contributed a great deal to the transition of Germany from an enemy to an allied state. My reaction that day was very much like that on 5 May 1945, when I heard the message on my radio that "All troops will halt in place and not fire unless fired upon." I felt a real sense of closure, the end of an experience that had begun with Edward R. Murrow's words from London on 1 September 1939 that World War II had started that morning with Germany's attack on Poland. For seventeen years the German experience had determined the broad outline of my life. On that final day I did not comprehend that the moment was just the beginning of more than four decades of reflection, attempting to better understand what World War II, including my unique postwar experience in Pullach, had meant. Most surprising about my experience is the extent to which the past four decades have been a period of continuing discovery of information, most of which I did not know when I left Nikolaus on that late afternoon.

I told the sergeant on duty to pack up the flag and the few papers on his desk and then close the office. I got in my car, parked just in front of the White House, and drove down the cobblestone drive to Heilmannstrasse, turning right to exit Nikolaus through the Pullach gate. Regardless of the reason, the occasion slipped by unnoticed, except for my solo personal "retreat" ceremony. Perhaps the founding of the BND on 1 April 1956 was intentionally permitted to go by unnoticed. I was told that Gehlen was traveling to Bonn for ceremonies marking the occasion. When I returned to the Pullach compound on 1 April and called on Horst Wendland to symbolically turn over the key to my office, he seemed surprised that I had departed at the close of business the previous day. He seemed somewhat embarrassed, but in typical Wendland style he remained discreetly silent. Looking back I think it was probably a mistake on my part to have moved so promptly on 31 March; the two flags coming down had suggested it. The compound was to become the property of the German government on 1 April. Would it still be appropriate to fly the American flag over the compound?

So 1 April passed without any ceremony in Pullach, probably because Gehlen had not been able to get a firm idea from the chancellery on what was to transpire that day. Gehlen had made it clear to his staff in Pullach that there was nothing to be done to celebrate the event until they heard from Bonn. I have no recollection of hearing or seeing in print anything on the founding of the BND at that time. In any case, the first day of April passed without notice. I assume that on the basis of the cryptic Adenauer cabinet record of 20 February the BND was legally founded on 1 April, and Gehlen was given an interim appointment until the many legal and bureaucratic requirements had been met. Forty years later I read a short history of the BND that recorded Gehlen's appointment as president on 20 December 1956, not nine months earlier.

I heard nothing directly from Gehlen when he returned to Pullach, nor in those first few days of April. As a footnote to history I can report that my former office at the head of the stairway up from the main foyer of the White House has been the office of the president of the BND for the past forty-five years. My mission in Pullach was at an end. The agency and I both agreed that it was time for me to move on to other things, and I began making plans to depart Germany in early summer after the school year came to an end. The CIA had accepted my recommendation that Tom Lucid replace me as the senior CIA officer charged with developing a liaison relationship with the new German service. Lucid was a dedicated professional intelligence officer. An outgoing, party-loving Irish Catholic with a fine tenor voice and an attractive Irish wife who fit gracefully into his gregarious lifestyle, Tom had a talent for bringing out the always illusive lighter side of his German colleagues. On the rare occasions when we enticed Gehlen to appear at an informal party, I would provide improvised piano accompaniment to Tom's rendition of "Wienerlied," always ending with "Wien, Wien, Nur Du Allein"—an act that we had developed during our shared days in Austria. Gehlen was a congenial and pleasant observer of this kind of nonsense. In the years that followed my departure from Munich he was exposed to a regular dose of it from Lucid and even seemed to enjoy it.

No dramatic reduction in the size of the CIA staff was contemplated. Lucid was developing specific proposals for members of the American staff he wanted to keep in the liaison staff after my departure, and I aided the German station regarding assignments for members of my staff who were prepared to move on. As each day passed it became more apparent in Nikolaus that legalization was in process. The administrative plan to accomplish our part had long been submitted. To Gehlen's credit he did everything necessary to ensure a smooth transition. Lucid assumed responsibility for working out his new relationship with the BND, and Gehlen appeared entirely preoccupied with establishing an appropriate BND presence in Bonn while maintaining his principal headquarters in Pullach.

In May Gehlen invited my wife and me for afternoon coffee with Herta and him at their home in Berg. It was an entirely congenial affair; our conversation was filled with expressions of mutual satisfaction about our accomplishments and good wishes for the future. Gehlen presented me with a gold medallion engraved with the figure of Saint George slaying the dragon. At some point Gehlen had settled on Saint George as the patron saint of the Gehlen Organization. I assumed the gesture had to do with the founding of the BND on 1 April 1956, but the engraved date, "3/31/1956," was the final day of the CIA's sponsorship of the Gehlen Organization. Also engraved on the back was the number four; I do not know who received numbers one, two, and three. Just before we departed the Gehlens asked a favor of us: their eldest daughter, Katharina, was enrolled in Hunter College in New York City, to begin studies in September. Would we help look after her? We knew and liked Katharina and assured the couple that as long as she was in the United States, our home would be her home and we would expect her to be with us during school holidays. That conversation started a long and close relationship with Herta Gehlen and her four children. Katharina spent time with us at our country home in northern Virginia and became part of the family.

Our plans to depart Munich at the end of the school year suddenly changed. A personal tragedy marked the end of my assignment in Munich, just as one had marked its beginning with the sudden death of my wife Connie in 1948. In early

June our son Jimmy, age twelve, lost an eye when a colleague of mine permitted his son to take a German pellet gun on a Boy Scout outing. The gun had an odd-shaped projectile, which can do terrible damage to anyone hit by it. One of the boys had seen too many Westerns and was enacting his version of a shootout at high noon when he hit my son in the eye. I spent almost ten days at the Army General Hospital in Stuttgart while surgeons struggled to save some of Jimmy's vision or at least the eyeball. In the end the eye was removed. After that ordeal we finally departed Munich in August and sailed out of Bremerhaven aboard a U.S. military transport.

In the weeks prior to my departure I spent many hours with the Germans I had worked with over the previous eight years. The American staff in Pullach had become a closely knit group. They did all possible to make the last months in Munich a time of pleasant memories, and saw us off at the main train station in Munich with a champagne "Aufwiedersehn" organized by the always upbeat and ebullient Lucids. Several things lent additional poignancy to memories of that summer. Some of our closest friends, including Virginia and Henry Pleasants, who had moved on to Bern, were back in Munich when Jimmy and I returned from the hospital in Stuttgart. The Pleasants had also shown up in Munich after my arrival there in the late summer of 1948 after the death of Connie, whom they had known well from our days in Vienna. I think it is accurate to say that we had truly become a family, as Americans living abroad are likely to do in such circumstances.

After ending my involvement in European operations at the end of the 1950s I had no further official role in the CIA's relations with the BND, but did maintain ties with many individuals who had shared the Pullach experience—many of them maturing into genuine friendships. Not until 1968, when Gehlen made a retirement visit to Washington, did he (for reasons unknown to me) "revise" his position that I had been involved in the hostile G-2 actions taken against him in late 1955. During the several days of his stay in Washington he saw many acquaintances within the CIA and in other elements of the U.S. intelligence community. By that time I was chief of the CIA Near East Division and preoccupied with sorting out the aftermath of the 1967 war. The only time I saw Gehlen on that visit was an afternoon sailing trip we took on Chesapeake Bay as Ed Petty's guests. I later learned that Gehlen sent a letter from Washington to the BND office in Germany, in which he stated, "I was wrong about Marshall. He was, after all, all right and supportive of us." Four years later I was invited to a private celebration of his seventieth birthday at his home in Berg, attended only by members of his family, Annelore Krueger, his lifelong secretary and assistant, and me. Two years later I received in the mail a silver bowl from Gehlen, inscribed with the words "Mr. James Critchfield, zur Erinnerung, an langjaehrige Zusammenarbeit, Reinhard Gehlen 24.12.74" (in memory of long years of cooperation). It appears that in his later years Gehlen wished to make amends for his attitude toward me at the end of my time in Pullach. After both our government retirements I dropped in on Gehlen from time to time. He and Herta were still living in the small prefab house. He was a changed personality—friendly, warm, and almost affectionate in recalling our shared experiences. Once, when my wife and I had afternoon tea with the Gehlens, he grasped me by the arm, sat me down on a small sofa beside him, and asked that we be photographed together. This was a Gehlen I had never known.

Through our numerous ups and downs my unofficial relations with Gehlen and his family were always congenial. By some curious process I think Gehlen came to regard me as a friend who had played an important role in his life. This warmth was evident during my late visits to his home and, above all, my last visit in 1979 when I found him terminally ill with cancer and barely able to talk. After a half hour of sporadic conversation he had become silent and closed his eyes. Turning to Herta sitting in a chair at the foot of the bed, I said I thought I should leave. With his eyes still closed Gehlen reached out to me with an emaciated hand and said in German, "Wait." After a minute or two he opened his eyes, turned his face toward me, and with some difficulty and, continuing to speak in German, he said: "Before you go, I want to thank you for helping me achieve the dream of my life, the Service." He then settled back and closed his eyes. I took his hand, murmured a farewell, and departed. That last time I saw Gehlen left no doubt in my mind about his purpose and priorities during those years in Pullach. Several days later I received a message, while traveling in a remote part of the Arabian Desert, that Gehlen had died. I was unable to get back to Munich in time to attend the funeral. After Reinhard Gehlen's death Herta brought the family even closer, and she lived for years as a healthy and happy matriarch of the family.

In May 1998, fifty years after my first contact with Gehlen, I was invited to Pullach to talk with BND officers about the early origin of their organization. A day or two later I attended a private luncheon given by a friend of many years, Val Rychly's widow Hannelore, at which the four Gehlen children were present. After lunch, standing at the center of the living room surrounded by the Gehlen's children, I raised a glass of champagne to the memory of their father and in thoughtful and carefully selected German told them how I viewed the legacy of their father. I credited him with giving the now reunited Germany a modern and well-conceived national intelligence service to which he had brought a large number of dedicated and talented associates—many from his days in the German General Staff. In my toast I did not gloss over my opinion that he had made mistakes, but fully acknowledged that he had lived through dangerous and difficult times. I recognized the unique quality of his contribution, and the dedicated service he had rendered to Germany and to my own country in the fifty years since I had first met him in Pullach. I told them about my last meeting with their father just shortly before he died. My meeting with the Gehlen children was a most rewarding experience.

Reinhard Gehlen almost single-handedly and with clear vision and audacity had conceived and carried out the delivery to General Eisenhower's G-2 an almost intact Fremde Heere Ost in the summer of 1945, thus becoming the first German officer to take a step in the direction of the eventual alliance with the United States. By late 1948 he had developed a detailed concept of the intelligence service that he would offer to a future German government: a primarily civilian service attached and reporting directly to the head of the government (the chancellor), and subject to oversight by the German parliament. The service would provide the foreign intelligence requirements of all elements of the federal government. Gehlen was supported by Adolf Heusinger in the view that the service should not be subordinated exclusively to the military, a situation that had contributed to the intelligence failure at Pearl Harbor. The intelligence service would have neither internal investigative or police authority. Initially, because of the divided character of Germany, Gehlen had been somewhat ambiguous about its role in dealing with subversion from East Germany.

Whatever else he might have accomplished, Reinhard Gehlen did not emerge as a role model for future leaders of German intelligence. He was at times quite controversial, and had taken too many risks (quite unnecessarily, in my opinion) in recruiting politically tainted persons into the Gehlen Organization. Later, as president of the BND, his involvement in West German internal political affairs had continued to be controversial. In his retirement years he had become more concerned with the possibility that communism would win out over a Western society incapable of either understanding or dealing with it. His book, *Der Dienst, The Service,* had gone far beyond my own perceptions that had been moving in the opposite direction after observing Moscow's failures in Western Europe and the Middle East. In *Der Dienst* Gehlen displayed a continuing obsession with the danger of a communist victory over the West, possibly an unfair criticism made with the hindsight of the collapse of Soviet communism, which came as a surprise to most of the world.

The central fact is that Gehlen built a modern, well-organized, centralized intelligence service. Organizationally it looked much like the Central Intelligence Agency, but in reality Gehlen had quite independently arrived at the same conclusions on national intelligence that had guided the United States in creating the CIA. The principles and concepts that governed the design and creation of the BND remain remarkably intact more than four decades later. The BND has lived within the political and philosophical boundaries of a firmly democratic German society and state that dates back to the decade immediately following the end of World War II. Like all intelligence services from this era, the BND has been to some degree politicized while maintaining its essentially independent character. That Reinhard Gehlen was the central force in conceptualizing and creating this modern German intelligence service is without a doubt his principal legacy to the German nation.

GERHARD WESSEL AND THE HISTORY
OF GERMAN INTELLIGENCE

Excluding Reinhard Gehlen himself, Gerhard Wessel was, I believe, the man who played the most important role in every phase of the Pullach story. He was a central figure in Fremde Heere Ost during the war. In 1945, when Gehlen was removed to the United States, Wessel assembled and held together the surviving Fremde Heere Ost and later was one of the inner circle around which Gehlen developed the Gehlen Organization in Pullach. He joined Hans Speidel in Paris in 1952 and accompanied him to SHAPE in late 1954. He resumed a military career and built an intelligence and security effort in the defense ministry and the Bundeswehr. Deeply involved in NATO matters, Wessel was assigned with the rank of lieutenant general and served for two years as the German representative on the NATO Military Committee in Washington. When Gehlen retired in 1968 the chancellor called Wessel home from Washington to replace him as president of the BND, a position Wessel held for ten years until he retired.

Wessel was a reserved, quietly dedicated man, always remarkably in control of his own situation. He and Gehlen were not close and I rarely saw them together. Wessel avoided involvement in any of Gehlen's political affairs, but he gave Gehlen his loyalty and support as a matter of principle after his early involvement in the plan that was hatched in 1943.

I met Gerhard Wessel on my second day in Pullach and an enduring friendship grew out of that first meeting. When he was notified in 1968 that he had been appointed head of the BND, I invited him to lunch in Washington and gave him a long and candid description of my observations since he had left Pullach in 1952. I told him that relations between the CIA and the BND had been damaged by lack of trust that dated back to Gehlen's suspicious and at times paranoiac nature. The successful Soviet penetration of the organization and the KGB's detailed knowledge of personalities had permitted the Soviets to conduct disinformation operations employing a wide range of KGB assets all over the world. They had successfully planted information that cast suspicion on individuals in the BND who were close to Gehlen. The move had generated an enthusiasm within the CIA for hunting down suspected spies in the BND. The convictions of Felfe, Clemens, and Tiebel in 1963 had simply magnified the problem. With many other services—the British, the Canadians, and several of the small northern European ones—we had dialogues, separate and tightly controlled, that were based on a trust that had developed over time. Such trust had not developed with the BND, except between a few individuals at the Pullach level.

Wessel accepted the observation that establishing trust with the CIA had always been a problem in Pullach. He understood that the KGB exploited this distrust. I told Wessel that, although I no longer had any responsibility for the CIA in Germany or Europe, I had discussed my concerns with Dick Helms and separately with Jim Angleton. Both favored creation of separate operational channels to get to the bottom of unresolved CI cases of common concern. It was agreed that Horst von Buttlar, one of the most respected old hands from Pullach, and I would be working at the ends of a special channel under the technical control of Angleton. We also agreed on a well-informed CI specialist on each side who would assist the effort. On our side the working expert would be Ed Petty, who had an encyclopedic knowledge of the German service and its history of counterintelligence problems. It took roughly two years to go as far as possible in this effort, but a whole new level of trust emerged and did resolve most of the outstanding cases. Gerhard Wessel's total cooperation in this effort went far in creating this new atmosphere of trust.

As far back as 1948, whenever I asked Gehlen who he saw as his replacement were he to become ill or die, he promptly answered: "Why, Wessel, of course." In the later years whenever I asked him this same question, I always got the same reply. In 1985 Wessel wrote a brief history of Gehlen and the BND, and in it gave Gehlen full credit for the creation of the German Federal Intelligence Service. After his retirement from the BND in 1978 Wessel had no further active role in the Service but did choose to maintain his residence in Pullach. Thereafter I frequently visited him and his wife Rosemarie, and in his later years we became quite close. Wessel died in 2002 in his home in Pullach. I felt a tremendous personal loss at the end of our relationship, which spanned a half-century and had produced such a significant change between our two countries.

17

An End and a Beginning for
German Military History

BUILDING THE BRIDGE FROM THE WEHRMACHT
TO THE BUNDESWEHR

THE BUNDESWEHR, under a series of laws passed by the German parliament, became officially recognized in March 1956—one of the success stories of the fifty-year postwar era. From the very beginning, those responsible accorded their highest priority to bringing the new armed forces into active and sensitive participation with the government, the parliament, and the public. Reforms were directed at developing the image of the Bundeswehr among the German public and its increasingly integrated and exposed relationships with the armed forces of other NATO countries.

The Bundeswehr undertook a unique process of introspection and reform called "Innere Fuehrung," or inner leadership. The officer most identified with this sustained reform was Maj. Graf Baudissin, one of the youngest of the fifteen military experts in attendance at the secret meeting at Himmerod in 1950. Baudissin was from the beginning an advocate of a reformed culture and a profound reorientation of attitudes and relations between the soldier and the officer, and between these two and the German citizen. Still, controversy and debate arose over the extent of reform needed before the first German soldier donned a uniform. The issue had been clearly defined by Gen. Alfred Jodl, one of only four senior officers of the Wehrmacht who individually had been named, indicted, and convicted by the International Military

Tribunal at Nuremberg in November 1945. Jodl said, "As a soldier I obeyed and I believed my honour required me to maintain the obedience I had sworn. I have spent these five years working in silence, although I often entirely disagreed and thought the orders I got were absurd and impossible. I have known since the spring of 1942 that we could not win the war." His comments reflected the thinking of many of the 130 senior officers of the Wehrmacht, most of whom had been unwilling, for the same reasons, to become involved in any effort to overthrow Adolf Hitler. By avoiding personal involvement, the integrity of the loyalty oath they had taken and the principles of obedience and honor they possessed remained intact. The reforms, initiated by Baudissin and supported by those involved in organizing the Bundeswehr, were meant to address these very issues.

Chancellor Adenauer served Germany and the Bundeswehr well by his action in turning to Heusinger, Speidel, and Foertsch in his first realistic examination of the national security problems confronting Germany. These generals, known as three of the most formidable military intellectuals that had come out of the Army General Staff, had spent much of the five years after the war in thinking through a way for Germany to be accepted in the Western community of nations. They had developed the blueprint of a German national security system, including its armed forces, that would be needed if the Federal Republic were to be accepted in some kind of a security alliance within the postwar Western European community of nations. The men and women who have since served in the Bundeswehr are the beneficiaries of that legacy.

Heusinger became the first inspector-general of the Bundeswehr in June 1957; in 1961 he was elected chairman of the highest NATO military body, the Military Committee, in Washington. But the most remarkable and important element in the legacy of Adolf Heusinger was the role he played between 1945 and 1955, the decade before he returned to uniform and before the existence of a defense ministry in Bonn and the formal acceptance of the Federal Republic into NATO. His carefully thought-out plan to create a national security system and gain Germany's acceptance into NATO marks Heusinger's unique and principal legacy.

By late 1948, when Heusinger had become the head of Gehlen's evaluations staff in Pullach, the staff's intelligence analysts concluded that the Soviet strategic ambitions had clearly been advanced at least as far west as the English Channel. Communist ideologues were still talking of "world revolution." President Harry Truman, while going along with the rapid withdrawal of U.S. forces from Western Europe, had confronted Soviet expansionist moves toward Greece, Turkey, and the Persian Gulf with a military aid program known as the Truman Doctrine of 1947.

Nevertheless, with the coup d'état in Prague in 1948, the Soviets had consolidated their control of pro-Soviet regimes throughout Eastern Europe.

In light of these events Heusinger joined forces with Hans Speidel and Hermann Foertsch in an intensive effort to think through all that was transpiring in Europe. The Gehlen Organization, with its comprehensive intelligence operation being conducted on the Soviet Union, provided Heusinger with the only German institution in West Germany that could give him the necessary support. Gehlen's information network became even more critical when communist North Korea launched a conventional full-scale war against South Korea in 1950. Heusinger concluded that Soviet strategic ambitions had reached beyond Europe to become global in character and eventually became a contest between two superpowers, the Soviet Union and the United States, and he saw the future of Germany within this larger context. Heusinger, Speidel, and Foertsch reached an agreement on the broad outline of a defense and foreign policy (described below) which, they had concluded, would serve the interest of the new German Federal Republic:

1. The security of Germany and all of Western Europe could not be achieved by the Western Europeans acting alone; the European system of nation states had demonstrated in the long history since the Treaty of Westphalia in 1648, including the history of two great wars in the first half of the twentieth century, that it was not only unable to avoid wars in Europe but had actually provoked them.

2. Because of its separateness from Europe, its unique history, its size and resources, and its character as an undivided nation on a vast continent reaching from the Atlantic to the Pacific, the United States offered Germany and Europe its only hope for a secure future.

3. Germany should seek security only within an Atlantic strategy and within the North Atlantic Treaty Organization. The alternative, a Western European defense concept, was not, for both military and political reasons, viable.

4. A forward strategy, that is, meeting the Soviet threat at the Elbe, was a prerequisite for Germany's participation in an Atlantic defense alliance. U.S. strategic nuclear power would give real credibility to a conventionally armed NATO force facing the Soviet forces at the Elbe.

5. Defense and related foreign policy planning within the German Federal Republic must be shared between the Adenauer government in power and the opposition SPD, led by Dr. Schumacher. Toward this end the generals had conferred with and believed they had the support of the SPD leaders.

6. The creation of a new German armed force within the developing German democracy would involve the sensitive and complicated process of examining the German military past in order to preserve the institutions, traditions, and customs that were judged to be both useful and acceptable in building a new force.

Starting with our conversations during my first year in Pullach, I had followed with growing interest the evolution of the thinking of Heusinger and his two colleagues. Considering Heusinger's long and uninterrupted position at or close to the center of Army General Staff planning for most of the German campaigns in World War II, it is truly remarkable that he had the inner strength, the wisdom, the integrity, and the will to place himself at the absolute forefront of the small group of former officers who dared and were able to turn away from the recent catastrophe of World War II in order to capably address the future.

When Heusinger ended his tour as chairman of the NATO Military Committee and prepared to return to Germany to retire, I hosted a small dinner party for him at my home in northern Virginia, attended by CIA officers Allen Dulles, Dick Helms, Gordon Stewart, Bronson Tweedy, and John Bross. Responding to my farewell toast over a glass of Mosel wine, Heusinger, with some humor and the familiar glint in his eyes, remarked that we who had shared those early days in Pullach had accomplished much about which the world would never be informed. In fact, the official record in the Defense Ministry has nothing on the three years he spent with the Gehlen Organization as chief of its evaluations staff. To my knowledge there are no published accounts of this time in German history.

The Defense Ministry in Bonn, Heusinger's contemporaries in the Bundeswehr, and the fraternity of officers that shared the early days of NATO have been lavish in giving recognition and praise to Heusinger for his role as the leader and guiding spirit in shaping the character of the Bundeswehr. On Heusinger's seventieth birthday a collection of testimonials from his contemporaries in NATO was published. Excerpts from some of these illustrate the level of respect for him.

A man who in his position had a full knowledge in all of the military planning of the war until 1944 covering the length and breadth of Europe . . . and yet did not lose his inner freedom and the integrity of his conscience—such a man could simply not disappear from history.

—Professor Hans Herzfeld, noted German historian of the nineteenth and twentieth centuries.

Dear General Heusinger,

On the occasion of your anniversary, I should like to convey my warm congratulations. The great family of nations allied in the cause of peace will not forget your distinguished name. The German soldier stands high among the armed forces of the Alliance and has earned a fine reputation as a dedicated representative of a democratic country and as a faithful servant of the Alliance. In great part this achievement reflects your own qualities and results from the example you have set. We are all greatly indebted to you for your service to the cause of peace and security.

—Lauris Norstad

Gen. Lauris Norstad was Supreme Allied Commander Europe in the decisive years when the German Bundeswehr was undergoing its initial buildup.

It has long been the tradition of the German General Staff to develop a breed of coolly analytical intellectual soldiers. Heusinger is the archetype of a school which has influenced generations of military thinkers. . . . The experiences he had amassed as master of operational planning remained and he was able to use them later for a better purpose in the resurgent army of a new democratic Germany.

—Brig. Peter Young (Ret.), head of the Military History Department at the Royal Military Academy at Sandhurst.

It is in accordance with his nature that he kept a cool head in interpreting and assessing the circumstances in which he had to carry out his task. It was therefore not only the existing circumstances but also his own personality that caused him to take considered action step by step. He respected those powers, which exercised influence on the new armed forces from the field of politics. His principle was we must not run our heads against a stone wall!

—Gen. Ulrich de Maiziere, Bundeswehr Inspector-General in 1966.

German historian Dr. Karl Demeter, whose book spans the history of the German military from the seventeenth century to the early years of the Bundeswehr, described the challenge that faced Adenauer, his advisors, the Bundeswehr, and, ultimately, German society in sorting out and selecting the traditions, principles, and values of the past that should be preserved. Demeter summarized it all well, ending with a level of optimism that I share:

The history and sociology contained in these pages may, perhaps, help rediscover the authentic tradition of the corps of officers and sift the timeless elements in it from the rest. It is, however, the task of those who would follow in their place to search the rubble of the recent past, pick out and try the stones that can be used again, and judge where they can best be inserted in the new structure of today. But the useful stones should not be made to serve only the new edifice of Germany's defense. That structure cannot stand save as part of an ordered plan for the State and for the wider association of which the State is part. If this be done, then time will not be slow to reveal that the value and the living strength of the German tradition of arms are rooted in the universal principles of human decency, and can serve no other end than the peace and freedom of the human race.

Professor Demeter was clearly describing the legacy of Adolf Heusinger.

I suppose there is some irony in the fact that I, an American officer who had responsibility in leading hundreds of American soldiers in combat against the soldiers of the Wehrmacht, had come to regard Adolf Heusinger as one of the great military leaders I have known. No professional officer in NATO contributed more to the evolution of the NATO military alliance.

After years of reflection on the transition of Germany into a trusted ally and member of the Western community of nations, I have concluded that, for all its faults and flaws, the policy pursued in Germany by the United States at the end of World War II was a remarkable success. In no part of Germany's democratic society is this success more evident than in the German armed forces that became the much-respected bulwark of the NATO defense that successfully contained the threat of Soviet-led Warsaw Pact forces in the three decades before 1989. In reviewing the developments of the decade immediately after World War II, in which I was both a participant and an observer, I am impressed with how narrow was the bridge linking the German military before 8 May 1945 to that which followed. The Bundeswehr was first given shape and character in a meeting of a small number of former Wehrmacht officers at Himmerod Abbey, the birthplace of the Bundeswehr. Equally remarkable is the fact that the same three former generals who dominated the work at Himmerod had, just two months earlier, provided Chancellor Adenauer with a memorandum on how he might proceed in developing a national security system. To say that German military history ended on 8 May 1945 and then started all over again would be an exaggeration and simplification that under scrutiny could not stand. I think this essential truth becomes evident if the history of the decades that followed the end of World War II is painted in bold strokes of the brush.

It was Adolf Heusinger who described the Halder era as that of the "last German Army General Staff." Halder's decision to establish an advanced headquarters of the Army General Staff in East Prussia at the beginning of the war against the Soviet Union gave the younger generation of General Staff officers who assembled there the means to coalesce into a group that later became a cohesive and influential force within the Western community of nations after the war.

Chancellor Adenauer was at the center of a very small circle of Germans—Adenauer, State Secretary Hans Globke, Heusinger, Speidel, Foertsch, and Gehlen—whose individual initiatives and actions during the six months after the start of the Korean crisis essentially redirected Germany's interrelated foreign and defense policies; their efforts eventually led to the creation of a German defense ministry, German armed forces to serve in NATO, and a German national intelligence service.

In the months immediately after the outbreak of the war in Korea the Allies were preoccupied with their own differences and gave little attention to Adenauer's concerns. Adenauer was simply preparing to sit down with the Allies when invited. During the five years in which uninterrupted diplomatic negotiations continued over how Germany would participate in the defense of Europe and the Atlantic community, Germany had no defense minister and not one military man in uniform. An ongoing debate within Amt Blank, among veterans of the Wehrmacht, and within various political groups during these five years produced an evolving consensus over the creation of the Bundeswehr. The rapid integration of German officers into NATO that began in 1956 lifted the level of debate on traditions, customs, obedience to orders, and loyalty oaths out of a historic German context into an international military environment.

The postwar history of Germany and Europe could have been different. Germany could have become a communist or neutral state. Gen. Lucius Clay had repeatedly warned of the dangers of just this possibility in the critical summer of 1948. In 1952 the Soviet Union conducted a major diplomatic and propaganda campaign designed to create a neutral Germany under Four-Power aegis. Adenauer and his advisors remained firmly tied to the West. Had the Soviet initiative succeeded, the global history of the past fifty years would have been quite different. The German armed forces emanating from either a communist or neutralist Germany would have had a character quite different from that of the Bundeswehr. The Bundeswehr that developed in the late 1950s was a part and parcel of the evolving German democracy, and it has contributed in a positive way to the image of the German Federal Republic within NATO.

Germany has acted as a major contributor to the peace, prosperity, and stability of Europe and its officers and soldiers are among the most respected and appreciated in the international community of military men and women. The influence of the Bundeswehr is now being cautiously extended to export Europe's stability to the east under the changing character of NATO. The Bundeswehr was conceived and its character defined by former Wehrmacht officers. The difficult challenge for these men to address was the problems of traditions, customs, a legal code to regulate obedience to orders, and the relationship of the new armed forces with the democratic society that was rising out of the ashes of World War II. The Gehlen Organization was not created to preserve any element of the German General Staff, nor was it meant to provide a support base for planning Germany's remilitarization. One can debate whether Heusinger, Speidel, and Foertsch could have achieved what they did without Gehlen's support. It is clear, however, that the initiatives and actions of the small circle of Germans sitting in the Gehlen Organization went far in shaping the defense and foreign policies that Germany has followed so effectively the last half of the twentieth century.

A history that occurs as a chain of events and actions by individuals usually exhibits a dynamic of its own. Germany's transition from an enemy to an ally of the United States and the West was probably destined by broader forces. This remarkable transition clearly represented the will of the Western alliance and of the German people. But the ultimate success of this pivotal moment in history should be credited in no small part to Reinhard Gehlen and the small circle of former German Army General staff officers at the center of the Gehlen Organization.

Appendix: The Principal Players

The German Side

Konrad Adenauer: Germany's first chancellor after World War II. He led Germany's transition from enemy to ally and its eventual entrance into NATO.

Hermann Baun: After heading the Abwehr's agent operations on the eastern front throughout the war, he immediately made an agreement with Reinhard Gehlen to re-create the information-collection operation against Soviet forces. While Baun met his commitment and for two years provided critical support to Gehlen, their relations deteriorated and eventually produced a break. He played no role in the emergence of the BND.

Ludwig Beck: Chief of the German Army General Staff from 1934 to 1938. Ideologically and intellectually opposed to Hitler, he exerted a great influence on young officers entering the German General Staff during this period.

Theodor Blank: A leader in the labor wing of the Christian Democratic Union. He headed an office responsible for defense planning and negotiations with the Allies in the years 1950 to 1955, and became defense minister in 1955 only after sovereignty was granted and Germany was accepted into NATO.

Herbert Blankenhorn: The principal advisor to Adenauer on foreign policy. He initially identified with the British and with Graf Schwerin, but with Hans Globke's ascendancy in the chancellory in late summer 1950 his role was diminished. He continued to be prominent in Germany's diplomatic relations with NATO and the Western Allies.

Eberhard Blum: A member of Gehlen's inner circle for several years after the war. Raised in Holland and having no General Staff background, he contributed in the effort to broaden the image of Gehlen and of the BND. After serving a remarkable twelve years as the BND representative in Washington, he was called back to succeed Wessel as president of the BND.

Heinz Felfe: A former SD officer who was recruited by the KGB and positioned within the Gehlen Organization for a full decade after 1951. An almost legendary figure in the intelligence world, he inflicted enormous damage to the BND and to Gehlen's reputation.

Hermann Foertsch: Commander of the German First Army at the end of World War II. He joined Heusinger and Speidel in developing the concepts and plans for Germany's rearmament and the early planning stages of the Bundeswehr.

Reinhard Gehlen: A General Staff officer who, under Franz Halder, headed Fremde Heere Ost, the intelligence department of the General Staff stationed on the eastern front. He emerged in the postwar era as president of the BND, Germany's first intelligence service.

Dr. Hans Globke: As state secretary in the chancellor's office he was the most powerful figure in the early Adenauer government, shaping the foreign and defense policies that took Germany into a close relationship with the United States and NATO. He brought Heusinger, Speidel, and Gehlen into key positions in Adenauer's national security system.

Franz Halder: Chief of the German Army General Staff from 1938 until his final break with Hitler in 1942. He was arrested by the Gestapo and taken to Berlin for interrogation after the 20 July 1944 coup attempt against Hitler. It was in his General Staff headquarters in East Prussia where the Gehlen Organization was born and where the relationship between Heusinger and Gehlen developed.

Heinz Danko Herre: A General Staff officer intimately associated with Gehlen from their early days in Fremde Heere Ost and during the entire postwar period leading up to creation of the BND. He was with Gehlen in the United States immediately after the war and emerged as the member of Gehlen's closest advisors, the one individual who demonstrated a personal responsibility for the American connection, regardless of his assignment.

Adolf Heusinger: A lieutenant general and chief of operations in the General Staff under Franz Halder and his successor, Kurt Sietzler, from 1940 to 1944. He was arrested and interrogated by the Gestapo after the 20 July 1944 coup attempt against Hitler. After the war he emerged as the primary figure in the early development of the Bundeswehr.

Conrad Kuehlein: A General Staff officer who twice served as Halder's personal adjutant on the eastern front and for a brief period on Gehlen's Fremde Heere Ost staff. After the war he became head of the operational staff of the Gehlen Organization and one of the most important figures cementing the relationship between the Gehlen Organization and American intelligence.

Graf Schwerin: A recognized commander of armored forces in the war who briefly emerged (under British sponsorship) as a military advisor to Adenauer in the summer of 1950. He was not an influence beyond 1950.

Kurt Schumacher: Head of the opposition German Social Democratic Party during the immediate postwar period.

Hans Speidel: A lieutenant general who in 1944 was chief of staff on Rommel's Group B. He was also brought to Berlin for interrogation by the Gestapo after the 20 July coup attempt. He shares credit with Heusinger for creating the Bundeswehr and developing the relationship with NATO.

Horst von Mellenthin: A General Staff officer who headed the Abwehr station in Berlin and later headed Germany's prewar military attaché service. He was a major influence in both Gehlen's efforts in developing an intelligence network and in Heusinger's efforts at remilitarization.

Horst Wendland: A General Staff officer on the eastern front who late in the war served as head of the organizational department of the General Staff. He joined Gehlen's staff in 1948 and rapidly emerged as one of the most respected and capable members of the inner circle, ultimately named Gehlen's general deputy.

Gerhard Wessel: A General Staff officer who shared Gehlen's entire experience on the eastern front and who was for much of the time Gehlen's deputy. Late in the war he succeeded Gehlen as head of Fremde Heere Ost. He was the central figure in the FHO staff assembled by the U.S. Army G-2 at the end of the war. He later succeeded Gehlen as BND president.

Eberhard Wildermuth: A member of the Free Democratic Party in Adenauer's coalition government who aspired to be the minister of defense. A friend of Hans Speidel, it was he who initially brought Heusinger, Speidel, and Foertsch and their ideas to the attention of the chancellor. After 1950 he played no further role in military affairs and died in March 1952.

The American Side

John Boker: The U.S. Army officer who discovered Reinhard Gehlen in the Wiesbaden interrogation center and introduced him into the U.S. Army G-2 system.

Lucius Clay: The most influential American general in Germany during the postwar period from 1945 to 1949. He exercised his power from Berlin as U.S. military governor, as commander in chief, U.S. Forces–European Theater, and finally as commander in chief, U.S. Command–Europe.

James Critchfield: A U.S. Army officer during World War II who remained in Germany and Austria as an Army intelligence officer and subsequently joined the newly formed CIA. From 1948 to 1956 he was the principal CIA officer working with the Gehlen Organization until its emergence as the BND.

Thomas Wesley Dale: An expert on international communism and a talented operations officer, he was the key Army counterintelligence corps officer in Germany during the early to mid-1950s. He ran a top secret operation to penetrate the Adenauer government, including the Gehlen Organization. The product from this operation, known as Operation Campus, was never shared with the CIA.

John Deane: Officer in charge of the Gehlen group at Oberursel.

Allen Dulles: Director of the Central Intelligence Agency who had a colorful career in OSS operations during World War II. After the war he emerged as a supporter of the U.S. association with the Gehlen Organization.

Dwight D. Eisenhower: Supreme commander–Allied Expeditionary Force, then commander in chief, U.S. Forces–European Theater, and president of the United States.

Richard Helms: CIA director of operations during the period of the evolving Gehlen Organization. He provided the support from Washington needed to keep the activity alive.

Tom Lucid: He came up through Italy with Mark Clark's Fifth Army and was the chief of the 430th counterintelligence corps before transferring to Pullach in 1949. Before the war he had been an attorney in the district attorney's office in New York City. A party-loving Irish Catholic, he was liked and respected in the Gehlen Organization. In 1956 he replaced Critchfield and assumed the new role as head of CIA liaison with the BND.

John J. McCloy: A prominent New York lawyer appointed by President Truman to replace General Clay. He became the U.S. high commissioner in Germany in 1949.

Henry Pleasants: After serving in Army Intelligence during World War II, he had a long and impressive tour of duty in postwar Vienna before joining Critchfield in Pullach as a member of the CIA. He was a major figure in dealing with the Gehlen Organization and later as the CIA's representative in its dealings with top levels of the Bonn government.

Edwin Sibert: Eisenhower's G-2 representative in Frankfurt in the summer of 1945. His unilateral decision to take over the Gehlen Organization gave Gehlen the support he needed to survive.

Truman Smith: From 1935 to 1939 he was the military attaché in Berlin. As a retired colonel he supported the Army G-2's efforts to block Adenauer's plan to take over the Gehlen Organization.

Gordon Stewart: Chief of Station–Germany during the formative years of the Gehlen Organization as a CIA-supported activity.

Arthur Trudeau: The head of the U.S. Army G-2 in Washington who, beginning in 1954, unsuccessfully opposed Adenauer's policy on the Gehlen Organization.

Eric Waldman: A U.S. War Department intelligence officer who worked with the Gehlen group at Fort Hunt in 1945 and 1946 and in Germany from 1946 to 1949.

Glossary

Abwehr	Intelligence service of the German General Staff and High Command
Amt Blank	Precursor of the German Federal Republic Defense Ministry
BfV	Bundesamt fuer Verfassungsschutz, Federal Office for the Protection of the Constitution
BK	Office of the Chancellor
BND	Bundesnachrichtendienst, Federal Intelligence Service
Bundestag	Parliament of the Federal Republic of Germany
Bundeswehr	Postwar German armed forces
CIC	U.S. Army Counterintelligence Corps
CIG	Central Intelligence Group
EUCOM	European Command
FHO	Fremde Heere Ost, Foreign Armies East
G-2	U.S. Army General Staff officer heading section dealing with intelligence
Gestapo	Geheime Staats Polizei, Secret State Police of the Hitler regime
GV L	General Vertretongen L, General Agency L (formerly Dienstelle 114)
KGB	Soviet Committee for State Security
MfS	East German Ministry for State Security
OKW	Oberkommando der Wehrmacht, High Command of the German Armed Forces, Hitler's supreme headquarters
OMGUS	Office of Military Government, United States
OPC	Office of Policy Coordination
OSO	Office of Strategic Operations
OSS	Office of Strategic Services
RSHA	Reichssicherheitshauptamt, Reich Security Head Office
SD	Sicherheitdienst, Security Service of the RSHA
SHAEF	Supreme Headquarters–Allied Expeditionary Force
SHAPE	Supreme Headquarters–Allied Powers Europe

SS	Schutzstaffel, Protection Detachment in charge of Gestapo, SD, and RSHA
SSU	Strategic Services Unit
USFA	U.S. Forces–Austria
USFET	United States Forces–European Theater
VOPO	Volkspolizei, People's Police, in East Germany
Wehrmacht	German armed forces under Hitler

Bibliography

Abshagen, Karl Heinz. *Canaris: Patriot und Weltburger.* Stuttgart: Union Deutsche Verlagsgesellschaft, 1949.

Adamic, Louis. *A Nation of Nations.* New York: Harper and Brothers, 1945.

Adenauer, Konrad. *Memoirs, 1945–1953.* Chicago: Henry Regnery, 1966.

Bailey, George. *Germans.* New York: Avon Books, 1972.

Boldt, Harald. *Adolf Heusinger, Reden 1956–1961.* Verlag: Boppard am Rhein, 1961.

Bor-Komorowski. *The Secret Army.* London: Victor Gollancz, 1951.

Bower, Tom. *The Pledge Betrayed.* New York: Doubleday, 1982.

Boyle, Andrew. *Ring Der Verrrater.* Hamburg: Albrecht Knaus Verlag, 1980.

Brandt, Willy. *A Peace Policy For Europe.* New York: Holt, Rinehart, and Winston, 1968.

Bullock, Alan. *Hitler and Stalin.* New York: Knopf, 1992.

Carter, Violet Bonham. *Winston Churchill: An Intimate Portrait.* New York: Harcourt, Brace and World, 1965.

Clay, Lucius D. *Decision in Germany.* New York: Doubleday, 1950.

Conant, James Bryant. *Germany and Freedom: A Personal Appraisal.* London: Oxford University Press, 1958.

Conot, Robert E. *Justice at Nuremberg.* New York: Harper and Row, 1983.

Cookridge, E. H. *Gehlen: Spy of the Century.* New York: Random House, 1971.

Demeter, Karl. *The German Officer Corps in Society and State, 1650–1945.* New York: Frederick A. Praeger, 1965.

Dulles, Allen. *The Secret Surrender.* New York: Harper and Row, 1966.

Eisenhower, Dwight D. *Crusade in Europe.* New York: Doubleday, 1949.

———. *Mandate for Change 1953–1956.* New York: Doubleday, 1963.

Fest, Joachim. *Plotting Hitler's Death.* New York: Henry Holt, 1994.

Gehlen, Reinhard. *Der Dienst.* Mainz, Germany: Hase & Koehler, 1971.

———. *The Service.* New York: World, 1972.

———. *Verschlusssache.* Mainz, Germany: Hase & Koehler, 1980.

German Denazification Law and Implementations with American Directives Included, 15 June 1946. Bavaria, Germany: Special Branch, Office of Military Government.

Gilbert, Martin. *Churchill: A Life.* New York: Henry Holt, 1991.

Goerlitz, Walter. *The German General Staff.* London: Hollis and Carter, 1953.

———. *Der Zweite Welt Krieg 1939–1945.* Stuttgart: Steingrueben-Verlag, 1952.

Goldhagen, Daniel Jonah. *Hitler's Willing Executioners.* New York: Vintage, 1996.

Goodspeed, D. J. *The German Wars.* London: Orbis, 1977.

Grose, Peter. *The Life of Allen Dulles.* New York: Houghton Mifflin, 1994.

Henke, Klaus-Dietmar. *Die Amerikanische.* Besetzing, Germany: R. Oldenbourg, 1995.

Heusinger, Adolf. *Befehl Im Widerstreitt, Gedruckt in der Deutschen.* Stuttgart: Verlags-Anstalt, 1950.

Hoene and Zolling. *The General Was a Spy.* Hamburg, Germany: Hoffman and Campe, 1971.

Holborn, Hajo. *American Military Government: Its Organization and Policies.* 1st ed. Washington, D.C.: Infantry Journal Press, 1947.

International Military Tribunal Secretariat. "Trial of the Major War Criminals before the International Military Tribunal." Nuremberg, 1947.

Irving, Clive. *Axis.* London: Hamish Hamilton, 1980.

Irving, David. *The German Bomb.* New York: De Capo, 1967.

Jackson, Wayne G. *Allen Welsh Dulles as Director of Central Intelligence, 26 February 1953–29 November 1961.* Vol. 2: *Coordination of Intelligence Released through the CIA Historical Review Program 26 April 1994.* HRP 91-2.

Jones, Barry, trans. *General A. Heusinger, Security and Reduced Tension.* Cologne: Markus-Verlagsgesellschaft, 1967.

Kahn, David. *The Codebreakers.* London: Weidenfeld and Nicholson, 1967.

Keegan, John. *The Second World War.* New York: Viking, 1990.

Kimball, Edward, ed. *Churchill and Roosevelt.* Princeton, N. J.: Princeton University Press, 1984.

Kozaczuk, Wladyslaw. *Geheimoperation WICHER.* Koblenz: Bernard und Graefe, 1989.

Krieger, Wolfgang. *General Lucius D. Clay und die amerikanische Deutschlandpolitik 1945–1949.* Stuttgart: Klett-Cotta, 1988.

Krieger, Wolfgang, and Juergen Weber. *Spionage fuer den Frieden?* Tutzing, Germany: Akademie fuer Politische Bildung, 1997.

Large, David Clay. *Germans to the Front.* Chapel Hill: University of North Carolina Press, 1996.

Larrabee, Eric. *Commander in Chief Franklin Delano Roosevelt, His Lieutenants, and Their War.* New York: Simon and Schuster, 1988.

Lochner, Louis P., ed. *The Goebbels Diaries 1942–1943.* Garden City, N.Y.: Doubleday, 1948.

Loftus, John. *The Bebarus Secret.* New York: Alfred A. Knopf, 1982.

Manvell, Roger, and Heinrich Fraenkel. *Hitler: The Man and The Myth.* London: Granada, 1978.

Mayntz, Renate, and Fritz W. Scharpf. *Policy Making in the German Federal Bureaucracy.* Amsterdam: Elsevier, 1975.

m.b.H. *General Adolf Heusinger.* Cologne: Markus-Verlagsgesellschaft, 1967.

Mee, Charles L., Jr. *Meeting at Potsdam.* New York: Dewell, 1976.

Meyer, Georg. *Adolf Huesinger, Dienst eines desutschen Soldaten 1915 bis 1964.* Hamburg: E. S. Mittler & Sohn, 2001.

———. *Vom Kriegsgefangenem zum Generalinspekteur Adolf Heusinger 1945–1961.* Potsdam: Militaergeschichtliches Forschungsamt, 1997.

Meyer, Georg, et al. *Herausgegeben vom Militaergeschichtlichen Forschungamst, Anfaenge westdesutscher Sicherheitspolitik, 1945–1946.* Munich: R. Oldenburg, 1982.

Ministry of Foreign Affairs of the U.S.S.R. *Correspondence between the Chairman of the Council of Ministers U.S.S.R. and the Presidents of the U.S.A. and the Prime Ministers of Great Britain during the Great Patriotic War of 1941–1945,* Vol. 1. Moscow: Foreign Languages Publishing, 1957.

Model, Hansgeorg. *Der Desutsche Generalstabsoffizier.* Frankfurt: Bernard und Graefe, 1968.

Morgenthau, Henry, Jr. *Germany Is Our Problem.* New York: Harper and Brothers, 1945.

Murphy, David, Sergei Kondrashev, and George Bailey. *Battleground Berlin.* New Haven: Yale University Press, 1997.

Naimark, Norman M. *The Russians in Germany: A History of the Soviet Zone of Occupation, 1945–1949.* Cambridge, Mass.: Belknap Press of Harvard University Press, 1995.

Neumann, Franz. *Behemoth: The Structure and Pace of National Socialism 1933–1944.* New York: Oxford University Press, 1944.

Nicolson, Harold. *The War Years 1939–1945; Volume 2 of Diaries and Letters.* Ed. Nigel Nicolson. New York: Atheneum, 1967.

Paris, Erna. *Unhealed Wounds.* New York: Grove Press, 1985.

Paul, Gerhard, and Klaus-Michael Mallmann. *Die Gestapo: Mythos and Realitaet.* Darmstadt, Germany: Primus, 1996.

Pechel, Rudolph. *Deutscher Widerstand.* Zurich: Eugen, 1947.

Prittie, Terence. *Germany Divided: The Legacy of the Nazi Era.* Boston: Little, Brown, 1960.

Quinn, Lt. Gen. William W. *Buffalo Bill Remembers.* Fowlerville, Mich.: Wilderness Adventure Books, 1991.

Reese, Mary Ellen. *General Reinhard Gehlen: The CIA Connection.* Fairfax, Va.: George Mason University Press, 1990.

Ruge, Friedrich. *Buendnisse.* Frankfurt: Bernard & Graefe.

———. *In Vier Marinen.* Munich: Bernard & Graefe, 1979.

Sanders, Jim, Mark Kirkwood, and R. Cort. *Soldiers of Misfortune: Washington's Secret Betrayal of American POWs in the Soviet Union.* Washington, D.C.: National Press, 1992.

Sayer, Ian, and Douglas Botting. *America's Secret Army.* London: Grafton, 1989.

Schwartz, Thomas Alan. *America's Germany: John J. McCloy and the Federal Republic of Germany.* Cambridge, Mass.: Harvard University Press, 1991.

Seaton, Albert. *The German Army 1933–1945.* New York: Meridian, 1982.

Servan-Schrieber, Jean-Jacques. *Franz Josef Strauss, Hefausforderung und Antwort.* Stuttgart: Seewald, 1968.

Seventh U.S. Army in France and Germany. *Report of Operations. Vol. 3: 1944–1945.* Heidelberg: Aloys Graf, 1946.

Shirer, William L. *The Rise and Fall of Adolph Hitler,* 1st ed. New York: Random House, 1961.

Shulman, Milton. *Defeat in the West.* New York: E. P. Dutton, 1948.

Smith, Jean Edward. *Lucius D. Clay: An American Life.* New York: Henry Holt, 1990.

———. *The Papers of Lucius D. Clay: Germany 1945–1949.* Vols. 1 and 2. Bloomington: Indiana University Press, 1974.

Snyder, Louis L. *Basic History of Modern Germany.* Princeton, N.J.: D. Van Norstrand, 1957.

Strauss, Franz Josef. *The Grand Design: A European Solution to German Reunification.* London: Weidenfeld and Nicolson, 1965.

Supreme Headquarters, Allied Expeditionary Force. *Arrest Categories Handbook.* Germany, April 1945.

Thorwald, Juergen. *The Illusion: Soviet Soldiers in Hitler's Armies.* New York: Harcourt Brace Jovanovich, 1974.

Trevor-Roper, H. R. *The Last Days of Hitler.* New York: Macmillan, 1947.

Troy, Thomas. *Donovan and the CIA.* Putnam Valley, N.Y.: Aletheia Books, 1981.

Truscott, Lt. Gen. Lucien King, Jr. *Command Missions: A Personal Story.* New York: E. P. Dutton, 1954.

Turner, Henry Ashby, Jr. *Germany from Partition to Reunification.* New Haven: Yale University Press, 1992.

U.S. Senate Committee on Foreign Relations. *Documents on Germany 1944–1961.* Washington, D.C.: U.S. Government Printing Office, 1961.

Van Bergh, Hendrik. *ABC der Spione.* Germany: Ilmgau Verlag Pfaffenhofen/Ilm, 1965.

Von Bittenfeld Herwarth, Hans-Heinrich, and S. Frederick Starr. *Against Two Evils.* New York: Rawson, Wade, 1981.

Von Lang, Jochen. *Der Sekretar: Martin Bormann: der Mann, der Hitler beherrschte.* Berlin: Zeitgeschichte, 1990.

Walde, Thomas. *Die Rolle der Geheimen Nachrichtendienste im Regierungssystem der Bundesrepublik.* Munich: R. L. Piper, 1971.

Waldman, Eric. *The Goose Step Is Verboten.* New York: Free Press of Glencoe, Canada, 1964.

Wannenmacher, Walter. *Epoch der Angst.* Frankfurt: Ullstein GMBH, 1971.

Werth, Alexander. *Russia at War 1941–1945.* New York: E. P. Dutton, 1964.

Wessel, Gerhard. *Generalleutnant a.D. BND—der geheime Auslandsnachrichtendienst der Bundesrepublik.* Deutschland, Sonderdruck aus "Beitraege zur Konflikt-forschung" 15.Jahrgang, Heft 2/1985, Seiten 5-23. Koeln: Markus-Verlagsgesellschaft mbH., 1985.

West, Nigel. *MI-5 1945–1972: A Matter of Trust.* London: Weidenfel and Nicolson, 1983.

Westphal, Siegfried. *Heer in Fesseln.* Bonn: Athenaum, 1950.

Whiting, Charles. *Gehlen: Germany's Master Spy.* New York: Ballantine, 1972.

Wickert, Erwin. *Dramatisch Tage in Hitler's Reich.* Stuttgart: Steingrueben, 1958.

Williams, Charles. *Adenauer: The Father of the New Germany.* New York: John Wiley and Sons, 2000.

Wilmot, Chester. *The Struggle for Europe.* New York: Harper, 1952.

Winks, Robin W. *Cloak and Gown: Scholars in the Secret War 1939–1961.* New York: Quill, 1987.

Winterbothman, F. W. *The Ultra Secret.* New York: Harper and Row, 1974.

Wolgin, Alexander. *Hier sprechen.* Russen, Germany: Kraussfopf-Verlag, 1965.

Index

About the Author

James H. Critchfield joined the Central Intelligence Agency in 1948 after serving in the U.S. Army in the European theater during World World II. He held various positions in the CIA, which included acting as the principal U.S. officer responsible for overseeing the creation of the new German intelligence service. He also served as chief of the Eastern European, Near East, and South Asia divisions and as the national intelligence officer for energy, and, in 1973-74, was an energy policy planner at the White House.

Mr. Critchfield is the recipient of the CIA Distinguished Intelligence Medal, the CIA Trailblazer Award, the Officer's Cross of the Order of Merit of the Federal Republic of Germany, as well as the Silver Star, Purple Heart, and Croix de Guerre during his Army career.

After his retirement from the CIA in 1974, Mr. Critchfield served as president of Tetra Tech International, Inc. He died in 2003 and is survived by his wife, Lois.

The **Naval Institute Press** is the book-publishing arm of the U.S. Naval Institute, a private, nonprofit, membership society for sea service professionals and others who share an interest in naval and maritime affairs. Established in 1873 at the U.S. Naval Academy in Annapolis, Maryland, where its offices remain today, the Naval Institute has members worldwide.

Members of the Naval Institute support the education programs of the society and receive the influential monthly magazine *Proceedings* and discounts on fine nautical prints and on ship and aircraft photos. They also have access to the transcripts of the Institute's Oral History Program and get discounted admission to any of the Institute-sponsored seminars offered around the country.

The Naval Institute also publishes *Naval History* magazine. This colorful bimonthly is filled with entertaining and thought-provoking articles, first-person reminiscences, and dramatic art and photography. Members receive a discount on *Naval History* subscriptions.

The Naval Institute's book-publishing program, begun in 1898 with basic guides to naval practices, has broadened its scope to include books of more general interest. Now the Naval Institute Press publishes about one hundred titles each year, ranging from how-to books on boating and navigation to battle histories, biographies, ship and aircraft guides, and novels. Institute members receive significant discounts on the Press's more than eight hundred books in print.

Full-time students are eligible for special half-price membership rates. Life memberships are also available.

For a free catalog describing Naval Institute Press books currently available, and for further information about subscribing to *Naval History* magazine or about joining the U.S. Naval Institute, please write to:

Membership Department
U.S. Naval Institute
291 Wood Road
Annapolis, MD 21402-5034
Telephone: (800) 233-8764
Fax: (410) 269-7940
Web address: www.navalinstitute.org